Intentional Communities

The International Library of
Group Psychotherapy and Group Process

Therapeutic Communities Section

Section Editors

R. D. Hinshelwood
Consultant Psychotherapist
St Bernard's Hospital, Southall, Middlesex

Nick Manning
Lecturer in Social Policy and Administration
University of Kent

Intentional Communities

Ideology and Alienation in Communal Societies

Barry Shenker

Routledge & Kegan Paul
London, Boston and Henley

First published in 1986
by Routledge & Kegan Paul plc

14 Leicester Square, London WC2H 7PH, England

9 Park Street, Boston, Mass. 02108, USA and

Broadway House, Newtown Road,
Henley on Thames, Oxon RG9 1EN, England

Set in 10/12 pt Linotron Times
by Input Typesetting Ltd, London
and printed in Great Britain
by T. J. Press (Padstow) Ltd,
Padstow, Cornwall

Library of Congress Cataloging in Publication Data

Shenker, Barry, 1944–

Intentional communities.
(The International library of group psychotherapy
and group process. Therapeutic communities series)
Bibliography: p.
Includes index.
1. Collective settlements—Case studies.
2. Hutterite Brethren—Case studies. 3. Kibbutzim—
Case studies. 4. Therapeutic community—Case studies.
5. Alienation (Social psychology)—Case studies.
6. Ideology—Case studies. I. Title. II. Series.
HX632.S54 1986   307.7'7'0926   85-14244

British Library CIP data also available
ISBN 0–7100–9961–4

Contents

Preface

This book has its roots in my doctoral thesis written at the London School of Economics. Prior to writing the thesis I spent many years living on a Kibbutz, during which time I read widely on the subject of communal societies. Since its completion I have developed new interests, particularly in mental health and public relations. In preparing this book I have therefore not confined myself to my academic studies, but have drawn upon my personal experiences, occupational activities and general intellectual interests. The result is that this book is not so much a description or a general theory of 'intentional communities', although there is some of both, as an essay, an argument, a conception about their nature.

I would like to thank those at the London School of Economics who guided my research, Dr (now Professor) Michael Hill and Professor David Martin. Funding for research and travel came from the United Kibbutz Movement (Ichud), the Leverhulme Foundation and the University of London Senate. I would also like to thank my many friends in the Kibbutz movement for their support, and particularly the members of Kibbutz Tzorah, and also my friends at the Richmond Fellowship. My hosts at Crystal Spring Colony, and in particular Rev. Jake Kleinsasser, were extremely warm and friendly. The editors of this series, Nick Manning and Bob Hinshelwood have been most helpful and have displayed enormous reserves of patience.

Finally, there are those closest and dearest to me who, in ways I am not sure I can explain very clearly, made the completion of this book possible.

Barry Shenker
London, 1985

Part A

Chapter 1
The study of intentional communities

Interest in communal societies

In recent years communal societies have aroused much public interest. This interest has been active and, more commonly, vicarious. Many people see communal living as an appropriate response to the materialism and alienation of present-day society. Others are simply fascinated by the practical steps some people take to make communal life a reality. Communal societies, it seems, appeal to that part of us which is idealistic and romantic.

Contemporary interest in communal societies, at least since the 1960s, stems from a combination of optimism in the power of social experimentation and cynicism in the ability of social institutions to make the world we live in a better place. This arose partly from new attitudes towards political activism and social roles, and from a quest for social liberation. The economic upsurge of the 1960s and the concomitant release of social energy gave communalism a new spurt. Now, as we live through the economic difficulties and global dangers of the 1970s and 1980s, with the attendant perception that society has 'lost its way' – under these circumstances many people see communal experiments as a lone star of idealism and commitment.

Each age produces its own generation of communal adherents. There has hardly been a period in western history when some group or another has not invoked communalism as an answer to their needs and beliefs, indeed as *the* answer to the crisis of the time. The vast majority of these communal experiments achieve no more than footnote status in history. Despite this record of social marginality and historical failure, a new generation emerges each time, determined to attempt its own communal experiments.

It seems, therefore, that the 'communal urge' is not primarily a historical legacy nor simply a response to immediate circumstances. Rather, it appears that within every (western) society, just as there will be those who wish to be marginal, deviant, intensely individualistic or eccentric, so will there be those who seek comprehensive integration of the society as a whole, or of groups within it, groups which carry the society's 'true' meaning and purpose. No prompting is required for this trend: it is intrinsic to human society.

Why study communal societies?

Shortlived and unmomentous as most communal societies are, there are nevertheless a few which can rightly claim more than transient, historical status. Although they have not left an indelible mark on the course of human history, they can justly argue that they have had a significant impact on their surrounding environment. Are there lessons to be learnt from these communal societies?

The study of communal societies can be useful for four distinct reasons. One is that as self-contained 'total communities' and distinct social groups interacting with their environment we can see them both as micro-versions of large societies and as social groups with unique characteristics. Their internal structure and their external relations contribute to our understanding of social processes generally and of social movements in particular. Questions of belief and commitment, ideology, alienation, integration, deviance, the functioning of sub-groups in a society, economic rationality – to mention but a few – are all issues which are reflected in microcosm within communal societies, so that the latter can serve as 'case-studies' for wider social phenomena. They are, equally, historical phenomena, acting out a role in certain times and places. It follows that by analysing their historical and social context we can gain insight into the wider trends of the time. A third value is that some practices of communal societies can have direct application in other contexts – economic, organizational or social. Discrete, unique and non-conformist as communal societies may be, they too need to survive and do all the things that any society is required to do if it is to function efficiently. The point is that in view of their ideology they choose to do many things in non-conventional ways – yet still manage to survive. Particularly in the case of long-lasting communities, the wider society may have much to learn from them. For this reason there is ongoing interest in such matters as family relationships, bureaucratic structures, child-rearing practices and industrial management.[1]

And finally, but no less important, the response of non-communards to the existence of communal societies – whether from those who live close by and are directly affected by them, or from those who are distant and know hardly anything about them – can be quite revealing about 'human nature'. The existence of communal societies often evokes a powerful and emotional interest, even among people who have not the slightest intention of joining one and indeed never even come into contact with one. Communal societies appear to touch a raw nerve in our psyches, generating a gamut of reactions ranging from, at the one extreme, vicarious admiration and sometimes naive, romantic idealism, to, at the other extreme, hopelessly ill-informed and irrational hostility – frequently tinged in both cases with a degree of sexual fantasy.[2] These responses can give us a wealth of insight into our own beliefs, values, social sensitivities and psychological processes.

An approach to communal societies

It would be more than foolhardy to attempt, within the confines of one short book, to analyse communal life with a view to benefiting from these four uses. There is, though, one question about communal societies which, if answered satisfactorily, can contribute to our understanding of what they are 'really' about. That question is quite simply this: why is it that in the long and never-say-die history of communal experimentation, there are a few or, to be precise, a few groups, which have persisted over lengthy periods of time and seem well-ensconced for the foreseeable future? This is not an issue of 'success', since success is self-defining. A small group of ten people setting up a commune which disbands after two years may have achieved all they wanted: in their terms they were successful. Yet some communal societies exist for long periods. For them, persistence and growth are ends in themselves (albeit not the only ones); from their own point of view, they too are successful. (What price they have to pay for such success and how they frequently manage to avoid paying it are issues we shall be examining.)

What follows is an attempt to understand the lives of three types of communities. It should be clear from the outset that no particular sociological or psychological model is drawn upon. A variety of theoretical influences is present and freely used as appropriate – phenomenology, existentialism, Marxism, functionalism and others, such as P. A. Sorokin. The approach is eclectic but not, I hope, in the pejorative sense of the word. I have drawn on any available source to serve my primary aim – to paint a picture of communal life which is accurate, logical and, perhaps above all, I hope, sensitive.

My approach, put simply, is to analyse communal life by looking at two dimensions of it: the 'external' factors (e.g., relations with the environment or forms of social organization) and the 'internal' factors (e.g., belief, meaning and commitment). This approach may be better understood by injecting a personal note. While living on a Kibbutz for many years I read widely about communal societies. However, much of this reading left me with a feeling of unease, a sense that outsiders, for all their 'objectivity', were often more concerned to impose their own abstract models and private values on their material than to understand those of their subjects. Then, there were many nuances of daily life in communities which outsiders often failed to notice, or misinterpreted entirely. In a word, I did not have the feeling that they were talking about me or anyone I knew. So, many of their conclusions hardly seemed consonant with the facts as they are or as insiders see them. For example, to see commitment as primarily a matter of imposed, external (to the individual member) authority, or as a consequence of social processes and mechanisms over which the individual has little control, or as a result of psychological weakness, was to me both personally unacceptable and logically faulty. This seemed to contradict the voluntary nature of the communal life I was living (and in which I had now developed an academic interest), and it did not tell me much about the Kibbutz and others' ability to persist and to achieve what they have. If many of the interpretations of communal life were correct, then even the minority of communities that are well-established should have died out; yet it is their persistence which needs explanation, not why they should have collapsed. Of course the history of communal movements is fraught more with failure than with persistence, and it is only too easy for the insider to over-roman-ticize, distort, apologize or be defensive within his own frame of reference. It seemed to me though that without an understanding of the insider's perceptions and motivations, no analysis could be complete. Yet this could not be a self-sufficient level of under-standing. The objective consequences of their viewpoint and a whole variety of external circumstances seemed equally necessary to explain the nature of life in these communities and the reasons for their persistence.

I have, therefore, tried, in addition to drawing on a variety of sources, ideas, perspectives and ad hoc observations, to combine two approaches – call them 'subjective-objective' or 'inner-outer' if you will – to give a picture of communal life which is, I hope, consistent with the facts as the observer knows them and as insiders relate to them.

The 'problem' of intentional communities

What precisely, then, are we trying to understand about communal societies or, as I prefer to call them, intentional communities (defined below)? We are apparently dealing with two separate issues. One is – how and why do intentional communities persist? Put crudely, what makes for communal 'success'? The other is – how does the individual perceive his life in the community? What is commitment? What are the inherent tensions between the individual and his community? In short, why should an individual want to live in an intentional community?

In fact our analysis of these two issues – communal persistence and individual commitment – are very closely related. One could reasonably ask why any society – not only intentional communities – persists, and equally why anybody lives in the society they do. The difference between asking these questions in general terms and asking them in relation to intentional communities is that in the latter case the answers are dictated by the fact that we are dealing with societies which exist for a specific purpose: they are ideological creations. This makes the ability to answer our ques-tions more problematic. Nobody asks why Great Britain or Green-land exist: they simply do. Nor do we ask why people choose to live there: they simply do. How these societies change and what people in them make of their lives are extremely important questions. But they are only important given the fact that they are already going concerns. Not so with intentional communities. People in these communities are anxious to preserve both their communal existence and their collective purpose. The two go hand in hand. To do both simultaneously is by no means easy; indeed they could be in outright conflict.

So, in answering our two questions – on collective persistence and on individual meaning – we are in fact dealing with the same issues since they are not really separate questions. How the community deals with its collective needs and how the individual creates and sustains a meaningful community existence – these are one set of complex processes, each influencing the other. This, the reader will discover, is not to say that there is some neat consistency in everything the community or the individual does. On the contrary, conflict and inconsistency are rife – but so too are integration and consistency. It is precisely this issue – how both the community and the individuals that comprise it continue to make the whole thing hang together so that it works simply as a going concern and as an ideological vehicle, warts and all – it is this issue with which we are concerned.

Put another way, we are asking three questions: How do intentional communities persist organizationally? How do individuals find life in the community meaningful and satisfying? And how does each succeed in doing this within the framework of an ideological belief-system? Then – the really crucial question – how do they do all three simultaneously? The answers to these questions show that communal life is complex and that there is no simple formula for success. Indeed, if there is one single answer it is this: that those communities which do persist themselves realize, perhaps unconsciously, that there is no simple formula; that life is complex; that ideological needs are one thing and organizational or individual needs are another, and that very often one can do without the other very well; but equally that they can support and reinforce each other, and that their particular ideologies have it within them to do so; that ideological consistency and social change are not necessarily antithetical; and that communal adherence and individualism need not be in conflict. What *their* understanding of these issues is, and how they actually go about managing them, is the topic of this book.

This brings us back to the approach I have adopted in analysing intentional communities. In the Note on Sources at the end of this chapter I note various theories on the subject and point out that most emphasize one of two approaches: either that the community has learned to adapt to changing circumstances and to sustain organizational viability, or that it has so socialized its members into accepting social norms and beliefs that the community can demand of them whatever is required to ensure survival. Both are important arguments, but each on its own is insufficient; even when taken together we are still left with an inadequate understanding of our subject.

I think the one school is too concerned with seeing commitment in terms of external control, while the other is too concerned with finding the right formula for success. The thrust of my own discussion will be to see what living in the community means from the perspective of the insider and how specific aspects of it relate to this perspective. I also try to see how the community goes about meeting its basic needs, with special emphasis on the relation of these considerations to ideology – which, after all, is what intentional communities are purportedly all about. Commitment will be seen not so much as a matter of control as of personal identity, self-perceptions, self-defined needs. Meeting basic necessities will be seen not so much in terms of 'you need more of this and less of that' but rather of mutual compatibility between, at one level, the means chosen and, at another level, between the means as a whole and the ideology (so that there is no *inherent* reason to be, say, democratic or authoritarian, involved with the environment or withdrawn from it, and so on).

We can perhaps understand this better through another consideration. The Hutterites and Kibbutzim, the two main groups of communities we examine, both believe very much that they are democratic and egalitarian societies. The point here is two-fold. For one thing, their concrete expressions of democracy and equality are very different, yet this does not stop them from believing that they are democratic and egalitarian. But, more than that, to the Hutterite Kibbutz economic equality bears no relation to what equality is 'really' about, while to the Kibbutz member Hutterite democracy is no democracy at all. So there is no point in saying that intentional communities, if they are to persist, should be egalitarian or democratic since these terms can mean almost anything. What is crucial though is what they mean to their adherents, how they implement them and how they perceive the relationship between practical implementation of these principles and their abstract belief-system. This is done first by abandoning the idea that, to ensure persistence, an institution must have this-or-that form; rather, we need to examine the relationship between whatever form does exist and the other institutions of the community, and also what that form represents in the conscious-ness and perceptions of the members themselves.

What are intentional communities?

The term 'intentional communities' is not an everyday one, hence some definition is needed. Intentional communities share certain features with organizations, sects and social movements, yet are none of these. An intentional community is a relatively small group of people who have created a whole way of life for the attainment of a certain set of goals. The two elements of the term are equally important. They are *intentional* communities in that they are not like, say, a tribe or village which has arisen or developed spontaneously over the years. Intentional communities have emerged as a result of a number of people consciously and purposefully coalescing as a group in order to realize a set of aims (although the founders may have existed as an informal group prior to declaring their 'intentionality'). These aims are not partial: they attempt to create an entire way of life, hence, unlike organiz-ations or social movements, they are intentional *communities*.

Their being a community has two further qualities: they are characterized by face-to-face relations and they embrace commu-nalism as an ethical end in itself (apart from its instrumental value). Clearly there can be degrees of intentionality and degrees of 'community-ness'. To what degrees these must exist in order to qualify as intentional communities I cannot say since this is an undertaking in itself but the foregoing gives us the essence of an intentional community. Without specifying quantities, I suggest that an intentional community exists if, 'by and large', the following conditions are met:

(1) It was founded as a conscious and purposive act;
(2) Membership is voluntary and based on a conscious act (even if the member was born in the community);
(3) The group sees itself as separate from and different to its

environment and relates as a group to (or withdraws as a group from) its environment;

(4) The community is relatively self-contained – most members can potentially live their entire lives in it (or for the period during which they are members);

(5) Sharing is part of the community's ideology;

(6) The community has collective goals and needs and expects members to work towards their satisfaction;

(7) The ideology claims that the goals of the community, even if orientated to the benefit of the individual, can only be obtained in a collective framework;

(8) Ultimately the community, or people appointed by the community, but not the individual, is the source of authority;

(9) The general way of life of the community is considered to be inherently good, i.e. is an end in itself over and above its instrumental value;

(10) The community's existence has a moral value and purpose which transcend the time-span of individual membership.

We should emphasize that these qualities can exist not only in varying degrees, but in various ways. Sharing, equality, self-containment and so on can be interpreted in many ways and, as we shall see, this is an important factor in the persistence of intentional communities. The point is that where these qualities exist in the eyes of both the outside observer and the members themselves, we have an intentional community. This helps to underline why it is so important to see what members themselves define as, say, sharing. A rigid definition may exclude many groups from being intentional communities along this dimension. What we are concerned with is if the community sees itself as based on sharing, how it defines sharing, how sharing governs its members' behaviour, how the definition of sharing relates to other aspects of their lives, how that definition changes over the years and how the ideal definition is or is not expressed in reality.

The term 'intentional community' is, I think, preferable to two rival terms – 'utopian community' and 'communal society'. The former is inapplicable for two reasons. One is the pejorative nature of the term, which is in some cases valid, but often does not do justice to the community concerned. In, particular, some communities – especially those we are discussing here – do not see themselves as being utopian, and (I argue later) this very quality has helped them to persist. Utopianism has connotations of a perfect society, of the perfectibility of human beings, and of the end of history or, at least, of a total break with the historical past.[3] While an element of this has existed in our communities they have by and large adopted a far more sanguine view of the possibilities inherent in their life-style. The term 'communal society' is of course appropriate in view of the characteristics I mentioned above, but this does not indicate their intentionality, only their communality, and the latter is only one aspect or consequence of their overall intentionality. Further, it is the tension between their intentionality (or 'pure ideology' to use a rough term) and their actual attempts to persist in the world which concern us here and not only their communality. For these reasons I prefer the term 'intentional community'.

The persistence of intentional communities

Why did we choose these three communities – Hutterite colonies,[4] the Kibbutzim and the therapeutic communities – for this study? Our main purpose is to understand how intentional communities manage to persist. This entails two tasks. One is to see how they have managed specific operational problems; the other is to see if there is anything in their general interpretation and application of the defining qualities mentioned above which has contributed to their persistence.

Now, it is particularly difficult to define the term 'persistence'. As I have already mentioned, there is a distinction between persistence and 'success'. I am not concerned here with defining the latter, except insofar as the communities we are discussing define it for themselves. Persistence, too, can be difficult to define. We can define persistence chronologically, ideologically or structurally, but none is entirely satisfactory. If we define persistence *chronologically* we need a rigid cut-off time to divide between persistence and failure. If we define it *ideologically* we need to see whether the communities' intentions have in fact been realized, but this is difficult because their intentions have often been far from clear. The original intentionality has often been characterized more by enthusiasm than by clarity. Furthermore, as we have already said, it is difficult to define sharing, etc. in a clear enough fashion to ensure a test of consistency. From a *structural* point of view we need to take two approaches. One is to see whether the community sees itself as being *essentially* consistent over the years. Despite specific or ad hoc or cumulative changes, do the members feel that they are a continuation, in essential respects, of what went before? The other approach is to examine whether, historically, there have been any radical changes, so that whatever the community itself thinks, the observer finds it difficult to recognize a common element to present and past practices or beliefs. This may be extremely difficult. I mentioned earlier how the observer's own frame of reference can influence his judgement regarding even 'objective' facts, and this is a case in point. This is complicated by the problem of having to define the essential or fundamental characteristics of the community. We need to know whether any particular institutions are *in themselves* fundamental or whether they are *expressions* of something else which is fundamental.

For these reasons it is perhaps best to combine all three approaches – the chronological, the ideological (members' viewpoint), and the structural (observer's viewpoint). This is what I have done. The two major communities chosen for study definitely see themselves as being the same community as their forebears, structurally and ideologically. As the observer I see numerous changes that have occurred, yet it seems that many of them have taken place within a consistent ideology and within a single historical orientation.

In her own work on communities in America, Kanter (1972) opted for the chronological approach. She, like so many other observers, wanted to find reasons for success and failure. She took as her criterion the persistence of a community over twenty-five years (one generation). Her chronology also stopped if there was a radical and unarguable change in the community (such as Oneida – a communal society founded in 1848 and dissolved in 1880 into a joint stock corporation). She studied ninety-one communities founded between 1780 and 1860. Eleven were successful, seventy-nine unsuccessful and one uncertain. As examples of the successful ones, we have the Shakers (nearly 200 years, at their peak 6,000 members in eighteen villages), Harmony (100 years, 800 at peak), Amana (ninety years, 1,800 at peak), Zoar (eighty-one years, 500 at peak) and Oneida (thirty-three years, 288 at peak).

By comparison we have three other communal movements in western society: the Hutterites, the Kibbutzim and the monastic movement, against which even the 'successful' American ones seem gross failures. The Hutterites have persisted for over 450 years and now have over 30,000 members in some 230 colonies. The Kibbutzim have existed for over seventy years and have 116,000 members in some 260 communities. Indeed, it has been calculated that the present population of Hutterite communities and Kibbutzim represents 90 per cent of all nineteenth- and twentieth-century western communes.[5] Neither group looks like fading out in the near future; on the contrary they are continually expanding. For this reason it is useful to study these two groups. They are both intentional communities, and by all the criteria of persistence they have persisted.

There is a further reason why it is useful to study these two communities. This relates to my earlier comment that many of the nuances and self-perceptions within communal life are often missed by observers and that to a large extent these are crucial to the persistence of the communities. There are also other factors which are not measurable yet need to be analysed, e.g. the communities' *approach* to education, not simply its external form. In short, my arguments about persistence do not lie only in a comparison of organizational details but, more important, in trying to grasp the 'essence' of life in each community.

There is another consideration here. I do not mean this metaphysically, but it is easier to explain death than life. If a community disintegrates it is easy to say 'they couldn't attract members' or 'they failed economically' or something similar (which may be true). But the questions we need to ask are: *Why* could they not attract members or succeed economically? And *even if* they had done so would they have persisted? In short, to know the overt reasons for failure does not tell us what is needed for persistence.

There is a distinct advantage to studying more than one group of communities. If we studied only one, we would be able to pinpoint certain factors which would seem to be a recipe for success but we would not know if these were specific to that community only or if they were generally applicable. On this basis there is no limit to how many communities one should study but it is clear that it must be more than one. The Kibbutzim and the Hutterites are therefore appropriate because, while they share many characteristics, they also differ in so many respects. If we can find consistency in this diversity then perhaps we have the basis for generalized conclusions. To study only one community is to open oneself to the danger of mistaking form for principle. If we examined only, say, the Kibbutzim, we might well conclude that their form of democracy is a necessary ingredient for persistence. By examining other communities I have concluded that different forms of democracy are equally relevant to persistence and that democracy may not even be necessary at all, depending on a variety of conditions. It is therefore the general conditions that I am seeking, of which institutions are a specific expression, and I wish to avoid confusing the two.

Finally, why did I decide to include a brief look at therapeutic communities? For one thing, as already said, the more communities we can look at the better. Then, even though a therapeutic community qualifies as an intentional community, it is, in many respects, different to the other two types: it is smaller, more limited in aims, has a shorter time-span (for the individual member) and a different ideological basis (emotional health as opposed to secular humanistic socialism or religious fundamentalism). In particular, it is not a 'total' community in that although for the period that one resides in a therapeutic community one's life in it is nearly all-encompassing, this phase is shortlived. Not only is it not a lifetime commitment, the ideology requires that one's life in the community be transient. The consequence is that the essential components of intentional communities such as sharing, and other things such as style of personal relationships and the management of external relations, can take on a different form in therapeutic communities to that seen in our two major communities.

A note on sources

This book is not based upon any single theoretical model of social processes. The ideas and arguments presented are culled from a variety of approaches, leading to a 'model' which is eclectic but, I hope, no less consistent for that. Space does not, unfortunately, allow me to elaborate on these sources, although the notes and bibliography should prove adequate indicators.

For the sake of clarity, though, I would like to refer to four bodies of theory which have particularly influenced my general thinking about social change, ideology and its relation to social structure, and alienation.

These are phenomenology, in particular the work of Berger and Luckmann, and also of Schutz; the theories of P. A. Sorokin, and especially his notions of sociocultural unity, social solidarity, identity and change; functionalism, as expressed chiefly by Levy and Parsons, and also by Goldschmidt and Johnson; and some aspects of Marxist theory, especially Marx's theory of alienation, which has particular relevance to intentional communities.

There are also a number of general theories regarding the nature and persistence of communal societies. Broadly speaking, some emphasize commitment and control as the central mechanism of operation – Abrams and McCulloch, Cornfield, Coser, Gide, Goffman, Kanter and Zablocki fall into this category; others emphasize the satisfaction of operational, 'functional' necessities – Conkin, Fellman, Goodwin and Taylor, Infield, Kramer, Mumford, Wagner and Whitworth are relevant here. There is, of course, some overlap between the two; others, such as Erasmus and Hall, emphasize factors such as mutual trust and the creation of shared meanings, respectively. Particular theories about the Hutterites and about the Kibbutzim are also appropriate. Bennet, Boldt, Clark, Eaton, Hostetler, Infield, Serl and Sorokin all provide theories to account for the historical survival of the Hutterites. As regards Kibbutzim, we find a variety of explanations as to their relative popularity and success: Bettelheim, Buber, Cnaani, Cohen, Diamond, Etzioni, Gazit, Golomb, Krook, Rosner, Spiro and Talmon-Garber have all contributed to this debate. Again, I have drawn freely and in an ad hoc manner on these and other observers to create, against the broad theoretical background, a general conception as to the nature of intentional communities or, more prosaically, what makes them 'hang together'.

Chapter 2
A theory of alienation

In order to understand the nature of intentional communities we need to develop our concepts about two central elements in their existence – alienation (and its denial) and ideology. Questions of social system, identity, conformity and deviance, commitment, the relationship between belief and reality – these are all crucial to our understanding of intentional communities.

The nature of systems

Our starting point is that the primary task of a social unit, whether an individual or a group, is to sustain its ability to function as a system. Only by being a system can it function at all, and to be a system it needs an identity (for the individual) or culture (for the society). The arguments here apply equally to the individual and society, not because one is a reduction of the other but because they are both systems; in order to function and persist, they both need to meet the same conditions.

A system is formed when two or more entities in the universe exist in such a way that the existence or operation of any one of the entities is linked to the existence and operation of the others. Defined otherwise, we may say that if an entity ceases to exist or to function adequately, or continues functioning but in a different way and as a result some other entity is affected, then the two entities formed a system. The more direct the influence of one on the other, the more integrated the system. Individuals, groups and societies are all systems because they consist of elements which in themselves have no value or purpose, but derive these from operating with other elements to form a functioning whole or system. Each system can then form part of a wider system. Identity is the set of meanings or basic principles around which the constituent elements of the system cohere.

Identity may be thought of in terms of 'self' – personal, group, societal. There is no objective or a priori definition of self or essence, that is, of the unit's identity or of what qualities the unit 'should' display. What its identity consists of is those aspects of its existence which enable its constituent elements to operate as a system, i.e. allow it to be an ongoing unit within a consistent frame of reference (meaning). These elements consist of physical-biological, emotional, cognitive and interactional factors. What the 'existential thread' or meaning is that allows them to 'hang together' is a matter of observation, not of a priori definition. There is no such thing, I contend, as the 'essential' nature of human beings or groups, that is, a priori characteristics which transcend individual variations or exist whether persons or groups actually display them or are aware of them (so that if they do not display them they are somehow deficient or deviant). Identity is the abstraction of an existential condition and the condition itself; it is not a metaphysical assumption.

The two defining characteristics of a system are order and meaning. *Order* refers to the *integration* of the system's biological, affective, cognitive and relational elements; to the *regularization* of behaviour patterns, expectations and reactions; and to *control* over oneself and one's environment. *Meaning* refers to the fact that the individual or society has conceptions about the nature of the universe and its (self's) place in it, attributes worth to itself and its environment, and possesses criteria for evaluating specific elements in them. Unless there is a degree of order the self, by definition, could not be a system; it would be unable to adapt to changing circumstances or meet its needs in any way. Equally, the strain of not knowing what to expect from other selves and the inability to assert any control over what one needs to do in order to persist would lead to the collapse of the system or its total assimilation into another.

However, a contrary situation can be equally destructive to the persistence of the system. Over-integration, over-regularization and over-control can be as damaging as their opposites, as they too do not allow for adaptation and change. Just as the system requires the social and psychological 'economy of order', it also requires – if it is not to degenerate – a degree of tension, instability, uncertainty and openness to influence by others upon it. Every need requires its opposite.[1] Homogeneity requires heterogeneity, regularity requires spontaneity, security requires challenge and uncertainty. Too much of either side of the balance can be destructive to the system's persistence.

The same arguments apply to the system's meaning. Unless the system has a set of meanings it would never know how to go about attaining order; all aspects of self and environment would appear equally relevant or irrelevant; the system would have no guides to action, no criteria of importance, no guidelines to behaviour. Two aspects of this should be stressed. One is that what the meanings a person or society adopts is not a matter of a priori definition, *even though the self tends and needs to think it is*. The other is that, just as with order, too much meaning can be harmful. The system can be bogged down in over-rigid definitions of importance, can be too inflexible in assessing situations and reacting to them, too concerned with permeating every single element of its existence with worth or lack of it. Such oversaturation of meaning creates social and psychological strain, and leaves the system unable to change and adapt as circumstances demand. So, fundamental to the idea of a social or personal system is that it has meaningfulness – but equally fundamental is the characteristic of meaninglessness. Once again, too much of the one will vitiate the other and, as a result, the capacity of the system to persist.

Meaning and order are not only necessary to the system's existence and persistence; they also serve to define each other. We have seen that the self's set of meanings 'tells' the system how to attain order. This does not mean though that the set of meanings is somehow autonomously arrived at and then imposed on the elements of the self and its environment to create a system ex nihilo. Nor, to take the other extreme, do a number of elements of the universe simply 'happen' to work together successfully with a person or group coming along later to contrive meaning out of it all. Order and meaning stand in a dialectical relationship. Human life and institutions consist of groping in the dark, not to *find* meaning (since there is no meaning 'out there' to be discovered) but to *create* it.

Yet they do not grope randomly. Their meaning is given to them from birth, and even if, as adults, they create institutions, they begin with a vast and complex set of 'pre-given' ideas (even if only implicitly understood). As the system manages in the world so, in its reflexiveness, does it 'see' what its meaning is and, given the principles of its meaning, it can proceed to operate in the world by applying them to other elements of itself and its universe. This is not a chicken and egg argument, since that would be futile. What we are saying is that up to a point the meanings we possess exist independently of what we actually do or experience, and vice versa. Yet to a very large extent the two shape each other – we act in certain ways because our meanings indicate that it *is* necessary; conversely, because certain actions happen to have been an appropriate means of managing in the world, we come post hoc to invest them with meaning. Yet the comments we made about order and meaning each needing to be characterized simultaneously by closure and openness apply equally to the relationship between them. If meaning and order were so closely interlocked that they could not act autonomously in any way, the system could not hope to survive. If the self is to be a unique system (and to be a system means to be unique, otherwise it is simply a sub-system of a larger system *and no more*), then it needs to be able to play around with its meanings, to test them, to be creative, to question them. Similarly, if it is to function adequately it often needs simply to get on with whatever needs to be done without reference to the meanings, and even perhaps in defiance of them. While order and meaning must clearly exist in large doses of mutuality there is also a limit beyond which such mutuality hinders the system's operation and threatens its sense of identity.

A definition of alienation[2]

To have a sense of identity means that the individual (i) operates as a coherent system; (ii) has a meaning in terms of himself and his environment; (iii) is stable; (iv) feels at home in the world; (v) is a discrete entity in the world. Alienation is a condition wherein a person is unable to maintain a sense of identity, hence there is a breakdown in that person's ability to function satisfactorily. The person may be self-consciously aware of his identity but need not necessarily be so, that is, he may simply *be* alienated or non-alienated. A breakdown in identity occurs when any one of the above conditions ceases. Any social unit can possess these five characteristics (in which case we may refer to culture instead of identity). When in the collective context any of them are lacking, we refer to an alienating situation. Collectivities can be alienating; only individuals can be alienated.

A state of alienation exists whenever, and insofar as, a sense of identity is lacking; conversely, a state of non-alienation exists to the extent that a sense of identity (even if only tacit) exists. No person is entirely lacking in the above-mentioned conditions (by definition) nor do we possess them absolutely (as will be shown below). Hence, all individuals are partly alienated and partly non-alienated. Alienation is not defined by the fact of a person or group having doubts about its identity, but in being unable to function satisfactorily *as a result* of having these doubts. Alienation, then, does not simply mean having a problem; it means being unable to cope with it, being unable to continue as an ongoing system in terms of one's identity. When referring to 'breakdown' I do not mean only psychotic or neurotic cases (or anomie in relation to society). I mean any instance where the individual feels anything less than totally at ease with himself. He may feel fear, loss, tension, doubt, uncertainty, lack, guilt, resentment, threat or anything else whereby who he is, what he is, what he is doing, where he is going or what is happening to or around him is not clear. There is a state of anxiety between the emergence of a problem and its resolution – in that period the individual is alienated. The moment the problem is overcome and the sense of ease is regained, the individual ceases to be alienated. Yet since living daily life requires the continual solution to problems, life is a constant shift from one problem to another and successfully (or not successfully) overcoming them. Hence being able to overcome them in a way which reinstates stability, control and continuity means being able to sustain an identity, that is, not to be alienated.

When I refer to 'problems' or 'threats' or to identity 'crisis' I do not wish to paint a morbid picture of human life. These words are in a sense more intense or dramatic than they are intended to be, but are nevertheless appropriate. What I mean can be understood from our earlier consideration that the basic aim of all human activity is the perpetuation and development of the individual's identity. Conversely, we say that individuals do not engage in activities which are likely to disrupt their identity. This is not necessarily an egoistic standpoint since the meanings which identity hinges on may include extra-individual or other-worldly values or goals. In fact, all human beings include within the framework of their identity some sets of non-egoistic considerations, yet ultimately these can be 'reduced' to the means an individual 'appropriates' to sustain his identity.

Whatever identity he possesses it is that which sustains him as a human being, hence whatever threatens his identity is a threat to his existence as he has defined it. Our lives consist basically in sustaining our individual existence within a framework of meaning, that is, within a conception of our identity. Most of our activities, and especially our major undertakings in life, are designed to sustain and preferably to expand that identity, or at the very least, not to contradict it. We certainly do not consciously perceive our work, our family relationships, our cultural interests and so on in that light. We act by and large in 'natural' ways, natural because they fit in with our identity, and we stop to reflect on them only when some threat to the ongoingness of the system or the consistency of meaning emerges. Anything, no matter how small, can be a threat; the size of the threat does not depend on its external 'appearance' but on its relation to our ability to overcome it. So we go through daily life doing things which, seen in a wider perspective, are all attempts to sustain our identity. Each attempt is thus a problem and each problem is a threat unless it is solved. Each of our daily tasks, no matter how small, is part of our need to sustain our identity, and each is in its own right a problem and a threat.

We do not perceive most of them as a threat since we have learnt to cope with daily life; we manage to move from problem to problem and threat to threat in instinctive or habitual ways, or simply through rationally assessing how best to cope with the task at hand, which then comes to be seen as small and easily manageable. So in terms of identity every act is a matter of sustaining or at least not contradicting our identity. For this reason we have argued that alienation is not a matter of having problems, although it is that originally, but of the ability or otherwise to overcome them. Problems are endemic to daily life. We invariably move rapidly from problem to solution but between the two there is a state of tension, no matter how infinitesimal, which is the condition of alienation. We have learnt to accept such tension and not to feel over-concerned with it, which is why it might not even appear to exist. Nevertheless, it does exist, in however small a scale, at any particular time. From time to time the scale may be very much greater and the problem, with its concomitant threat, may now consciously be perceived as such. We may say that since normal daily life has a built-in tension, the need to redress this tension, that is, to satisfy our identity needs, is what motivates our activities. The 'normal' person then is not one who does not have problems but one who has learnt to cope adequately with them, that is, can sustain an identity with only minimum alienation.

The structure of identity

We need now to distinguish between two levels of personal identity. They are closely related in that being co-existent in the same individual one supports or threatens the other, but they can be analytically separated. It is important to do so, since the form taken at one level does not necessitate, within limits, the form taken at the other.

The first level of identity is related to answering questions like 'who am I, what am I, what is my purpose?' At the second level one answers questions such as 'what kind of person am I, how do I relate to other people, what are my likes and dislikes?' The first level (the *societal* level) refers then to broader and possibly more stable issues; it seeks to locate the individual at a generalized level in relation to his society and to determine what his overall values and goals are. The second level (the *private* level, even though it has societal referents) refers to his personal traits, his manner of conducting daily living, his attitude to others, his reactions to daily situations. We can say that the societal level refers to social roles and extra-individual values (in that they are seen to have a transcendent nature) while the private level consists of personality traits and personal values.

The two levels together make up an individual's identity. It is important to distinguish between them. They obviously overlap considerably and in daily life we seldom stop to differentiate between them or even to reflect on them at all. They also stem from each other to a large extent, *although not necessarily*. The individual must find some congruity within and between the two, but they can conflict. For example, one may wish to relate to others in a certain way but cannot do so because one's public role does not allow it. (I may as a father wish to respond to my child's behaviour in certain ways, but cannot do so because fathers 'aren't supposed to act that way'.) Or there might be conflict within any level (between, say, one's ethical beliefs and the demands of one's public role). In both cases a crisis of identity emerges, that is, there is alienation.

To some extent we all live with these contradictions since they are inevitable: were we to attempt to be consistent in every single matter, that is, to try to align perfectly our societal and private levels of identity, the task would undoubtedly prove to be beyond most people's reach. The attempt to attain a 'perfect' identity would lead to more rather than less identity crisis. Conflict between the two levels of identity means tension, hence alienation; yet to resolve the tension absolutely would require a degree of consistency which would be socially and psychologically impossible to sustain, and hence would also create alienation. So we once again conclude that alienation is endemic to human existence.

A second reason to distinguish the two levels of identity is that while the societal level is possibly more stable and more rationalistic (in that society may reflect on and articulate the nature of public roles, values, social goals), the private level is more concerned with daily interactions, personal reactions, one's ability to handle situations, one's attitude to others and so on. This is a much less predictable level of existence. At this level there is never complete stability. We are constantly faced with fear, anxiety, tension, disappointment (but note, as earlier, that we see these conditions as built in to daily life, hence hardly perceive them in such grave terms). This was one reason for postulating a state of chronic alienation. At times too we question the societal level consciously and directly. In any event, there is in our lives a permanent degree of identity crisis, therefore alienation is universal.

One significant conclusion here must be that no amount of social reconstruction is capable of removing alienation. The only question in terms of social policy is whether there will be more or less of it, whether there are aspects of society which generate greater or lesser degrees of alienation and whether – given the ontological nature of alienation – society is willing or able to minimize it.

Identity and society

One problem for individuals is that they are not entirely free to 'choose' their identity (or conversely to decide what is problematic or not). Our 'self'-definitions are to a large extent made for us by society, and individuals who challenge the definitions of what is normal, i.e. what one's identity 'should' consist of, are considered deviant, abnormal, insane, rebellious and so on. The same applies to social groups who choose identities other than those given by society. To define or choose an identity means to seek to overcome alienation. Now, in all societies it is perfectly legitimate to overcome alienation, only some ways are more legitimate than others. So groups may coalesce in a number of individuals seeking personal identity through criteria other than the accepted ones, or through proposing different criteria for society as a whole (in which case they may exist as a group in order to change society as a whole or may be satisfied with withdrawing from it and existing independently). These groups too are considered deviant, etc.

In terms of alienation the point I wish to make is that individuals who accept the criteria of identity as provided by society, *and* manage to continue existing as an ongoing system within the confines of those criteria, are not alienated. *Equally*, those who reject the socially given criteria but nevertheless continue as an ongoing system through having found what is for themselves an adequate alternative identity – these people too are not alienated. The alienated ones are those who accept the given criteria but cannot internalize them to the point of continued smooth functioning (e.g. they accept in principle the virtues of communality but in practice find it goes against their temperament), or who reject them but cannot find a substitute (hence also fail to function adequately), or are thwarted by society from access to the means of attaining the accepted identity.[3]

If a person functions continuously with a stable identity, *for whatever reason*, then he is not alienated. If his identity breaks down, *for whatever reason*, then he is alienated. What the individual must do, or what qualities he must possess in order not to break down, is decidedly not a matter of abstract definition: the permutations are potentially endless (we shall return to this later). The criterion for a successful identity is whether it allows for the system to be ongoing, and whether it will be ongoing depends on both the inner logic and the operational efficiency of the elements which constitute an identity (and not, as we have said before, whether the identity conforms to an a priori essence).

Clearly our identities are shaped and limited by their relation to other identities. In order for system A to operate as a system, it needs to make adjustments to systems B, C, D . . . etc. The ability to adjust to the demands made by others in the operation of their systems – the expression of their identities – is part of the condition of non-alienation. But I would like to emphasize that one's identity is not limited by others simply for pragmatic reasons. More important is the fact that to a very large extent we look to others in order to 'decide' what identity to adopt. In having identity problems we do not opt for particular solutions simply because functionally we are limited in our choice (important as that may be) but because in the totality of possibilities open to us we need guidance, and it is in the ways which others have already chosen to act that we seek such guidance. Even within the range of options open to us there is much flexibility and we have little idea in advance as to how to act. We rely on the behaviour of others – just as they rely on us – to guide us. If we had to choose entirely of our own accord how to handle every situation, we would no doubt be overcome by uncertainty and even fear. Having precedent and example to go by helps us overcome this. Hence we are not simply 'forced' to act in certain ways in order to prevent chaos or in order to show consideration and tolerance. We choose to act in ways consistent with the behaviour of others in order simply to provide ourselves with some consistent guidelines *for the sake of having guidelines*. In short, I make my actions consistent with those of others *not so much because I fear chaos in society but rather because I fear chaos in myself.*

This helps to explain the phenomenon of reification. We all exist in a state of uncertainty as to how to behave. Just as I look to others, so they look to me for guidance. Implicitly we realize that this guidance is rooted in and based on human weakness and dependence and on a man-made consensus. This makes the consensus highly vulnerable, which is the root of the uncertainty surrounding it. This uncertainty is largely overcome by assuming that the ways we have chosen to behave are pre-given, since pre-givenness makes these ways more stable and more possessive of authority than ways which have developed simply by groping, testing, trying, accommodation, adjustment or chance (which is *in fact* what happened). Put otherwise, it is not enough that there simply be order (integration, regularization, control) in the sense of having a number of elements which operate together success-fully. The expression of order must be legitimated – and this is the function of meaning or ideology. The origins or basis of order must seem to us to be natural, inevitable, objectively necessary. If not, we would constantly be questioning, doubting and hesi-tating. This would have the dual effect of imposing on us great psychological strain and an inability to act with minimal efficiency. By reifying meaning we overcome this problem, even though there is no inherent reason to construct order one way or another.

We have mentioned people who withdraw from society but we are mainly concerned with those who are involved in their soci-eties, that is, who seek to maintain their identity through relating to others, and in conventional society. They seek to *identify* with their societies since through this they strengthen their *identity*. We have seen that identification with others means to find, develop and express one's identity. The way this is done is crucial to the question of alienation. There are two levels of analysis here, which parallel our concepts of private and societal identity.

The individual has needs which are of a private nature, that is, they focus on his body (though not only in a biological sense); he also has needs which he sees in a more transcendent manner, i.e. he believes that his identity can only be maintained if the social group of which he is a member lives as a whole according to certain rules or standards or has a certain structure. By his being part of such a structure his identity is maintained or attained. So the individual has private needs and societal needs. Very few individuals are totally oblivious to one or the other. We need certain things 'privately' – sexual gratification, entertainment, affection, material goods, not to mention basics like food and shelter – irrespective of the type of society we live in. Yet we also 'need' to live in a certain type of society. We seldom say: 'As long as I have what I want I couldn't care *at all* what goes on around me.'

Naturally, what type of society we 'need' to live in is considered as pre-given as how we 'need' to talk to our children or seek sexual gratification. Whether we accept these means of need-satisfaction unreflexively or reflexively or whether we create a new society or sub-society in accordance with our perception of what needs to be done, the conclusion is the same from the viewpoint of alienation and identification. We identify with our societies to the extent that they satisfy our needs, and since what our needs are and how they are to be met is part of our identity, identification with our society is basic to our identity.[4]

Commitment

From here it is only a short step to a theory of commitment. Commitment is the conscious, deliberate and voluntary act which leads to identification with one's society. Commitment is therefore the process through which a social identity is established. Conversely, we may say that identification is a state in which the motivations for the act of commitment are implicit and routinized. Commitment is essentially active; identification is passive. In being active, commitment is a creative act designed to avoid alienation and to strengthen one's identity. Identification is a state where, having already established a framework of meanings, we are content to take it for granted, to act in a variety of 'obvious' ways and to behave with a degree of mechanical, unreflective regularity, indeed even to be apathetic to one's meanings and environment.

Commitment is the conscious act of asserting, questioning, revising, reconstructing and creating a universe of meaning. Commitment leads to identification, although the person who identifies with his society need not necessarily have gone through the act of commitment. He may have accepted unquestioningly all the taken-for-granted meanings of his society. Yet even the person who arrives at his identification as a result of commitment needs to be passive and to act unreflectively much of the time. We have already stressed that to sustain an identity requires both activity and passivity, spontaneity and regularity, tension and stability. Individuals could not take the strain of constantly affirming and reaffirming their commitment, since the act of commitment in itself requires questioning and doubting meanings and their concrete expression, and then resolving the tension generated. The individual would never 'get off the ground' as it were. Nor, having affirmed his identity, could he function adequately if he were constantly affirming and reaffirming its validity. A person who needs to do this is one who is basically having identity doubts. The person with a stable identity spends most of his time simply carrying on without reflecting on the nature of his identity – and if that identity is to be stable *that is the way it must be.*

Many persons, though, are not concerned with stability for its own sake: they prefer to go through the process of commitment, since for them this is a creative act through which they reaffirm the old identity or shift into a new one. At a collective level, societies can do the same thing, and in fact each society has members and institutions whose task it is to remind people of their identities; some societies also have people who take it upon themselves to question the basis of that identity or to seek new and more constructive ways of expressing it.

Commitment is not therefore necessarily a conformist or deviant act; it can be either. I can identify passively with my society and then continue that identification through a conscious act of commitment (and indeed there are rituals designed for that very purpose); or I can seek a new social framework for my identity; or I can simply continue passively my whole life without ever stopping to consider the nature of my identity. In any event, commitment and identification are opposites in some respects and in this the latter is necessary to the former. Commitment requires consciousness and emotional energy, but to translate commitment to permanent and stable reality, consciousness and emotional energy must become passive, implicit and taken-for-granted; commitment must become identification.

Identity limits

We need to explain what we mean in arguing that while 'on paper' there are no limits to the ways in which individuals can find their identity, such limits do in fact exist. I cannot state here what, in the totality of the human race, human beings are capable or not capable of doing, tolerating, wanting or believing. The history of the twentieth century has done enough to indicate how injudicious such generalizations will be. But in principle there must be limits to what any *particular* individual can do or tolerate without his identity suffering a severe crisis. So while within humanity as a whole identities may be infinitely varied (some will dispute this) each *individual* can tolerate so much and no more unless he undergoes so thorough a change that his entire past becomes totally and utterly non-existent for him.

The reason is that no individual could establish an identity and at the same time envisage an entirely open and infinitely varied universe. To establish an identity means to close the universe, to define *both* what one is and is not, what one is capable of achieving and incapable of achieving, ready to tolerate morally or unready under any circumstances to tolerate. Having an identity means to create stability and meaning, to define what is problematic and what is not, and how to handle what is problematic. There is no a priori reason for us to argue that there are universal limits to what we are capable of, but for each individual to have an identity he must conceive of such limits. *Identity* means creating a personal universe which is *identifiable*. One finds identity through being able to define for oneself a universe. Through locating oneself within it one identifies one's universe and identifies one's place in it and through thus identifying oneself one finds one's identity. A person who cannot identify himself, who cannot circumscribe the universe and his place within it, cannot have an identity (which is why societies who cannot provide their members with a basis for defining their identities are alienating societies). It follows that for *that particular person* there are limits to the extent to which his identity can be flexible; there are points beyond which he cannot conceive of himself as being otherwise; he cannot act or think beyond them without sabotaging his basic sense of identity.

Alienating societies

Some societies 'tell' their members (or have been so created by their members) that need-satisfaction means helping the society to attain its collective goals. The individual's private level of identity is to be sustained primarily by aligning it fully with the societal level of identity. The individual who does this is not alienated; the individual who refuses, yet finds for himself an alternative sense of identity (which is frequently based on the very act of refusing the demanded identity), is also unalienated. Those who wish to find their identity via conventional society or wish to find an alternative but succeed in neither are alienated.

Conversely, if we go to the other extreme, we have societies which formally or informally minimize their right to dictate to the individual what his needs should be, i.e. they emphasize private gratification to the exclusion of virtually all else. In societies which emphasize private material gratification (as opposed to those which emphasize private gratification in non-material ways), those members who accept that finding an identity means private material gratification *and* succeed in so doing (because they have access to material goods) are unalienated. Those who reject the accepted concept of identity but find an alternative which allows them to be an ongoing system are also unalienated. The alienated are those who, like the alienated in the other example, accept the definition of identity, but through their own inability or because of the impedimenta which society places in their way, cannot attain it, or wish to but cannot find an alternative.

The problem regarding the latter example (the individualistic society) is that the means of attaining gratification are scarce resources (wealth, beauty, fame, occupational success), which means that given this definition of identity, there are many who are going to be excluded from attaining it, hence will be alienated.

This then is one respect in which we can talk of some societies as being more alienating than others. People accept that there are necessary and desirable ways of finding an identity but society does not provide them with sufficient means of doing so. An identity crisis then arises and the individual is alienated. Thus to say that he is alienated from his society means that he cannot identify with his society, that is, he cannot find a sense of identity according to socially acceptable criteria, *nor* can he find an alternative. The individual who withdraws is *estranged* from his society, but if he finds a satisfactory alternative identity he is not alienated.

So a society is *alienating* when any of the following conditions prevail: (i) the society does not provide individuals with sufficient guidelines to establish an identity or guidelines as to how to cope in the world, that is, individuals have to search for an identity from scratch as it were; (ii) the society does provide a definition of identity but blocks members from attaining it; (iii) it does not allow for acceptable alternatives; (iv) and no provision is made for the individuals to attempt to minimize their alienation at the private level. A *non-alienating* society is that which (i) provides its members with clear guidelines to establish an identity; (ii) provides the means of attaining it; (iii) recognizes the inevitability of alienation within the private level of identity; (iv) recognizes the tension inherent in the relation between the societal and private levels of identity; (v) provides socially legitimate (whether formal or informal) means of resolving this tension within conventional society; (vi) is ready to allow its members to find alternative identities. Such a society would have a fairly clear but not rigid definition of its own culture. This definition would be explicit enough to satisfy the above criteria but loose enough to allow for a structure which encompasses a variety of fairly autonomous sub-groups, each of which provides a framework for the expression of different individual identities within the overall meaning of the society's culture.

In the matter of 'alternative identities' I would like to stress that I am not equating alienation with deviance. Any of the above situations can lead to personal deviance, but deviance may be the way the individual *asserts* his identity, in which case he is estranged from his society but in terms of personal identity is not alienated. It is where deviance entails a threat to identity that alienation is involved, but alienation can be the result of conformity as much as of deviance. Hence it is not the specific relationship itself (between the individual and society) which determines whether there is alienation or not. Where individuals identify and actually manage to conform to their society (because in this way they feel they are strengthening their personal identities), then clearly, by definition, they will be less inclined to deviate. But just as deviance does not necessarily mean the individual is alienated, so conformity does not always mean that he is not alienated. Where the individual conforms but finds that his identity is thus threatened, e.g. the approval of others or over-concern with doing 'the right thing' is so fundamental to his sense of identity that any sign of disapproval or even slight failure leads to great self-doubt and lack of confidence (so that the individual is in a chronic state of great tension) – in such circumstances conformity is contributing more to alienation than to non-alienation.

Alienating situations

We have argued that in all societies there are matters of societal identity and private identity. While the two overlap considerably they are also autonomous; they can never be identical and in fact to try to make them identical is likely to increase rather than decrease tension. There is always a degree of incongruity and tension between them, whether this is publicly recognized or not. Every society provides means of overcoming identity crises, both by demanding that the individual submits to the public definition of identity and by providing formal or informal means of defining one's private level of identity. In no society is one level absolutely ignored, nor can it ever be.

Now, in all societies there is a limit to which *society* (institutions) can help the individual in any formal way when alienation at the private level of identity occurs. What is also required is a certain type of response between individuals at precisely those levels where they most basically interact and respond to each other. Each type of social relationship can create its own identity crisis and each type requires its own kind of solution. So where problems arise at the most basic levels of human interaction, which are characterized by spontaneity, intimacy, directness and immediacy, solutions are required similarly characterized by spontaneity, intimacy, directness and immediacy. We shall call these unstructured interactions and unstructured responses or solutions. Just as each society needs (in order to prevent alienation) to provide a definition of public identity and guidelines both for the means of attaining it and for overcoming the tensions which this expectation creates, it also needs guidelines regarding how to interact and how to relate to others in an unstructured way as people sense crises emerging. There is no apparent connection between the solutions to the two levels of identity crisis. Any particular society may be more successful at overcoming crisis at one level rather than the other; some are relatively successful while others are relatively unsuccessful at both levels.

Hence, we are faced with a paradox. Individuals in society need to be given guidelines regarding the attainment of an identity, but if the guidelines are too clear, explicit or rigid then there will be too little room for individual variation, so the private level of identity will be frustrated and alienation increased. On the other hand, if the private level is 'over-respected', this means we will be left too much to grope for ourselves at the societal level and will once again face uncertainty and tension.

Let us put the argument this way. We seek and need both a public and a private level of identity. Yet there is an inherent tension between them since the one is necessary to provide security, the other autonomy. There are points beyond which the individual cannot surrender either without threatening his overall sense of identity, since both security and autonomy are basic to the definition of identity.

Now, let us imagine two extreme kinds of situation. In the first one the public level demanded of us is quite overbearing and we therefore feel there is too little room for private identity. Individuals then need to 'conspire' (not necessarily politically) against their society. Where the level of public identification is very high, whether demanded by others or *even when taken up voluntarily*, the individual seeks a counterbalancing situation. There are two ways he can do this. In one he can indulge in small acts of deviance. These are not simply means of satisfying an objective 'need': even if the need did not exist it would be created *for the very purpose of being deviant* – and this happens even if, and sometimes *because* the individual identifies with his society. It is not so much, if at all, the material object attained through deviance which is significant for the individual, but the act of deviance in itself. To act deviantly in such circumstances is to assert one's individuality, that is, the autonomy of one's identity. One can do so through minor acts of deviance since these do not upset the basic order or meanings of one's society (hence do not threaten our public identity). The unalienated member in such a situation is the one who can live with the tension between the two levels of identity; he satisfactorily expresses both levels of identity as they conflict and even at times *makes* them conflict, yet can keep them basically as a single system. Another way of asserting oneself 'against' society is, ironically, through the aforementioned expressions of warmth, intimacy, spontaneity and immediacy. These are interactions which are beyond the control of institutions since no institutional arrangements, however powerful or progressive, can substitute for them completely. To love one's neighbour is not simply a moral act, however noble. The person with a strong sense of public identity can 'afford' to indulge in positive, unstructured interactions; but he sometimes *needs* to do so in order to sustain and enhance the individuality and autonomy of his identity *vis-à-vis* public institutions.

The question is whether a sufficiently delicate balance is attainable so as to provide clear definitions of identity at both levels, yet still allow for individual variations and alternative definitions. No society, I contend, can find such a perfect balance. Hence there is bound to be friction between the two levels of identity, that is, there is bound to be alienation.

At the other extreme, we may have societies which officially proclaim the values of tolerance, openness and freedom. Yet, while legitimating individuality ('over-respecting' the private level of identity) they are not providing guidelines to the attainment of societal and private identity levels. Confusion arises between tolerating a private identity and helping a person to find one. Tolerance becomes an end in itself and the society fails to see that it needs to help individuals find their identities and *then* to tolerate individual variations. The point is that under free-for-all circumstances individuals do not necessarily feel satisfied. Just as much as they need individuality and 'conspiracy' so do they need a public identity. But society does not help them in this regard (read: they refuse to recognize the possibility of helping themselves). An 'over-open' universe is as much a threat to identity as an 'over-closed' one. Where society can only offer the former, they seek some of the latter and they can do so, once again, in two ways. One is in egoism and a general reaction against warmth, sympathy and 'conspiracy' against society (they have nothing to conspire against), replacing it with conspiracy against each other. Only in this way can they survive, that is, maintain *some* identity, and preserve themselves against total disintegration, total alienation. Having no society to turn to, no transcendental or supraindividual values to hang on to, the individual is left only to his own devices. He thus turns in on himself and by asserting the superiority of his very own existence, defends himself against his own disintegration. The other means is by frantically hanging on to every social fad and transient *Weltanschauung* that appear on the horizon, since these are the only overt sources of conformity, of identification with others or, in our terms, of finding a public level of identity.

Thus we arrive at two seeming paradoxes. The first is that altruism and egoism are not necessarily what they seem to be. Altruism, we now see, is not so much a denial of one's self as an assertion of its right to act independently. In altruism, the self recognizes its right to develop and stabilize an autonomous individual identity. Egoism, on the other hand, far from being a celebration of the ego is in fact a cry for sociality, a recognition of being lost in the wilderness and of the need for others to help one in escaping it, for others to 'be significant'.

The other paradox is that in certain circumstances deviance and conformity may also be their apparent opposites. In the one case, the individual may be deviant precisely *because* he identifies with his society (but still needs to assert his private level of identity);

in the other, the individual seeks to be a conformist precisely *because* he is allowed to be deviant in so many ways and he has nothing clear to conform to, and so he clings to every popular trend and passing morality because only in so doing can he find a public level of identity.

I suggest that modern, industrialized society is largely characterized by the latter situation (conformity as a response to 'overindividualism') and intentional communities by the former (deviance as a balance to strong identification). In both cases the individual, albeit in opposite ways, is trying to de-alienate himself and this he does, not by totally removing the tension between the private and public levels of identity, since this is impossible, but by balancing them and even, if necessary, seeking such tension yet nevertheless living with it constructively.

The implications for intentional communities

How is all this relevant to the persistence of intentional communities? In Part B we develop our empirical arguments, and here we can present only some pointers regarding what I intend those arguments to demonstrate.

Let us use an analogy to illustrate some of our points. One assumes that there is no such thing as a perfect marriage. If partners claim that they 'get on perfectly' one would not only be suspicious but would actually consider it a bad thing. The relationship would most likely be healthiest when the partners are both well-integrated *and* autonomous, and where there is much scope for flexibility. Even if discord arises, they are able to cope with it. The 'ideal marriage' involves mutual commitment and fulfilment, yet it also allows for and indeed encourages individuality and private growth. Under these conditions one assumes that each partner in the ideal marriage will be happy and contented. Equally, though, each is likely to experience personal pain. The ideal partnership is one that recognizes the inevitability of both personal and common pain and can cope with both. Pain, it can be argued, is an essential ingredient of a relationship: what makes the relationship good is the ability to overcome pain constructively and to benefit from the experience. More generally, the good relationship is one where the relationship is itself strong and creative and where each partner feels personal growth within and as a result of the relationship. This is not a question of submerging oneself totally in the relationship and giving oneself up to it totally: on the contrary, the strength of the relationship lies in it providing the partners with a feeling that as a result of the relationship their personal autonomy *grows*.

So it is with intentional communities.[5] They persist where social meanings and social practices are well-integrated but still respect the need for personal autonomy and even promote it. In this way individuals are able to feel a close identification with, and commitment to, their communities: on the one hand, they perceive the community as providing a meaningful ideological and social framework, while on the other, they perceive that they have scope for individuality. The universe is, for them, neither over-open nor over-closed. (This is not an objective fact: it is the member's implicit understanding and perception which counts, whatever outsiders may believe.) This does not mean that crises do not arise between the individual and the community. On the contrary, such crises are anticipated and can even be healthy. The social system, both in its organizational workings and its informal structures, recognizes and copes with 'the pain of communal life'. It works better for some than for others: the point is that in the communities we have been discussing it works sufficiently well to ensure persistence.

We are certainly not claiming that the communities we are studying are non-alienating societies. By definition there is no such thing. Rather, our communities have recognized that the attempt to create a perfect society is likely to produce more rather than less alienation and to threaten rather than sustain viability. We argue that they understand, albeit implicitly, the problems involved in alienation and have managed to sustain a balance between alienation and non-alienation. This means in practice that they recognize the two levels of identity, the public and the private. They recognize that *both* need to be satisfied, and that to satisfy the public level at the expense of the private is dangerous to commitment and identification, while to satisfy the private level at the expense of the public is detrimental to community solidarity and viability and to ideological consistency. They also recognize that the two levels can conflict, that the individual tends sometimes to assert his private level of identity against the public level, and that within limits such conflict is not harmful to the community and is therefore to be ignored (although it must be clear that the limits are relative to each community).

The communities have also recognized that the individual's identity consists (as we have said) of cognitive, biological, affective and interpersonal factors and that *all* of these need to be satisfied for identification to be sustained over any lengthy period of time. To put it 'formula-like': in a total community you need to satisfy a person's total identity, in all its dimensions and ramifications. To put it otherwise, it is not enough to exhort a person to strive for communal-moral goals, you need to satisfy his need, as he defines it, for food, friends and work-satisfaction too.

Regarding identification and commitment we will also argue that the communities are, by and large, satisfied with the need for identification. They recognize that too much emphasis on active and conscious commitment can be negative regarding both organizational efficiency and the individual's psychological threshold. We should also note that neither the individual's identity nor the community's culture are regarded as fixed, even though the underlying principles and their parameters are. Individual identity and community culture are not so much a given fact as a constantly emerging process – each in its own right and with each shaping, defining and reflecting the other, and all this within the aforementioned parameters.

We have a situation, then, characterized by balance and flexibility. The two go hand in hand since to attain balance, flexibility is necessary. This applies to the relationship between order and meaning (defined above), alienation and non-alienation, commitment and identification, public identity and private identity, the needs of the community and those of the individual. One of the key factors explaining the persistence of our communities is that they have accepted (sometimes consciously, sometimes implicitly and sometimes while proclaiming the very opposite) the need for such balance. They have 'granted' just enough autonomy to each side of the dyad, yet have ensured too that they are sufficiently integrated, to ensure stability and satisfaction, change and continuity. These, we should note, have also been achieved by taking into account both the basic functional requirements for viability and the 'demands' of the ideology, and (once again) by balancing the two. So it is to the concept of ideology we now turn.

Chapter 3
A theory of ideology

The structure of ideological systems

Definitions of ideology are notoriously varied, so I have developed a scheme which is relevant to our present purposes. It is a working model (sometimes known in sociological jargon as an 'ideal-type').

Ideologies, when fully comprehensive and fully explicit, contain two levels of thought, the one *cosmological*, the other *operational*. Each level is further sub-divided – the cosmological into *ultimate facts* and *ultimate goals*, the operational into *norms* and *institutions*.

Norms are descriptions of what *kinds* of acts or what *general* conditions of society will facilitate achievement of the ultimate goals, *plus* the prescription to act accordingly (or to desist from certain classes of action). There may be *primary norms*, i.e. those classes of action or general conditions which lead *directly* to the ultimate goals, and *secondary norms*, i.e. those which facilitate the primary norms. Thus norms are *instrumental*, i.e. they are or demand acts and conditions which are good by virtue of their promotion of higher goals.

Institutions are classifiable into *primary institutions*, i.e. the concrete forms of social organization or the concrete ways of acting which facilitate the norms, and *secondary institutions* – the gamut of rewards, sanctions or socialization processes concerned with ensuring that the other levels are accepted by members of society and that the primary institutions operate successfully. In other words, an ideology is concomitantly a perception of reality, an evaluation of it, a prescription for relating to it in a particular way, an exhortation to act accordingly and a plan for actually doing so.

In the 'complete' ideology the various elements exist as a hierarchy, i.e. logically they are legitimated in sequence. So, to give limited examples: given an irrevocable, irreducible and indisputable *fact* (God), men have certain *goals* which, when attained, are themselves *final* (salvation); there are definite ways (*norms*) which lead to this directly (prayer and the ways of Jesus), for which purpose certain forms of organization (*institutions*) are instrumentally appropriate (the Church, concrete forms of sharing, an authority system based on age, sex and religious status, pacifism, etc.). Similarly: it is a *fundamental fact* of human existence that all men are intrinsically good and have many capacities; to express one's intrinsic goodness and one's inherent capacities are the *highest goals* men can aspire to; to do all this they need *norms* such as collective living, equality, democracy, collective responsibility; and these are attained by having social practices (*institutions*) like the general meeting, budgets, occupational variety, etc. Finally: it is a *basic fact* that individuals require emotional health; their *chief aim* in life should be to attain personal growth and self-awareness; this can only be done if our lives are governed by *norms* such as open communication, honesty, caring and respect for others; one way of achieving this is by establishing certain institutions, e.g. small groups in the environment living a quasi-communal life-style.

This description of ideology is therefore meant to cover the legitimation of social institutions, *whether these be concrete or projected*. In both cases ideology is *prescriptive*, which could mean either that things should be as they are or should be otherwise.

Legitimation

An ideology, while existing conceptually in a logical hierarchy, may develop in a very different manner. In its logical form each element of the complete ideology is legitimated by the next higher element in the hierarchy, leading back to the first principle (the ultimate fact). In practice, however, two things may happen:

(1)   There is not always a leading back to first principles, so that each level may become an end in itself, the 'legitimator' in its own right of what comes below it – indeed the 'lowest' level (social practices), which logically is totally contingent

on the three 'higher' levels, may well be seen as an end in itself (because living the daily life of the institutions may be intrinsically satisfying).

(2) Legitimation of one level may not necessarily be derived from the next higher level, but directly from *any* other level (so that, for example, prayer can be seen as a means of communicating with God yet having nothing to do with salvation).

In short, all this means that any aspect of ideology may be, in the eyes of its adherents, self-legitimating, or if not self-legitimating, legitimated in a whole variety of ways within the conceptual framework presented.

A further point regarding the loose structure of an ideology is that whereas conceptually it could and should cover every aspect of social life without exception, in practice of course it never does, i.e. it considers certain activities 'ideologically neutral'; alternatively, we may say that there is a range of activities which are *social* but not *social-systemic*, that is, not relevant to the needs of the system, these needs being defined by the ideology itself.

So far we have considered ideologies in their logical structure and their comprehensiveness. We should also comment on their explicitness. Clearly, each level of ideology, whether its status is that of means or end or both, may be articulated with varying degrees of explicitness. It seems equally clear that the higher the level, in particular that of ultimate goals, the greater the degree of vagueness possible. The lowest level, that of institutions, is defined in operational terms, hence explicitness is necessary here, although this does not preclude flexibility. Norms are classes of action and general conditions of society with concomitant obligations. So, as in our examples, prayer or the idea of equality or honest communication is defined not so much in concrete terms but as *general guidelines* to direct the institutions in a way consistent with the desired ends. Yet the ends themselves are rather vague. Salvation, self-realization or personal growth are so generalized as to be open to any number of interpretations. It may happen that they are given a seemingly precise definition in the sense that if a person or group acts in the specific ways prescribed by the institutions and their covering norms he or they will have achieved their goal by definition – but the goal in itself is usually ill-defined. Ultimate facts, for their part, are in a sense precise (God exists, people are good) but what that fact *substantively* consists of is highly generalized or vague. There is one implication to this which is important to our overall discussion – that the adherence to ultimate facts and ultimate goals may be total and uncompromising, yet still be subject to a wide variety of interpretations, a fact which obviously has ramifications all down the hierarchy.

The tension between ideology and reality

However much a society may wish its ideology to be all-embracing and explicit, and to make provision for change in an orderly, pre-defined way, there is inevitably going to be tension between actual social processes and personal behaviour on the one hand, and what the ideology says should be happening on the other. There are several reasons for this.

(a) We suggested earlier that individual and social systems require order, stability, conformity, etc. *and* their opposites. This means that social interactions and social change are, up to a point, going to be unstable and unpredictable, hence beyond the 'control' of the ideology.

(b) No society, even the most 'heavily ideological', can prescribe how to conduct every detail of life, including even those aspects most relevant to ideological integration. Trying to do this would prevent adaptation to external influences on the society. We recall too from our discussion of alienation that there is an inherent tension between our private and public identities. In conducting daily life, there is an element, no matter how small, of individual discretion, independence of decision and freedom of action. We noted that whether this is officially accepted or not, individuals seek a degree of autonomy. It seems inevitable then that heterogeneity in actions and attitudes, including those most directly related to 'ideological integration' will occur. Subsequently, strain will arise among these actions and attitudes themselves, and between the actions and attitudes on the one hand and the prescribed norms and institutions on the other.

(c) Societies cannot attempt to go beyond the point where integration becomes over-integration, i.e. of attempting to control and systematize every activity, since neither the personality nor the social system could tolerate it. So in practice society has to recognize that its ideology – the principles on which order and integration are built – must be limited. It has to define those aspects of social life which need specifically to be ordered, i.e. to state explicitly which aspects of social life are to be integrated around which principles. In so doing it is in effect also defining those aspects of life not relevant to the ideology, so that if they are not actually inimical to the integrating processes and principles, they are legitimate. Yet it may also happen in fact that these 'neutral' activities interact with the 'relevant' activities and thus turn out to be not so neutral after all. I am not claiming that all social activities are interlinked, only that some are linked by ideological prescription, others not, and that even the latter may affect the former willy-nilly. The point is that because of the necessity to 'allow' activities beyond the ideological sphere, that sphere must itself be affected by them.

(d) A further reason for tension lies in an earlier consideration as to why ideologies are embraced in the first place. We have seen that there is a dialectical relationship between ideology on the one hand and experience and reality on the other. The two develop around each other, but experience, needs and circumstances often change in ways not reducible to or envisaged by the ideology. Invariably the ideology refers to a limited and specific set of needs and circumstances. The ideology cannot envisage all possible circumstances (nor indeed should it if there is to be adaptability). Hence the inevitability of social structures and their ideological underpinnings slipping apart. (The fact of ideologies meeting only a specific set of needs is particularly relevant in intentional communities as far as younger generations are concerned.) The putative logical relationship between the elements of the ideology is more a reflection of need than an unarguable deduction. This 'logic' is *in fact* only an assumption rooted in the experiences, life-situation, perceptions and personality of the believer. To others the connection may be nonexistent, since their experiences, etc. may have been considerably different. So the plausibility of these logical connections is derived mostly from its *appropriateness* in a particular psychological and social context, and where the latter changes so must the former.

(e) In all societies there are numerous practical problems vitiating goal-attainment. Economic needs, the degree of self-sufficiency, external hostility, organizational needs, problems of recruitment, demographic needs, relationship with wider social systems – these are some of the objective problems and conditions of existence which societies have to come to terms with in order to survive. It follows that the ways in which this is done may not always be compatible with the prescribed norms and institutions of the ideology. At any rate, even where institutions operate in a way consistent with the ideology, they may have unintended consequences which contradict the goals the institutions were intended to serve. In a word, once the system is operating some needs are determined by choice, as it were, and others by 'the nature of things', and the ways of meeting both simultaneously do not always coincide.

(f) Finally, in all societies, we have already said, there must be some relation between ideology and experienced reality – ideology must explain and 'organize' reality and 'be organized' by reality. In all societies, including intentional communities, this is at least in part an institutionalized process and is left in the hands of particular members of society for organizational reasons. Yet, as we have seen, everyone is free up to a point to evaluate and control reality, and how the official interpreters of reality, ideology and their relationship do their job may not coincide with the way others are interpreting the world. With various conclusions being reached by different groups, tension could arise between the official ideology and social reality.

Ideological change in intentional communities

While there is an inherent tension between a society's ideology and actual social processes, and while such tension is up to a point useful, it cannot become too great else the society will be unable to meet its basic necessities. It will become an alienating society and, in the case of intentional communities, it (the society) will lose its very purpose for existing. It follows that there must be considerable compromise and mutual influence between the pure and abstract prescriptions of the ideology and the business of organizing a society. We have said that there is no a priori way for a society to be organized: our ideology tells us what should be done but, equally, what ideology consists of must be influenced by what is operationally possible and psychologically tolerable.

It would appear then that the task of constructing or maintaining a society in accordance with an explicit ideology is indeed formidable. Yet intentional communities do exist, and often persist, and seem to do so apparently in accordance with an ideology. How then is this done?

It seems to me that the nature of ideology is such that a fairly wide range of actual structures is compatible with a fairly explicit ideology. The main reason for this is rooted in the multi-level nature of ideology and the process of legitimation within it. We have noticed that in 'total' ideologies institutions are prescribed in accordance with the 'demands' of the higher levels. It follows that the vaguer the higher levels the more open they are to varied interpretations and applications. This means that different, even conflicting, institutional practices can be legitimated without too much effort. It follows that if there is tension because of apparent departure from the prescribed institutions, changes can be accommodated by pointing out that as long as the actual institutions are compatible with the ultimate ends, they are legitimate. In this way, new processes or a multiplicity of institutions can be accommodated without the trauma associated with ideological failure. Naturally, the vaguer the first principles the easier the accommodation. In short, the nature of ultimate facts and goals is such that they are particularly difficult to define or describe explicitly and this lack of clarity with its consequent ambiguity has a strategic importance in accommodating to social change.

As we have pointed out earlier, ideologies are often not total in that they either do not explicitly contain all the possible levels, or legitimation of one level is sought by 'short-cutting' the 'proper' hierarchy. This too may facilitate accommodation to various or changing practices. Even where there is relative stability or a high degree of consensus, the members of the community, while sharing the ideology overtly, i.e. behaving in similar ways, may do so for very different reasons. Each may legitimate the same institutions by appealing *either* to their intrinsic value, *or* to their compatibility with norms, *or* to their compatibility with ultimate goals, *or* to their compatibility with ultimate fact, *or* to any combination of these. This means that 'operational consensus' may be possible even in a society composed of individuals or groups having somewhat different needs and perceptions. Even in relatively small and homogeneous communities a great variety of needs has to be met and different perceptions of reality must be incorporated in a unitary scheme. The different ways of expressing the ideology and legitimating those expressions serve this purpose.

Yet this may also be a source of tension in intentional communities. Change in an institution is justified in terms of the source of legitimation of that institution. So, if an institution is legitimated in its own right by the members of one sub-group, their attitude to changing it will be very different to the attitude of those who see it as only a means to a higher end and accept that other institutions could do the job equally well, since for them it is only the ultimate end that counts. The absence of higher levels of ideology, at least in explicit form, could have the same consequences. On the one hand, where institutions are legitimated simply because 'the way they are is the way they should be', it is difficult to legitimate changes in them. On the other hand, by leaving the first principles so vague as to be virtually meaningless, or by not enunciating them at all, one can invoke them when needed and in whatever way needed to justify change. It should be clear then that the variety of ways of legitimating institutions in a society can be a source of preserving the status quo and of justifying change in ideological terms; it can also help to satisfy the need for diversity within a single framework.

We should also note that the ideology is never so perfectly structured or so logically developed that it becomes a perfectly consistent system. On the contrary, it may well contain elements which contradict each other. This is one reason for leaving some parts of the ideology vague and ill-defined. Too much explicitness can lead to inability to adapt to changing circumstances, as we have already seen, and to the possibility of inherent contradictions coming out into the open.

I wish to emphasize that the entire ideological 'superstructure' of intentional communities is not merely a rationalization of actual social processes. Nor is the actual structure simply the practical application of a well thought-out and preconceived ideological system. This should be clear from our earlier discussion on meaning and identity and of the relationship between ideology and social process. In many cases the ideology and actual institutions work so closely together in daily life that members may be largely unconscious of the former. Neither is a rationalization of the other. Both may seem to members to be simple facts of daily life. It is then possible that over a lengthy period of time all the minor and ad hoc manoeuvrings a society engages in may lead to an ideology and actual social structure somewhat different from that with which the community began or intended.[1] Many changes are not conscious, just as the tenets of the ideology are often not conscious. Frequently both are the consequence of cumulative changes in attitude, circumstance and practices: each change may in itself be small and even unnoticed, but the final effect may be quite radical.

We should note that members of intentional communities do not necessarily see the ideology in the way I have presented: on the contrary, they may well believe the opposite to be true and this is significant to the question of commitment (we will discuss this further in our comments to Chapter 5).

All this serves to clarify the crucial dilemma (even if only implicit in members' minds) facing intentional communities, namely, the need to formulate and maintain an explicit and comprehensive ideology so as to ensure that the prescribed institutions are properly legitimated and 'realizable', with the equal need to recognize that such perfection is impossible and that change is inevitable. As we have tried to show, the structure of ideology with its diverse ways of legitimating institutions does make the resolution of this dilemma possible.

We can now turn to a detailed description and analysis of intentional communities. Our theoretical ideas on alienation and ideology can be applied (together with other considerations) to explain their nature and persistence.

Part B

Chapter 4
Origins and development

Struggle against the odds: the development of Hutterite life

The Reformation had its origins in complex circumstances. While the motives of the Reformers were ostensibly and primarily religious, their activities and proposals could clearly not be limited to theological dispute.

The Protestants called for a return to the origins of Christianity and invoked the idea of man's fundamental sinfulness. Yet the fact that ideological revolt itself was now legitimate, together with one of its key concepts, namely 'justification by faith' (i.e. that the basis of religious belief was not membership of the Church per se, but having the right personal relationship with God), meant that the beliefs held by the Reformers could themselves be questioned. Certain groups began to take the principles and aims of the Reformers to extreme conclusions. They expressed these in a variety of political, social and religious beliefs and practices. This is known as the Radical Reformation, consisting chiefly of three broad groupings: the Maccabeans, the Spiritualists or Mystics, and (the largest grouping) the Anabaptists. The Radicals all rejected the links Luther, Calvin and Zwingli made between Church and state; they demanded a return to the apostolic age (the days of the early Church), a religion based on inward authority and not on external coercion, no compromises with Rome, and the radical reorganization of social life. The Maccabeans expressed this by turning to military activity and emphasized the imminent End of Days; the Mystics, for their part, engaged in theological speculation and attempted to divorce man from society and history.

The Anabaptists rejected both these positions. There were six main Anabaptist groups. They were linked by the following ideas: adult baptism, rejection of the unity of Church and state, a literal acceptance of the New Testament, discipleship, pacifism, excommunication, non-swearing of oaths, freedom of conscience (for the community, not for the individual in it), no theocracy, and glorification of the simple person leading a simple life.

Among the Anabaptists was one group, the Hutterites. The Catholic and Protestant authorities and the Hapsburg monarchy all attempted to suppress the Anabaptists on both doctrinal and political grounds. A group led by Balthasar Hubmaier took refuge at Nikolsburg in Moravia. After his execution (1528) the group was led by Jakob Wiedemann to Austerlitz. On the way they began to practise community of goods and this is regarded by the Hutterites as their founding. Meanwhile Jakob Hutter became leader of a South Tyrolean group. When they too faced persecution Hutter joined the Austerlitz group.

Power struggles developed between Hutter and Wiedemann. Eventually Hutter triumphed (1533) and with great ability succeeded in organizing the group into a cohesive, disciplined and devoted community. These qualities served them well in the years to come. At first great persecution followed them and the Brethren were required to live in forests and caves. Nevertheless, they did much successful missionary work and, especially through the writings of Ridemann, developed a more articulate doctrine.

In the 1540s the Moravian lords were having their own troubles with the Vienna monarchy. They saw in the Hutterites a means both of showing their political independence and of improving their own economic status (owing to the Brethren's great skill and efficiency as artisans). So they granted refuge to the Hutterites who began to set up communities in Moravia called Bruderhofe. In 1548, however, the Emperor Ferdinand pressed hard enough for the lords to expel them, although they soon returned. This heralded their 'Golden Age' (1553–92). Conversion proceeded (but began to dwindle towards the end of the century), economic stability was strengthened, the forms of social organization crystallized and religious doctrine became increasingly articulated. At the height of this period they had forty to fifty communities numbering 12,000 to 20,000 souls.[1]

The Hutterites differed from the other Anabaptist groups in the extremity of their views. The other groups were prepared to compromise on some principles, the Hutterites on virtually none. The Brethren were also the only ones to establish total communities. At times the Anabaptist groups helped each other; at other times hostility was intense. What was the appeal of the Anabaptists in general and of the Hutterites in particular? They had greater success in areas of religious diversity and in areas where persecution was milder. They could offer economic security at a time of hardship and especially in areas where inheritance laws left people with little land. Their ideas on simplicity, pacifism and rejection of the state were appealing: to the converts war, property and the state helped the rich and powerful only. Hutterite communities provided material security – but for this reason preachers (fearing that people might join for that end more than for doctrinal reasons) often discouraged converts and could afford to accept only the most dedicated. Naturally their economic success made it easier for the Hutterites to send out missionaries; it also helped the Brethren to save for future migrations. We should also note that the sixteenth century was a highly religious age. In rejecting one system of belief people were not rejecting belief altogether; on the contrary, many sought an alternative which was intense and binding and held hope for the future.

Around the beginning of the seventeenth century the position of the lords *vis-à-vis* the Emperor was weakening: affluence had led to a degree of internal decline among the Brethren themselves; the Turkish invasion of the Empire (1593) and the Hutterite refusal to be conscripted seriously jeopardized their position; and in 1618 the outbreak of the Thirty Years War further eroded their position (their patrons backed the wrong side) leading to their expulsion from Moravia (1621–2).

The Hutterites began migrating eastwards and southwards, finding refuge in (what is now) Hungary and Romania. They suffered decline and even abandoned communal living (1686); but at other times strong leaders emerged to revitalize discipline and adherence to faith and the prescribed social forms. Towards the end of the eighteenth century they began to settle on estates in Russia where the lords once again exchanged freedom of conscience (pacifism, autonomous education) for economic returns. Despite political security and freedom from conscription (or perhaps because of them), internal decline set in and in 1820 communal living was again abandoned. In the 1840s and 1850s attempts were made to resuscitate it and different leaders appeared around whom communality was re-established. Three such groups (named after leaders) emerged called Leute (people) and persist to this day. They are called the Schmiedeleut, the Dariusleut and the Lehrerleut respectively. At the beginning of the 1870s conscription was imposed, so the Hutterites migrated to America where they settled primarily in South Dakota (from 1874). They were helped at this stage by other groups of Anabaptist origins, e.g. the Rappites and Mennonites. Some abandoned communalism and joined the Mennonites.

At the turn of the century fear of conscription made them investigate the possibility of refuge in Canada, where the federal government was interested in opening up the Prairies, and would grant them freedom of conscience. Nothing came of it then but in the First World War they were persecuted for being pacifists (among other things) and took advantage of the earlier Canadian offer. As the pacifism issue receded in importance and the Hutterites themselves began to seek compromise solutions, some were able to return to the USA but most stayed on in Canada. They are now concentrated in Alberta, Manitoba and Saskatchewan. While at first largely welcomed (because they helped open up the Prairies), attitudes towards them shifted here too and various accusations, resentments and fears were expressed by the surrounding population: this led to restrictions on land acquisition and expansion. Their total rejection of the state has also had to be compromised, e.g. regarding their desire for autonomous education. Signs are now that there is a move towards greater local tolerance of the Hutterites through recognition of their economic success and of their contribution to slowing down the depopulation of rural areas; there has also been increasing sensitivity towards civil liberties. This also stems partly from the Hutterites' readiness to adjust to prevailing needs and thought patterns.

In 1981 the Hutterites numbered 31,200 souls in 230 colonies.[2] A colony consists of up to 150–170 souls. On average, Hutterites have over ten children per completed family, the highest birth rate in the world. The rate of natural increase is 41.5 per 1,000 head of population: this means that the population doubles every sixteen to eighteen years.[3] Wives are taken from other colonies, usually from the same Leut, and join their husband's colony. A colony is headed by a preacher who is appointed through election and by lot (to emphasize that the final choice is God's will). He is elected for life but undergoes a lengthy probation before finally being confirmed in his post. Other senior positions are the *Wirt* or *Haushalter* who is overall treasurer-colony manager. Then there are the various branch managers. The German teacher (see section on education) is also a senior member of the colony. The colony has a Council of Elders, usually men who have retired (officially) from active work (at about 45 years of age). They decide on matters of policy and oversee the community's morality. Important matters are discussed and voted on by the adult male congregation.

There is a strict status hierarchy in the colony – older over younger, male over female, baptized over unbaptized, married over unmarried. Only baptized men can hold responsible positions for the colony as a whole. Women's work is confined to their own or the colony's domestic duties (cooking, child care). The head cook is usually the head woman of the colony. The chief seamstress is also an important figure. The women sometimes do gardening or painting but always under male supervision.

The colony economy is strictly agricultural. It maintains its own agricultural services and tries to be self-sufficient (carpentry, welding, building). Their agriculture is mixed and most men can work in a number of places.

When a colony reaches 150 to 170 members it splits in two. Already land has been acquired and buildings set up for a new colony – if possible, nearby. The colony is then divided into two lists; these are equal numerically and in terms of age, sex, occupation and personal compatibility. The night before the split the entire colony packs its bags. The following day the lists are drawn by lot because the decision must be in the hands of God. The list that is drawn gets on the lorries and goes; the others unpack their bags and continue on the same colony.

The colony is part of a network called a Leut (people). The Hutterites have three Leute. There are few formal links between them. Each Leut has its own Council of Elders whose task it is to decide on policy for the Leut as a whole (ranging from dress style to relations with the government) and to keep an eye on all the colonies in their jurisdiction.

The need for ideology: the Kibbutz movement's growth

Towards the end of the last century the Jews of eastern and central Europe faced certain threats to their existence. In eastern Europe persecution was on the upsurge, culminating in pogroms and actual plans for extermination. In central and western Europe the very opposite process, namely assimilation, equally threatened the continued existence of the Jews. Various responses emerged to these situations, one of which, influenced by political trends among European countries, was Jewish political nationalism.

The idea of an independent Jewish state emerged, the corollary to which was the need for Jews to migrate to Palestine, settle the land, build cities and create their own political-economic institutions. Only a very small proportion of Jews actually executed these plans and among them were the founders of the Kibbutz movement.

Settlement on the land had begun systematically during the first 'wave of settlement' (*Aliyah*), from the early 1880s until about 1904. The Second Aliyah (1904–14) saw a new generation who had been influenced in eastern Europe by socialist ideas and had rejected the colonial nature of the earlier settlement. At first these immigrants worked individually but, having had little agricultural or manual experience, found it difficult to find work, especially since there was a labour surplus and contractors preferred cheaper Arab labour. Illness, loneliness and poverty generated disillusionment and frustration. Gradually, the immigrants began to form small groups and contracted themselves out as such, thus giving themselves as a group greater bargaining power than as individuals, while personally they now had greater material and psychological security.

Primarily they wanted to settle the land, albeit in non-colonial fashion. Labour on the land, and Jewish self-labour at that, became cardinal principles of faith. They gained some experience of the contract system but still not enough to convince the appropriate Jewish authorities to hand over tracts of land to them. Eventually the authorities, whose aim was to settle the land quickly, efficiently and profitably, changed their attitude somewhat. A group of women working at Sedjera were given some land to work autonomously – and showed a profit. At the same time the dominant agricultural system – experimental farms with hired Jewish labour – was not proving effective. Some of the immigrants, particularly a group from a town in the Ukraine called Romni, revolted against this system and demanded their own land. The authorities had little choice and handed a tract at Um Juni on the banks of Lake Tiberias to the Romni group in 1910.

This became Kibbutz Deganya. Earlier attempts (during the First Aliyah) to do the same thing had failed because the settlers had had no backing for it. The official Zionist movement, with its political and economic backing, had not yet been established; there was then no trend towards co-operative ventures; religious groups, who viewed collective agricultural undertakings with great suspicion, were strong enough to upset the plans of the settlers; there was as yet no concept of settling the land or of Jewish labour on it as ends in themselves. Only during the Second Aliyah did these trends develop and only in that context could the Kibbutz movement be founded and have the necessary support and appeal to develop.

Initially the group worked together with a number of others at Um Juni. They were paid individually but pooled everything, including the profits that were eventually shown. The group had little conception of what type of society it wanted. They knew they were rejecting the life-style of the ghetto, the patriarchal family, the hierarchy of status, wealth and learning, the estrangement from life on the land, the narrow religiosity and the intense emotionality of the family. They knew they wanted to be 'natural' people – intimate, close to the land, simple and equal, and that their relations were to be governed by honesty, mutual aid and love. If they rejected the structure of the ghetto, then at least they wanted its communality, intimacy, warmth and intensity – but not in the forms they had grown up in. They knew too that in the long run they wanted a regenerated Jewish people and an independent Jewish state, but precisely what this meant in terms of institutions or political activity was undefined and even seldom contemplated. The initial experience of living on the land, a small undifferentiated group at that, was a source of intrinsic satisfaction.

Gradually, however, basic questions had to be answered. Couples wanted to marry and have children; the Kibbutzim then grew larger; as the number of Kibbutzim grew their relationship to each other and to the wider Jewish community had to be examined; the Jewish authorities had to be influenced regarding Kibbutz interests; from 1919 the British Mandate had to be tolerated, then fought, then ended; the Jewish community had to be developed, immigrants absorbed and defence against Arabs maintained. How was all this to be done?

The first few years were difficult. Inexperience, climatic

conditions, marauders, hostility from Jewish officials and the exig-
encies of the First World War all proved difficult to surmount,
but surmount them they did. The Zionist authorities for many
years had an ambivalent attitude towards the Kibbutzim. They
saw the way of life as infantile: eventually the youngsters would
live 'naturally' in semi-co-operative and more individualistic settlements. They were also wary of their atheism and communism
(which was in some cases Soviet-orientated and was a constant
source of friction within the Kibbutz movement until the 1950s).
There was also a fair amount of opposition to the Kibbutz from
the political labour movements of the time who saw the Kibbutz
as a quasi-mystical flight from reality, whose energies would be
better directed at mobilizing the proletariat into political activity.

The 1920s were a period of great expansion and saw the emergence of various trends among the Kibbutzim. The difficulties of
maintaining a small Kibbutz had encouraged some to develop the
idea of the large Kibbutz, up to as many as 3,000 people (although
it is rare for any to come near this size). The protagonists saw
in the large Kibbutz the source of economic success, individual
development, service to the nation. The protagonists of the small
Kibbutz favoured intimate relations and minimal formalization of
personal relations or social institutions. Another level of division
emerged regarding the wider purpose of the Kibbutzim. Some
saw it as a kind of spiritual élite, educating and leading the people
to socialist values; others saw it as the spearhead of the class
struggle in Palestine; still others (the influential Gedudei Ha-
Avodah, 'Labour Battalions') saw its purpose as service to the
nation (road building, defence, immigrant absorption, etc.), whatever the nation's needs.

So both to protect their own interests and to promote their
various views, the Kibbutzim in the 1920s began to establish
formal links, with three groupings emerging: Hever Hakvutzot,
Hakibbutz Hameuchad, Hakibbutz Haartzi. In the 1930s the
religious Kibbutz movement (Hakibbutz Hadati) was formed,
basing its principles on the socialist-humanist (as opposed to the
socialist-Marxist) principles of the other movements and on
various trends in Jewish tradition. At the same time the formal
institutions of Kibbutz began to emerge, such as systems of
education, consumption, decision-making and allocation of rights
and duties.

Although the Kibbutzim remained only a small proportion of

the Jewish population (a maximum of 7.9 per cent in 1947) their influence began to be felt. Many of the best immigrants went to Kibbutzim because the latter appeared to express the aims of Zionism most dramatically. The continued labour surplus in Kibbutzim, due to lack of land and means of production, meant sending members outside to work, and inevitably some (because of the education and motivation of the Kibbutz members) went into public service – Histadrut (Trade Union), underground defence or political activity. The Kibbutz also played a key role in absorbing immigrants (illegal or otherwise), in defence and in economic development. The Kibbutzim could most easily absorb immigrants, provide defence against Arab attacks, hide arms caches and train underground fighters against the British. The enthusiasm of the Kibbutz members meant they would undertake any task, while the quota system of (legal) immigration meant that it was mainly the most able immigrants who came, and they naturally gravitated to the Kibbutzim. For all these reasons the 1930s and 1940s saw the height of the Kibbutz's status and influence in the community, even though the Kibbutzim felt that they were discriminated against by official institutions. They frequently felt that the capitalist society they were rejecting was ready to ditch them as soon as it was convenient.

With the establishment of the State of Israel in 1948 the Kibbutz's status dropped somewhat. The main tangible goal of the Jewish community had been achieved, and in the Kibbutzim, who had sacrificed so much to this end, tiredness crept in, a certain desire to look after themselves. At the same time various factors militated against the Kibbutz's central role. Defence was now taken over by the army; new immigrants from oriental countries or war-torn Europe did not want to go to the Kibbutz; many of the best people now looked to the state's institutions for personal opportunities. To make matters worse, political splits which had been developing in the 1940s now reached a head, with the largest movement (Meuchad) splitting up, some going to Hakibbutz Haartzi and some to the Hever (renamed Ichud Hakvutzot Vehakibbutzim). Some Kibbutzim even split right down the middle. The image of the Kibbutz hero began to wane drastically.

Ironically, this was in numerical terms the period of greatest expansion of the Kibbutz movement (seventy founded 1947–52). The new state's lands were much larger than originally planned and many groups hitherto unable to settle because of Mandate policy were now needed to settle land, defend the new borders and provide food for the increased population. Hence the 1950s and 1960s saw an expansion in the number of Kibbutzim (despite a net population decline 1952–7), a partial withdrawal from wider Israeli life, a demand for increase in living standards and a further formalization in institutions. Many Kibbutzim faced economic difficulties but economic reorganization – especially the mechanization of agriculture and the introduction of industry – plus help from public authorities helped them overcome this. The period also saw a change in Kibbutzim to greater emphasis on the family and on personal career development. Inevitably, this, together with the economic changes, led to shifts in institutional patterns.

The period preceding the Six Day War (1967) saw the Kibbutzim bear the brunt of enemy attack. Following the war the Kibbutzim began to play a central role in new settlement policies and generally a more outward-looking orientation began to emerge. The Kibbutzim became more involved in politics and in various forms of social work, especially in the immigrant development towns near which many are situated. At the same time there has been a reassessment of the meaning of basic values, and particularly attitudes towards Jewish religion and tradition, although it is still too early to indicate if any radical shifts in policy will come about.

At the end of 1982 there were 264 Kibbutzim with a population of 116,000.[4] Kibbutz size is usually measured by adult membership. The average is 250–300, with a range of about eighty to 1,000. All posts are rotated after anything from one to three years. The chief functionaries of the Kibbutz are the secretary, farm manager, treasurer, work organizer. The Kibbutz has an executive committee consisting of these and non-functionary members. The executive is responsible to the assembly (*Sihat Haverim* or *Asefa*) which meets weekly. The assembly consists of all adult members. It is the highest authority and can overrule any decision made by an office-bearer or committee. It elects committees for specific purposes – health, education, culture, sport, security and so on. The committee's task is to initiate policy in its spheres and to prepare policy discussions for the assembly. Any member can take on any role in the community but certain posts are becoming increasingly specialized. Each Kibbutz belongs to a federation. There are three main federations manned (on a rotary basis) by members of the Kibbutzim. Their task is to provide specialist services, represent the Kibbutz to external authorities, co-ordinate policies and partially to exert economic control.

The Kibbutz economy is both mixed-agricultural and industrial. Each branch consists of a work team with a rotatory leadership. There is much emphasis on occupational training, which includes service work – cooking, laundry, teaching, child care. Services are usually run by women while men gravitate to productive work, even though there is no ideological prescription for this.

Society and mental health: emergence of a mental health organization

We need to understand the development of the Richmond Fellowship against the background of changes that had been taking place in conceptions about and treatment of mental illness and in public attitudes towards it.[5]

The houses of the Richmond Fellowship are both therapeutic communities and halfway houses. These are not the same thing; not all therapeutic communities are halfway houses nor vice versa. There were various processes affecting the development of each and in the case of the Richmond Fellowship they converged, thus creating a climate in which its emergence became possible.

One such development was the advance of psychoanalysis, which liberated mental illness from biological reductionism and claimed that, however irrational a person's behaviour appeared, there was a rational explanation which could be discovered. Some post-Freudians began to look to social factors in their work, e.g. H. S. Sullivan's 'interpersonal situation' approach and Erikson's theories of identity development. As an alternative to individual work some patients began to be treated in groups and frequently this proved to be more effective (Foulkes, Bion). At the same time, research into hospital settings showed that the structure was often more of a defence against staff anxieties (Menzies), or that staff conflicts were passed on to patients (Stanton and Schwarz), or that institutionalization produced its own neurosis (Goffman, Barton). Research also indicated that the high turnover of hospital patients, which had previously been taken as an index of therapeutic success, was frequently the consequence of only having treated the superficial symptoms of the problem, leading to much rehospitalization.

Ideas also developed about the individual not having learnt to communicate properly in his family or not having had the opportunity to be expressive. One line of thought saw mental illness as either a role (in the family or in society as a whole, e.g. Laing) or as a label (labelling the individual as deviant or immoral or defective, e.g. Szasz), with overtones of social control and moral judgement. It was against this background that social therapy developed. Whereas hitherto mental illness had been seen largely in biological or psychological terms, social considerations now entered regarding not only the origins of illness but also the actual therapeutic work.

The growth of therapeutic communities[6] was particularly influenced by the work of Maxwell Jones who, in his work with ex-soldiers, realized that it was therapeutically effective both for patients to acknowledge that their illness was psychosomatic and to discuss it in groups and try to help each other. From now on the patient was not only going to stop being passive regarding those treating him but also regarding his fellow-patients. Slowly the idea grew that therapy could be still more effective by changing the structure of the hospital ward – less patient-staff distinctions, more patient-involvement in helping patients and in decision-making, more expressive behaviour.

Other developments saw a more flexible and less mystifying approach on the part of the public and G.P.s to mental health. Aided by 'the pharmacological revolution' of 1950s, particularly the development of psychotropic drugs, they now saw that mental illness could be cured, that the sick person did not have to be segregated and that involvement with society, especially through constructive work, was therapeutically useful.

Another main line of development was the changing nature of social services in Britain and especially those relating to mental care. Mental health was incorporated into the newly-formed National Health Service (founded 1947). This meant that mental treatment was more accessible to the public and it was free. General practitioners who had often been cynical about psychiatry now came into closer contact with it. At the same time the provision of social security meant that a person who was limited in his functioning, and was just released from mental hospital, need not suffer starvation; the state would care for him.

Greater social mobility also had an effect. Families were becoming spread out and different values were emerging within them. Hence the assumption that a family was waiting to receive the ex-patient back proved neither true nor desirable. So, during the 1950s there was a rapid growth in after-care facilities, out-patient clinics, day hospitals, night hospitals and halfway houses. This is what the National Health Service had envisaged, but their execution fell far short of the necessary or desirable.

In 1959 the Mental Health Act was passed relating to mental health. It reaffirmed the right and need of Local Authorities to care for the mentally ill but it did not make such care mandatory. It also gave the patient greater rights than before and tended to relate to the mentally ill patient like any other. There was to be less compulsion and more informal admission. Most important of all from our viewpoint, it emphasized the importance of local and voluntary action in helping to promote mental health.

It was against this background of changing concepts, attitudes, treatment methods and social services that the first house of the Richmond Fellowship was founded. Given the above trends, it was only a short step to see the need for houses in which adults could grow emotionally, could be treated as individuals in their own right, and could live in the wider community. The Act, as we have seen, did not make Local Authority care mandatory, so there was confusion as to who had to do what regarding mental health after-care. Elly Jansen, a Dutch theology student in Britain, established a house in Richmond and took in people who had recently been released from mental hospitals. There was as yet no clear idea as to how the house should be structured, although the concept of the therapeutic community and the general principles of social psychiatry were implicit. However, there was no model as to how this would apply to an independent community living in a neighbourhood. The only idea was to create a climate in which the aforementioned aims could be attained. But they needed external recognition. Initially there was some hostility from doctors and Local Authorities. They found it difficult to accept the idea of such a community, especially in view of the residents' background. They needed to be convinced that ex-patients were free citizens. However, church leaders and professionals in the psychiatric field were amenable to the idea, and some Local Authorities were persuaded to help pay for residents from their areas.

Initially the house was planned only as a one-year experiment. However, Elly Jansen and her co-workers concluded that if that was all there was to it, there would be little point to the whole effort. For one thing, people needed more time in the house. More important though was the realization that if such houses were to become more widespread then each would have to face the entire range of teething problems, external and internal, from the beginning, thus reducing therapeutic efficiency. So the idea of a wider organization emerged, and help from charitable institutions made expansion possible.

In 1960 the organization became a registered charity and this enhanced its status with Local Authorities and other financial sources. As time went on the number of houses grew (in 1984 there were forty houses in the United Kingdom and a further twenty abroad); an official headquarters, apart from the houses, was set up; and the structure of the organization as a whole and individual houses in it became more formal and more standardized. Houses also became specialized, e.g. for adolescents, drug addicts, schizophrenics. At the same time, the Fellowship's activities expanded into running a full-time college, becoming active in public education, and establishing houses overseas.

Headquarters consist of the director and deputy director, training personnel, financial personnel, admissions officer, public relations officer, projects officer, and clerical staff. A house consists of up to twenty residents and four to five staff (warden, deputy warden, assistant wardens, trainees, college students). Policy is contained in the Staff Manual. This contains the philosophy of the Fellowship, therapeutic policy, technical guidelines to running and maintaining a house, the duties of each person at each level of authority and procedures for communication, complaints and formulation of policy.

The residents are chiefly people who have been hospitalized for psychiatric reasons and have now left hospital but are still under emotional stress. They are not yet ready to lead independent – which often means isolated – lives. The aim of the house is to provide a caring (but not in an over-protective or patronizing sense) atmosphere in a loosely structured group. Residents are encouraged to discuss their emotional problems and desires with staff and other residents. The residents themselves have responsibility for the running of the house. This is both an opportunity to learn some basics about cooking, cleaning, etc. and to learn individual responsibility (as opposed to the dependence which characterizes most hospitalization). Residents are encouraged to seek employment or voluntary service in the area and weekly discussions are held on the difficulties of doing this, such as psychological barriers, employers' prejudices or the unemployment situation. Group meetings are also held to discuss household matters, to clear tensions, to plan activities and to provide information. The staff are meant to serve more as guides and encouragers than as supervisors, although they are expected to ensure that guidelines, as developed at headquarters, are adhered to.

There are few rules but those that there are must be observed – no violence, theft, sex or drug-taking on the premises. Attendance at the weekly group meeting is compulsory. In addition, there are a number of expectations – participation in work groups, attempting (at the appropriate stage of rehabilitation) to find employment, readiness to help others and to be helped by them – in short, to use the house to maximum advantage to oneself and to the house as a whole, and not just as a convenient place to sleep.

Richmond Fellowship Houses are now only one among a great variety of halfway houses and therapeutic communities throughout the country and represent only one approach to the treatment of the mentally ill within a broad conception of social psychiatry.

It is important to note that many of the assumptions and hopes on which the background developments were taking place proved to be false. The most important features are:

(1) There is still much stigma attached to being mentally ill, especially if the person has been hospitalized.
(2) The effects on family and friends if one of them becomes ill – feelings of guilt, fear, anger, embarrassment, confusion – are as intense as ever.
(3) The general public have still not come to terms with the mentally ill, e.g. difficulties in finding employment.
(4) Local Authorities are still reluctant to shoulder the full responsibility for the ill in their midst, and especially at times of cutbacks in their spending.
(5) General practitioners still show some hostility to non-organic psychiatry.

Discussion: how intentional communities rise and develop

We can now make some general comments about the circumstances under which our communities were founded.

What is striking here is the existence of two contradictory phenomena. On the one hand, the communities were set up in opposition to the prevailing culture of the base society. Unless opposition existed there would be no point to having an intentional community. This opposition – which could range from simple non-co-operation through derision and interference and extending possibly to outright persecution – helped the communities to find greater cohesion, sense of identity, conviction in the rightness of their ways and confirmation of their uniqueness and historical mission. On the other hand, the communities had their roots very much *in* the prevailing culture. Their ideology and way of life were not totally incongruent with prevailing ideas. The uniqueness of the communities lay in their combination of existing ideas[7] and in the radical and perfectionist interpretation given them. The assumptions on which the communities were based were acceptable in many respects to the base society. It was the way in which these assumptions were handled that aroused opposition from certain quarters. Yet the base society should not be viewed monolithically. Because the ideology and way of life of the communities were rooted in pre-existing and acceptable trends, they could appeal to large numbers of people. To some people the communities seemed like treason or madness; but to many they seemed to be the logical conclusion to what they were thinking, believing, doing and being taught anyway. At the grassroots level, the beliefs and way of life of the communities filled a social and spiritual vacuum. Both the Kibbutz and the Hutterites appealed also to people who had lost and wished to re-establish community life. At the same time, the communities served certain material needs in the base society. So, while many individuals turned to the communities for personal reasons, others (in some powerful positions) saw them as useful economic and political instruments, despite ideological objections.

It is the co-existence of these contradictory tendencies – conflict with the host society on the one hand, yet support from it on the other – which made the emergence of these communities and their subsequent development possible. Total opposition would have meant (and this indeed happened on occasions) persecution, low numbers, struggle for survival. Yet 'over-acceptance' would have led (and this too has happened) to a declining sense of purpose, unselective membership, apathy, overconfidence.[8]

In order to persist, there is no a priori reason for an intentional community to be involved with or to withdraw from its environment, but the ideology (see Chapter 5) of each of our communities prescribes such involvement or withdrawal. At any rate, our communities have wanted to expand individually and collectively; also they have not been content with minimum economic viability but have wanted to provide reasonable living standards. (The 'need' for higher living standards has been partially a consequence of being involved with the environment.) All this has inevitably meant that the communities have sought a liaison with the wider society, have been dependent on it and have been 'sought out' by it – yet by the nature of their goals and beliefs must stand in some opposition to it. This delicate balance of acceptance-rejection has characterized the history of the communities, with negative consequences where one side of the balance has been upset. Instances of imbalance are associated with periods of crisis in the communities – and the communities themselves have sometimes taken deliberate steps to right it (through withdrawal, accusations, or compromise over divisive issues).

Related to this is the fact that none of our communities has been concerned to remain a single unit. Associated with the idea of outside involvement is that of being a wide-ranging and expanding movement. Basically members identify themselves as 'a Hutterite' or 'a Kibbutznik'. Belonging to one particular community is subsumed under the idea of belonging to a particular movement. *The former cannot exist without the latter.* First and foremost you want to be a Hutterite or a Kibbutz member or you identify with the Richmond Fellowship's ideas – *then* you look for or identify with a particular community. Even the most passive member sees his membership of the community as intrinsically linked to his community's belonging to a wider network.

The idea that a community should belong to a network of communities, and that there should be a number of networks, has consequences for individual identification and community viability. One advantage of a community belonging to a co-ordinated and fairly centralized organization, all of whose constituent members are very similar to itself, is that it (the organization) can assist individual communities, e.g. direction of manpower, financial assistance, advice on various matters. It can represent them in their dealings with the outside world, thus extracting more support from the environment than a community could do alone. Moreover, belonging to a communal movement can give individual members a feeling of dynamism and expansion, a feeling of not being alone in their endeavours.

There is also an advantage in having competing movements. On the face of it competition should weaken individual movements, and depending on circumstances this may well be the case. But frequently it can be a source of strength, for two reasons: (1) competition with similar movements can produce, over and above any sense of identification one already has with one's own movement, an added sense of pride and belonging, of uniqueness and sectarian worth; (2) having more than one movement, each of which is a variation of a basic theme, means that potential members can each choose that variation most suited to their personalities and outlook, thus leaving each movement more homogeneous than it might otherwise be and thereby reducing the chances of disruption.

The same arguments apply to individual communities in relation to their movement. No two communities are the same, even if only from the viewpoint of personalities. Invariably there are subtle differences in organizational details, in methods of education, in means of handling problems, in approaches to and expressions of living standards and so on. However small and subtle these differences may be, they frequently determine the individual's satisfaction in the community. *Given his readiness in principle to commit himself to that way of life, it is the minutiae of daily living that can well determine the member's subsequent readiness to remain committed to it.* If there were only one movement or one community, individuals who were not suited to that framework might join, so destroying its basic homogeneity. On the other hand, potential members might not join at all if the framework did not exactly fit their own needs, outlook and personality. With plurality a potential member can 'shop around' until he finds a particular movement, and in turn a particular community, suited precisely to his needs, outlook and personality. In this way he can find greater satisfaction – leading to better climatization and greater commitment – while the community, for its part, can sustain its homogeneity.

We should stress that these are only potential advantages. They can equally be disadvantages when these 'variations on a theme' turn to internecine conflict (see Chapter 5) leading to a direction of energies away from higher goals, to more inward-lookingness, to an inability to attract new members. We should note though that internecine conflict over apparently petty matters can be a product as much as a cause of internal weakness. All three of our groups of communities have enjoyed the advantages and suffered the disadvantages of having a confederation of communities and a network of confederations.

The idea of each of our major communities being units within movements within movements is illustrated schematically in Figures 4.1 and 4.2.*

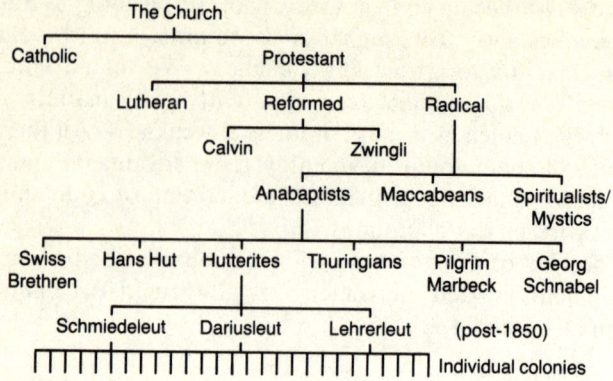

*Figure 4.1: Origins and development of the Hutterites**

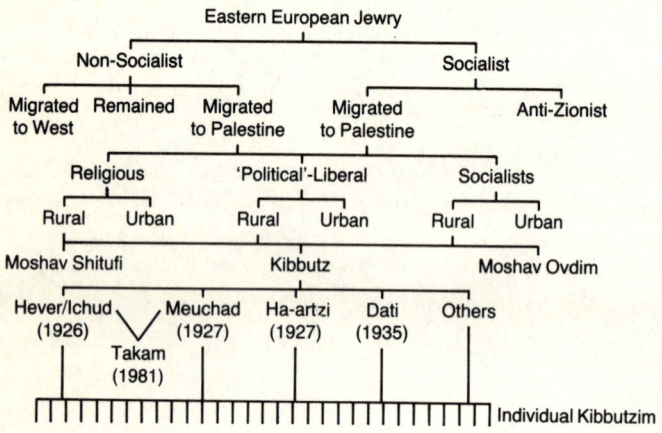

*Figure 4.2: Origins and development of the Kibbutz**

* Because I am trying to illustrate a general point both Figures 4.1 and
4.2 are very broad schemes and do not take into account all the
variations, permutations and combinations.

Chapter 5
Ideology

We can now proceed to examine the central fact of intentional communities – their ideologies. I say 'central' simply because it is around the ideology that the community's intentionality is constructed; it is the tension between 'pure' ideology on the one hand and the demands of the real world on the other, and the way in which the communities have resolved this tension – or at times encouraged it – which tells us much about their ability to persist.

One of the interesting facts about these communities is that despite the centrality of ideology and intentionality relatively little energy is expended on articulating them. This, as we shall see, has strategic advantages for the communities but makes the job of the observer more difficult, since he has to construct the beliefs, values and goals of the communities by himself.

The Hutterites are the only one of our communities to have a single and articulated doctrine but this was formulated more than 400 years ago, and while its general principles remain intact, account has to be taken of changes in Hutterite practices. The Kibbutz has no dearth of ideological writings and debates – but there is no single statement under which specific arguments and practices (and variations in them) can be subsumed. The principles of the Richmond Fellowship have found only a limited degree of expression.[1]

I have here tried to construct for myself the ideology of each group of communities. My aim has been to make the basic assumptions explicit, to link up the various levels of the ideology and to find in the life and beliefs of the community a systematic whole. (I have sometimes put the argument in the first person, since this is, I think, the way the committed community member would present it if he articulated his beliefs fully.)

Certainly the founders never articulated the ideology in this form: as we have seen, articulation only comes at a later stage. What I present here is therefore an ideal construct only under which specific variations and practices can be subsumed. What happens in practice will be discussed later.

Salvation through Christ's community: Hutterite ideology

There are three central beliefs to Hutterite faith. These are that God created and planned the universe in orderly fashion, that man is basically sinful (the fall of Adam) and that salvation is possible through a right relation to Christ. As we know the Hutterites were, when formed, concerned to re-establish the life of the early Christian Church. They embraced Luther's rejection of the notion that one could attain salvation by simply being a member of the Church and going through various external motions. As far as the Brethren were concerned, if the restitution of 'true' Christianity was their aim, the only logical step was to emulate the life of those who had created Christianity itself. Hence the Brethren do not regard themselves as only one form of Christianity among others, since this would imply that various interpretations are equally valid. As far as they are concerned, they are the Christians. (Yet one should respect others who, like the Hutterites, are prepared to suffer and die for Christ, since they too will gain eternal salvation. One should also respect people who live a life of 'all things in common'.) So their historiography divides the history of the Church into four phases: the pre-Christian period; the true Christian Church (until the conversion of Constantine and his fusion of Church and state 324 AD); the anti-Christ Church (meaning Rome); and the Restitution – the last being the period in which Hutterite beliefs emerge and eventually prevail. The Third Period is not simply a blot or deviation from the True Church. It is not the Church at all.

For the Hutterites time and history have special meanings. Time is non-material, beyond this world; it is eternity. For a brief period it is materialized in and on earth, but that materialization is subordinate to eternal time. The material period of time has a history. The Hutterites are therefore not concerned with chronology: what is important is not whether this event occurred before that, but what place it has in the divine scheme of things, what part it plays in building up or resisting Christ's True Church.

Man is basically sinful. Christ suffered for our sins but redemption is possible through emulating the life of Christ and his Disciples. That way of life and the principles underlying it are to be found in the New Testament. There is no need to interpret it: theology can only lead to pride, distortion, corruption, a feeling that man is more capable of understanding the Word than those who wrote it. It is all quite simply *there*.

When God created the universe he had two things in mind – order and purpose. It is not for man to question his purpose or to doubt the order he designed. God created all things, both the spiritual and the temporal. The temporal includes our own bodies; the spiritual is eternal and perfect. Our ultimate objective must only be to find salvation in the eternal, God. So our present lives must be directed to escaping carnality after death. Death is not to be feared; it is to be welcomed as the release from our carnal living of the eternal spiritual nature which God intended for us in his creation. So life in this world is not to be enjoyed for its own sake; nor are the creatures (things) of this world meant to be enjoyed sensually.

Yet we do of course live in this world, and while we do so we should live according to the Divine Plan. That means we must live the life of order that God intended. From the most mundane to the most sacred aspects of life order is to prevail. It is not for us to change, experiment, innovate or reconstruct. Order relates to everything: the relation between parent and child, husband and wife; the layout of houses; the plan of the day; the way in which we pray. There is a Right Way of doing everything. To live a life of order is to live a sacred life and to live the sacred life is to ensure eternal salvation.

However, future salvation will not come merely through living a prescribed way of life in this world. Overt motions are nothing if there is no sense of personal determination behind them. Man was created by God in his image, but Adam sinned and all men have subsequently been tainted by this. The sinner lies in all of us; in fact to sin, to be selfish, is our present natural inclination. Left to ourselves we shall end up in damnation, but this does not mean that salvation cannot be attained. On the contrary, salvation is possible on three conditions: we live according to the life of Christ; we live in community; we strive very hard to attain salvation and are prepared to suffer for our efforts. Christ appeared to save us from our sinful nature. This nature is not easily abjured but it can be if we try hard enough, both in the sense of personal determination and in the sense of collectively living according to the Word.

Even this is not enough, however. We live together with others otherwise life would be impossible. Hence the way in which we relate to others is highly important. Two principles govern our relations with others. One is the principle of order which we have already mentioned. The other is the principle of love. This means that we must relate to each other in the right way, this being the way Christ ordained. If we do this, order will prevail and love will permeate our relationships. So, for example, we will discipline our children because that is the duty of parents, because the concept of order means that children are subordinate to adults and because we love them and have their interests at heart. To relate to each other in the right way means relating to Christ in the right way.

God created everything for everybody's use. He wished to share his goodness with us; he did not intend some to have more possessions or more goodness than others. At any rate to gain for oneself invariably means to gain at somebody else's expense, which is certainly not what love is all about. Further, if one's actions are to be guided by the desire to gain, the selfish and sinful nature in us will come to the fore. Finally, to direct our minds and activities towards gain means to direct them away from our true purpose on earth – to attain salvation in the after-life. This means that we are required to live a simple life. To strive to gain more than we basically need leads us into the trap of enjoying the things of this world for their own sake. It also means that even in attempting to attain the minimum necessities for life on this earth, we are constrained. We may not engage in commerce as this is based on buying and selling for profit, which not only debases the nature of the goods involved but leads to greed and exploitation. (We should remember that Adam fell because of greed.) Perhaps most important of all, we are required to live in community of property, since in producing, consuming and acting together we create a true Christian community. God shared everything with the Son; the Son shared everything with his Disciples. Things gain their value from the purpose we put to them and the best immediate purpose we can put to them is the betterment of our neighbours. Hence community, fellowship, sharing, being of the Church, being of Christ's Truth – these are all one and the same thing.

So, only by living in a true Christian community is salvation possible. It is not simply a pragmatic necessity for people to live together in a divinely inspired way. To be part of such a community is to be part of a church or, to be precise, of The Church. God did not intend that we should each go our own way managing as best we can. He intended us to relate to each other in a particular way, to create a certain type of life. This type is the community of true Christians.

Yet to be a true Christian is not a formality. Christ is our personal Saviour. Hence to attain salvation one requires to be reborn, personally to accept Christ and his ways. Then, too, men have free will. We are capable of consciously accepting or rejecting Christ, of understanding the difference between good and evil. We are not forced to make a particular choice. The true Christian therefore needs to be personally saved and needs to be conscious of the fact that he alone can and must make the decision for himself. One must sincerely and consciously intend to live a Christian way of life. In short, one must actually *decide* to join the community in full realization of the consequences thereof. In joining the community we must accept its discipline and the superiority of the Church over our individual lives; we must realize that the forsaking of obedience to God is sin, that righteousness means obedience; we must accept the divinely ordained way of life in all its daily prescriptions and proscriptions; we must realize that to maintain such a way of life is hard and subject to the persecution of sinners; we must be aware of our inherent sinfulness and constantly attempt to overcome it; and we must understand that only the blood of Christ atones for original sin. So, to join the Church involves a very serious consideration and decision.

The act of joining is done through taking the baptismal vow. Clearly, this can only be done by adults. Children are quite incapable of joining the Church in this way: it is an affront to God to baptize babies and children who cannot comprehend the difference between good and evil or the enormity of joining the Church. It would mean that sinners could belong to the Church with impunity. Only so-called Christians, afraid of losing control over people's minds, would do this. The True Church of Christ does not require such artificiality. More than that, when a person joins the Church through true (i.e. adult) baptism, the Church is thereby strengthened. A church not based on the conscious, intentional and unflinching devotion of its members will be based on coercion.

For this reason the state exists. Sinners will not, by definition, live according to Christ's precepts – greed, selfishness and immorality dominate their lives. They require civil authority to regulate their lives. They cannot do this of their own accord. Force keeps the peace between them, not the true spirit of Christian love. Ideally, no true Christian will have anything to do with the state. To recognize the state is to recognize the legitimacy of force. The true Christian recognizes only the legitimacy of Christ's teachings and Christ taught not to use force, only to love. The attainment of spiritual perfection, which is our ultimate aim, requires spiritual not physical weapons. The true Christian does not use violence. Nor does he need to make oaths. The Christian always tells the truth; only sinners cannot be trusted, hence need to make or demand oaths. Also, states use force against true Christians because true Christians show up the sinfulness of the rest of mankind. This is because true Christians are part of the eternal Kingdom of Christ, which is antithetical to the temporal kingdom of sinners. Christians need no national nor civil church. Christ's church is The Church. One must expect to be persecuted; as long as sinners exist so will there be persecution. Christ's followers need not be afraid, however. They must not use force to resist persecution since this would be to recognize the legitimacy of force. The Christian *knows* that he is right; by being faithful to Christ's teaching he is guaranteed salvation. He can be secure in that knowledge; whatever the sinners do to him, eternal salvation is guaranteed. That is why being a Christian is difficult and why the choice to be one has to be heavily weighed.

Yet the state must be seen in its proper perspective. By imposing law and order on sinners it may thereby give protection to the faithful; it is, after all, God's creation. However abhorrent it may be to the faithful, God did intend it to serve a purpose regarding sinners, and for this reason alone it should be respected. Yet there is a limit to this respect – the faithful may not take advantage of it for material gain; nor must they accept any dictates of the state which are contrary to the Christian conscience, such as bearing arms; nor may they actively participate in the life of the state, such as holding public office. The state is at best a necessary evil, at worst an organized form of sin. Hence the faithful should not seek a confrontation with the state except where it is misused. Neither should the true Christian use force to resist the persecution that is inevitably used by sinners and the state against him. Christ prophesied persecution and as long as the righteous cling to their faith, they will be persecuted. But the true Christian is not afraid of persecution: he must be prepared to give himself up to Christ and take example from the 2,100 martyrs of Hutterite history.

The Brethren do not believe that they live in utopia (referring to life inside the colonies). Perfection will never be achieved, because man is basically imperfect. The Brethren come perhaps as close as they can to perfection, but are still a long way off. To think otherwise would be to indulge in self-idolatry, to place oneself on a par with Christ himself. Nor should it even be our aim to create a perfect society. Our aim is ultimate salvation. This is attained by striving to live the right path here on earth, by resisting temptation, by repenting sin. The person who genuinely does all these things is the one who will reach salvation, not those who are smug, self-righteous or self-satisfied. This means that life is a process of constant effort. Self-discipline must be consciously sought; no-one can strive hard enough to attain his aim, and no matter how hard one strives, one will never achieve perfection here on earth, but will be guaranteed it in the after-life.

Although persecution is a sign of sinfulness in the world, peaceful times do not make for good Christians either. In such times Brethren forget their identity because they become complacent; they forget the need to strive for salvation and allow themselves to succumb to the temptations of the flesh. So seduction is also a threat to the Hutterites, perhaps even a more dangerous one than persecution. The Brethren must constantly be aware of it and must strive to divorce themselves from the sinful, seductive world. The Hutterites' goodness stems from the fact that they are those who have perceived their carnal natures, have perceived the meaning of Christ's words, have understood the need for salvation, and have found the means of attaining it. They do not see themselves as inherently better than the rest of the world, only better because they have seen what they need to do and are acting accordingly. The rest of the world cannot tolerate it, so they try either to persecute or to seduce us and we must strive to avoid both.

None of this means that true Christians never stray from the true path. Sometimes our inherent sinfulness gets the better of us. Now, being Christians in a true community means that we are mutually responsible and mutually accountable, not only materially but also morally and spiritually. The spiritual well-being of our brothers is as of much concern to us as our own. So if one of us sins then it is the moral duty of others to point it out to him. But the way to lead him back to true righteousness is not by force; gentle persuasion must be used in a spirit of brotherly love. If this does not work then harsher methods, such as shunning, must be applied. Only if the erring member rejects all attempts to make him repudiate his sins should the ultimate sanction be applied – excommunication. Yet this is scarcely needed. In becoming a true Christian the member agreed to bow to the discipline of the community, a discipline applied fraternally and not harshly. He learnt that remorse, humiliation and debasement before God followed the recognition of his sins. Hence he is usually ready to recognize his sins, and this is made easier not only by the spirit in which he is rebuked but also by the knowledge that having repented he will be absolutely and totally forgiven by all fellow members.

In this connection, an important point about the nature of the community emerges. It is not up to individuals qua individuals to forgive others for their errors. They may well do so, but it is not that which leads to forgiveness. It is the Church that must forgive. The distinction is subtle but important. Each member of the community is primarily a member of the Church: it is through his giving himself up to the Church that he is a member of the community, hence it is as a member of the Church that he forgives the sins of others. Only when all members of the Church have forgiven the errant member is he forgiven. Similarly, only the Church can decide to excommunicate an individual. Quite simply, God is the source and the authority for everything. The individual can only seek salvation in God, so only in God is forgiveness possible. To ascribe to sources other than God the ability to provide salvation or forgiveness is idolatry.

One reason why members may sin is through bad influence from the outside. Therefore the true Christian should abjure the world. Within the True Church he cannot be contaminated, even though he may show occasional weakness. Sometimes, for economic reasons, contact with the world is necessary, but ideally this should be kept to a minimum. In one respect, though, the true Christian should seek the world and that is to convert it to the True Faith. The Bible specifically enjoins us to spread the Word, and this of course is absolutely necessary. Christ did not die for the sins of a few people here and there; he died for the sins of all, since all are sinful. This does not mean that we should accept lightly anyone who wants to join. While it is our Christian duty to impart the Word to sinners and innocent children, it is our equal duty to point out to them how hard the path to righteousness is. To accept 'reformed' sinners too lightly will do neither them nor us any good.

To commit oneself to the right way means not only to undertake an onerous obligation but to dedicate the totality of one's life to it. One cannot 'more or less' accept Christ. To be a Christian requires total dedication of one's total life through a total sharing of it with Christ. This is why the true Christian needs a true community, a total framework in which to act righteously. One cannot be righteous and live in a world of sinners. They contaminate and lure one into temptation. They represent carnal nature; the true Christian life represents eternal spiritual nature. The two are antithetical and must be kept apart. If all one's actions are premised on a dedication to God, then one requires to be with like-minded people and to create a way of life according to the precepts of the Word. Thus one needs the totality of a community to be righteous. This community is then a sacred community because it both shuns the world of sinners and acts in sacred ways. There is no distinction in such a community between sacred and secular. There is no place here for sinning during the week and praying on Sunday. The most mundane act is as sacred as the most significant because they all stand in a right relation to God.

Yet to be close to God not only means accepting his commandments or living formally in a community of saints. Equally, must one experience subjectively the joy of being a true Christian; one must enjoy the act of giving and taking, sharing, loving, obeying God's commandments. This is an additional reason for living in a small, intimate, closely-knit community, since only through such a community is true joy possible. The *feeling* of fellowship is no less important than the *acts* of fellowship. This explains the need for community of goods. To want goods for oneself is to try to glorify oneself; to share them with others is to put them to their proper use – the glorification of God. This also means that we must use goods simply and honestly, and not for sensual pleasure. There are two further implications to this. Since the righteous are destined to suffer, we will find it easier to bear our suffering in the knowledge that our fellows will look after our loved ones; in a world of selfishness there is no certainty that this will happen, but in a world of Christian fellowship it will. Second, simplicity gives wisdom. Once one tries, as sinners and the orthodox churches do, to go beyond the simple – with respect to the Word or with respect to God's creations – disobedience will appear. One should accept the Word as it is and God's creations as they are. Intellectualism leads to disobedience and idolatry. The closer we are to nature the closer we are to God who created it. Being close to nature also means we are less open to corruption, more self-disciplined and less sensuous. For that reason the Christian Church requires no marvellous edifices, no ornamentation, no musical accompaniment. To pray is to give thanks to God and to praise him sincerely. Doing so in a fine building has nothing to do with us; in fact, it would divert attention from the true purpose of prayer. Even our choice of where to live is not to be based on aesthetic considerations; equally, of course, we reject considerations of attaining ease, luxury, or profit. Our only considerations are first, how to divorce ourselves from the world of sinners, and second, how to live according to God's purpose.

This of course does not mean that our lives must be completely primitive. On the contrary, we may make use of machines for purposes of existence, even as a means of sufficient economic success to attain a reasonably modest living standard. The point is that our technological and economic activities are not directed to gain or luxury but simply to attaining a way of life which enables us to glorify God. As long as our real purpose on earth is constantly present in our minds, as long as that is the yardstick of whether our activities are good or bad, we will be faithful to the Church. Nor for that matter do we engage in activities, use machines or create artefacts for purposes of 'self-expression', 'self-fulfilment' or 'self-realization'. These concepts have no place in Christian mentality. Just as material creations must not be used for sensuous or idolatrous purposes, so must the individual not attempt to glorify himself.

This invokes the concept of *Gelassenheit*, or submission. Submission means giving oneself up totally to God; it means renouncing our carnal nature, always temptingly present in all of us in favour of our spiritual nature. This is both a state of mind and a set of actions. As a state of mind it means humility, obedience, dedication, sincerity, being at peace with oneself as a Christian with our spiritual natures, looking forward even to death in the knowledge that our spiritual natures will continue eternally. As a set of actions it means giving up our material possessions (hence community of goods), suffering, acting according to the spirit of the Word. (The ultimate expression of this is perhaps martyrdom; to be a martyr is the highest expression of one's voluntary commitment to the Church.)

The individual must break his will and deny himself mentally and materially. He aims at losing himself by giving himself up to God. The mystic also tries to do this but he forgets that he is a social being. He forgets that he lives in a material world purposely created by God, and he forgets the vice of intellectualism. No, the true Christian gives himself up to God by giving himself up to the Church, which means giving oneself up to the community in the totality of one's life. Only through the community, only with the help of one's brothers, is *Gelassenheit* possible. (To talk of the true Christian, the True Church and the Christian community as separate entities is to create false distinctions – one without the other is logically, materially and spiritually defective.)

We should remember that the community's authority on spiritual matters does not mean that the community goes about discovering, interpreting or elaborating a doctrine. There is no need for this, as the Word is there for all to see. It is also one reason for not having a professional clergy. Christ's Church requires no body of men specially trained in intellectualism or theology. No man is more spiritual or wiser than others by virtue of 'training'. The true community is a community of priests and saints. We all stand in equal relation to God; at any rate, to be spiritually perfect means to live a certain life with a certain intention in a certain attitude. No ecclesiastical authority is more spiritual simply because some so-called church has given him powers or, even worse, because the state has appointed him. One's spiritual nature is in constant tension with one's carnal nature. Each individual personally resolves the tension as best he can through the mediation of Christ as manifested in his community as a whole. All the members of that community are equally in that position and it is quite sinful to ascribe to some *within* the community greater spirituality or spiritual authority.

This of course does not mean that there is no authority at all. After all, God created order and, as we know only too well, men sometimes show weaknesses. What we need then is a guiding hand, someone (chosen by God, not by men) to act as a father-figure, to watch over the minds and actions of members of the community. He has no greater access to God than anyone else; he has no power to interpret holy texts; he is no less subject to the possibility of showing weakness than anyone else in the community; he is no less subject to the demands of a Christian life than others. To accept the choice God has made to be the spiritual watchdog of the community means that he has himself to be extra-careful in his ways and especially understanding of human nature. That is why he must undergo lengthy probation before the community, with God's help, can accept him fully and finally in his role. Having been accepted, it is his duty to remind us through the Holy Texts that our true nature is our spiritual nature and that there is only one order to the universe from which all else follows: God is omnipotent; God created man for a purpose; man, however, fell into sin; yet man can come to know his true nature; for this he needs to know Christ; to know Christ is to receive Grace from him. Finally, we must constantly be exhorted to be firm in our faith. This last is the function of the preacher.

The creation of Christ's Church was equivalent to the creation of man in his purity and perfection. Like Adam, the Church fell and became the church of sin, carnality and corruption. Just as man needs to be reborn, as expressed symbolically in his adult baptism, so the Church needs to be reborn; or to be precise, the rebirth of man and the rebirth of the Church are synonymous. Hence the Hutterites represent the Church of the Restitution; they are restoring Christianity as Christ practised it, which is the only Christianity through which man can attain salvation. It is the Christianity of faith, hope, love and *Gelassenheit*. It is the Christianity of obedience (Adam fell because he was disobedient). It is the Christianity of suffering (whoever accepts Christ must accept his suffering). It is the Christianity of saintliness and perfection because the Disciples of Christ lived as saints and perfectionists. The world will not be saved through technological advancement, education or 'moral reforms'. Only personal salvation through Christ can save it.

The goodness of self through communality: Kibbutz ideology

Kibbutz ideology rests on a number of assumptions about the nature of human beings and of society, and their inter-relationship.

Man (as a generic turn) has a number of inherent characteristics and a number of inherent desires. These, in fact, constitute the definition of man. Man is not to be defined biologically alone. Primarily he is to be defined in terms of his non-material qualities and aims. One is a person only to the extent that one expresses and realizes these qualities and aims. It is equally important to note that these are interdependent. They express a totality, and to manifest one quality at the expense of another is to vitiate the value of both, to negate the overall realization of one's inherent humanity. Hence it is not enough to say that people have qualities a, b, c, . . . etc: we need to show how they relate to each other. The point is not for a person to choose one quality or aim and to say 'this is what I want above all else', but to find the means of expressing all his qualities simultaneously and in balanced form. To ignore or overemphasize any one element is to do an injustice to the totality.

Man is fundamentally good and inherently social. This means that we are naturally kind and co-operative, concerned for the welfare of others, sensitive to the need for social justice. Each person, while having a number of universal aims, realizes that others too have these aims, and he is as concerned with their achievement of them as with his own. Co-operation and concern for others are instrumental (in that they help one promote one's own ends), and they are intrinsically satisfying. The two go together. The person who sees them as primarily instrumental will not gain intrinsic satisfaction from them; the person who gains intrinsic satisfaction will also find them instrumentally valuable.

We also aim to realize certain other qualities. These qualities should perhaps be called capacities in that we are naturally endowed with the possibility of realizing them and with the desire to do so. There are two primary capacities, creativity and self-mastery. To be creative is the same as self-realization, self-expression, self-fulfilment. It means that each individual has a variety of inherent talents and abilities. The fact of having such talents and abilities is what makes us human beings. The specific talents and abilities each of us possesses is what makes us an individual. It follows that one can only fully express one's humanity through development of one's individuality. It is also our inherent nature, as we have said, to want to develop fully in this way. Similarly, we have and desire the capacity for self-mastery. Clearly, if the individual is to express his individuality to the greatest extent he must not be subordinate to the dictates of others; he must not be in a position whereby he has to limit his capacity for individuality because others or circumstances force him to do so. So to be master of one's own life and to lead a life of creativity are synonymous.

Now, we have seen that man is also inherently good, i.e. concerned with the creativity, self-mastery and general welfare of others. Can a contradiction not arise between our own desire for self-fulfilment and our desire to see it in others? It would do, were it not for another of man's inherent qualities, namely his sociality. We have already seen one side of man's sociality in terms of his goodness – which means a concern for others. A further aspect of his sociality lies in the fact that only through society can man manifest his creativity and self-mastery. Man is not a member of society because of coercion; on the contrary, being a member of society is a necessary means of expressing his individuality. The claim that society limits one's self-fulfilment is merely a device for rationalizing the status quo, for justifying coercion, unpleasant conditions or injustice. Basically, society is the creation of men for the benefit of its members. Man is dependent on his society, but this is not the same as saying he is inherently limited or coerced by it. On the contrary, since it is man that constructs society, he will do so in a way that best satisfies his individuality. If this does not occur in practice then it is only because he has been misguided in his practical activities, or has been subjected to force, or is living a society designed to promote the welfare of some at the expense of others.

Man knows instinctively that only through co-operation with others can he meet his basic biological needs. Afterwards he may proceed – once again through society – to express his self-mastery in creativity. So the concept of self-mastery now takes on a double meaning: it means control over oneself and over one's society. Yet in fact this is one meaning. To control oneself one needs to control one's society; to control one's society means the potential to control oneself.

However, it would be naive to argue that man is so perfectly rational, consistent, self-conscious and omnipotent that his society accords exactly with his needs and aims. Given the fact that we were all born into pre-existing society and given the possibility of creating our own ideal society, we are subjected to influences not of our own making. This applies to individuals within the society and to the society as a whole. In short, man is as much a product as a creator of society. This has implications that we shall examine later.

Let us assume for the meantime that we are intent on creating a society in which our ethical natures and our desires for creativity and self-mastery are fully expressed. It is not possible to do this in *any* kind of society. Only if certain social conditions and forms of organization prevail will we attain our goals. The reason lies in the totality of our humanity, which we mentioned earlier. In almost any kind of society we may manifest *some* aspect of our inherent natures but, we have argued, to satisfy one element at the expense of others is to do an injustice to the totality, while to satisfy our own totality at the expense of others is to negate our inherent goodness.

We need a society in which all elements are equally satisfied, and for all people equally. So one may not satisfy one's creative capacities at the expense of other people's creative capacities since this will deny our ethical natures; nor may we negate our inherent self-mastery simply for the sake of social justice, such as may occur in a totalitarian society. The society we create must simultaneously and equally satisfy our capacities for goodness, individuality and self-mastery. This is the definition of a free society. A society which is not free is anti-social. It denies our true social natures and in so doing prevents us (or we prevent ourselves) from being true and full human beings.

For a society to satisfy such demands it must be democratic. This is a logical consequence of the demand for self-mastery. Only if all the individuals are able to participate directly in the decision-making processes; if they are able to delegate authority upwards (as at times they must) in the knowledge that those responsible will act in the way the electors themselves would act; and if all aspects of the life of the society, from the most trivial to the most profound, are subject to the scrutiny and direction desired by the totality of the membership – only then can we say that self-mastery has been attained. Democracy also means that the community acts as its own collective conscience. Since all members are involved in making decisions, all are required thereby to ask themselves if these further the basic aims and principles of the community or vitiate them. If decisions are left to a minority, one can never be sure what thoughts will guide their decisions; and to make matters worse, the rest of the members will be apathetic to those thoughts, waking up to them only when their own personal interests are affected or when a crisis hits the community as a whole. Individuals may sometimes show weakness but the community as a whole cannot, since there will always be some members to remind us of the community's true purpose. Only if there is total involvement can we be sure that our moral sensitivity will be maintained.

The need for democracy implies the need for equality. It is clear that if power in a society, or the control over those in power, is not spread out equally among members, then some members will have less control than others over the society's structure and operation, which in turn means less control over oneself. Yet equality also stems from recognition of individuality, paradoxical as this may at first seem. Equality does not mean that all have the same capacities for self-expression nor that they can or should express themselves in the same way. It means that we all have *some* inherent capacity for self-expression. Our inherent equality lies not in the extent of that capacity nor in its specific manifestation. Equality lies in the fact that we all possess the capacity for self-realization and self-mastery. The scope of these is relevant to our individuality but not to our equality. This means that equality between us is an intrinsic quality of our sociality and our very humanity.

While equality is a moral quality we possess irrespective of the actual condition in which we live, life can surely only be of value if equality exists in practice as well. How then are we to ensure that actual as well as moral equality prevails? For one thing, all people must be given the opportunity to find self-expression to their maximum ability and in ways appropriate to their individuality. This is possible by virtue of the fact that we control our own society, so we may construct it in any way we choose. We must also ensure that materially there is a more or less equal distribution of all our possessions. Because of our intrinsic equality there is no reason why some should have more and others less. Unequal distribution of material goods (which are often a necessary means to self-expression) will entitle some to find self-expression to an extent which others cannot. There is no desire here to limit people for the sake of limitation, an equality of poverty. On the contrary, we aim to provide as many opportunities as possible to all to express themselves. But to give some more opportunities than others is to negate the essence of our sociality, that of both the advantaged and the disadvantaged. This does not mean that all must receive exactly the same. To do that would be to deny individuality and that is to deny the essence of our humanity. A society should be organized in such a way that we are self-conscious regarding our moral equality, that we distribute our material provisions equally and that we recognize that there will and must be variations of a limited kind within that framework.

For this reason we are not opposed to increasing living standards. On the contrary, such an increase will enable us all the more to achieve our aims, but there are two limiting conditions. One is that the increase should be equal between members; the other is that high living standards per se should not be our aim. Not only would the latter detract from more profound means of self-expression, but would also lead us into immoral activities (such as exploitation of others) and vitiation of other aims we have chosen (such as building up the Jewish State).

There is a further reason to have equality, which leads us on to the next condition for our new society. Such a society requires certain sets of conditions for its institutions to operate efficiently and for its moral aims to be manifested. These conditions are interdependent. So in addition to democracy and equality we have the concept of an organic community, i.e. one which is characterized by intimacy, honesty, co-operation, fellowship and solidarity. These are conditions to be valued both for their own sake and as means to other ends. In themselves they are important because only when the artificiality of external appearances and many social conventions of bourgeois society are removed can we really understand what or who a person really is. If our aim is to satisfy our capacity for self-expression, self-mastery and goodness, then clearly this can best be achieved by opening up, both to oneself and to others, one's 'true' self, and not by hiding behind clothes, money, position or the ability to put up a front. One's true self lies in one's ability to relate meaningfully to others, to help them and be helped by them, to love and be loved – to have an 'I-Thou' relationship. Only a small society whose members are intimate with each other can achieve this; only a society whose members relate to each other in a spirit of openness, honesty and frankness can attain meaningful relationships. At times this may hurt since no-one enjoys being criticized, but the fact that criticism is made in a comradely fashion with the aim of making relationships more meaningful, makes its acceptance so much easier.

This presupposes that the members of the society identify with each other. One is hardly interested in having meaningful relationships with people with whom one has nothing in common. Even more important, one can only identify meaningfully with people who share one's aims and are conscious of one's inherent human qualities, just as one is conscious of theirs. Now clearly, in a society not characterized by democracy and equality, such mutual attitudes will not prevail, since the basis of relationships there will indeed be self-mastery and self-expression – but *at the expense of others*. In such a society people, both the haves and the have-nots, are denied their true humanity; life becomes a matter of survival or at best a competition for power and material goods – and in a competitive society one cannot, by definition, identify with one's fellow members. Nor will one want (or even be able) to enter into meaningful relationships with people who are basically not concerned with them.

It follows that an organic community only has value and is only able to operate if it is a voluntaristic one. To force people to join would be to arrogate to oneself power over them, which is hardly consistent with our conception of goodness. Nor could one sustain meaningful relationships with people coerced into them or coming into them by chance. Rather, we should be highly selective in accepting new members, i.e. we do not want people 'to do the right thing for the wrong reason' since the person who joins for any egoistic reason will be incapable of entering into the spirit of democracy, equality or meaningful relationships. This means either that he will ruin it for us or we will have to control him, and both these are unpalatable possibilities. We should choose people who understand their true humanity and are both willing and able to contribute to the enhancement of its practical expression for themselves and for others.

If the principle of non-coercion regarding outsiders is valid, it is equally valid regarding people who have already joined the community. Strictly speaking no conflict of interest should arise between the individual member and the community as a whole.

We have partly obviated the possibility of this happening through the selectivity of our membership. Yet we have seen that the principle of individuality is fundamental; so too are the principles of equality and solidarity. What if a person feels that he has needs that require his being given some form of preferential treatment? The way not to go about this, we have seen, is to apply rules of mechanical equality. First of all, the problem must be discussed in a spirit of frankness and comradeship. Then, the request must not entail a significant departure from the broad principle of equality. Third, the request must not be made or granted in a way which would upset the community's spirit of solidarity. To grant a request, *however trivial*, because a member has, say, threatened to leave or to strike, is inconceivable; to grant one, *however great*, because of concern for the member's welfare, because of a feeling of genuine need, because of the knowledge that the request has been made in comradely spirit with, ultimately, comradely intentions, is legitimate. Finally, the request and subsequent decision must be made in democratic fashion. In this way no conflict should arise between the individual and the community. (There is a distinction between conflict and a difference of opinion.)

Provided everything is requested, considered and decided upon in accordance with all the principles of the community, held equally by all parties to the discussion, no problem is insurmountable. If the individual feels that there is a conflict of interests between him and the community, then he must bow to the will of the community or leave. Self-mastery in this context means self-control. He cannot begin to act independently of the authority of the community. Not only will this lead to chaos, but to act in wild-cat fashion means to deny democracy, equality and solidarity – and to deny these is to deny one's essential humanity. For the community to acquiesce in wild-cat action is not only to upset its basic efficiency but even to deny its very nature.

Hence all decisions must be made and accepted voluntarily. To coerce members into accepting decisions (through some form of penalty) will mean to say in effect, and rightly, that they have denied their humanity; but in coercing them we are establishing power over them which, after they have already denied *their* own sociality, leads us to deny *our own*. To have power means that the principles of voluntarism, democracy and equality are secondary to the formal actions, however important and right such actions may be. Either the community is based on these principles or it is not. The individual either accepts them or he does not. If he does not, the community cannot force him to do so (although it can and should try to convince him in comradely fashion) without sacrificing the very bases of its existence. So the choice for an individual within a community is either to accept the way of life of the community or to leave it. But only a person who is not aware of his true human nature would do so. The self-aware person acts within the community in such a way that the community becomes an expression of his own personality.

All this means too that if the community is to function successfully then it must serve as a home in every sense of the word for its members. A home is a place to which one feels a sense of belonging; where one feels completely at ease; where one's needs are met; where one has close and satisfying relationships; where one has friends. The person living in a true community feels that it is home. Although one usually associates the idea of home with the family there is no reason why a group of previously unrelated people should not recreate for themselves that atmosphere and set of relations one usually associates with the ideal family. While there are no parent-figures for the community as a whole, the members are dependent on each other economically and emotionally as in a family; there is mutual support and concern, a feeling of blood, however symbolic, being thicker than water. Yet home is not only people but also a place, and the only place one can really strike roots is on the land. This leads to the importance of labour.

Man, we have seen, is naturally creative. Creativity does not of course refer to art and poetry and the like only – it refers to every sphere of human activity. One sphere of activity fundamental to all social life is labour. Now, to see labour merely as a necessary evil, as a means of attaining subsistence, or as a means of material gain for its own sake, is to mistake its true importance. Only people who fail to realize their true humanity or who are coerced into activities they do not like will think this. The fully conscious human being realizes that his labour is fundamental to his self-expression and self-mastery, to his very sociality. It goes without saying that whatever form labour takes the basic principles of the community must be maintained. Further, since from both a time and an economic point of view, labour is the single most important of our daily activities, it is essential to maintain our principles within it. If our principles do not operate in the sphere of labour, what hope is there for the rest of our activities?

There are of course many types of labour. The most fundamental of all is labour on the land. Everything we use or possess or simply look at is ultimately derived from the earth. So the most fundamental activity one can engage in is work on the land. This does not mean though that we need to be primitive in this activity. For one thing we are concerned with our *relationship* to the land and there is no inherent reason why the person pushing a wooden plough is closer to the land than the modern tractor driver. Furthermore, we wish to use the land as a means of attaining our aims and expressing our principles, and to limit ourselves to primitive means of production would probably vitiate our ability to achieve this. If technology can help us, let us enhance technology. Once again, it is not what instruments we use but what our relationship to the land is and what we want out of their use which is important.

The significance of the land is that it is nature. Now, if man wants to find his own true nature then he needs to be close to physical nature. This does not mean that in any metaphysical sense one's human nature is an extension of physical nature. It means that the elements of human nature can best be expressed in a framework of natural landscape. While agricultural activity is perhaps closest to this, only a small proportion of members of the community are actually engaged directly in working the land or raising animals. This does not mean that all the others are alienated from the land. As long as one's activities in the community take place within the physical elements of nature, and as long as one subjectively identifies with the land per se, one is able to relate as meaningfully to nature as the person who actually drives the tractor and tends the flock. Furthermore, each person, as we have seen, expresses his essential nature in and through his community. The point therefore is not necessarily for each *person* to be actively engaged in agriculture but that the community *as a community* should have a direct relation to the land.

The fact of being surrounded by nature also enhances one's ability to be simple, direct and honest. And of course the land means home, a place which is easily identifiable and has aesthetic qualities, a place with which one identifies. If we have argued that what is natural (*truly* natural, that is) is good, then we must conclude that man should literally enjoy both his own nature and his surroundings. So nature has both a moral and an aesthetic quality. There is no reason for us not to gain aesthetic satisfaction from eating, to limit it purely to a biological necessity. But we should always remember that there are limits to sensory satisfaction – to enjoy luxury foods while others are starving is to be aesthetic at the expense of our other principles, a situation we cannot abide by.

What of the actual work-activity itself? Given the advantages of living in a community based on the land, work has three further functions. First, it is a means of self-expression. Work, we have mentioned, constitutes the single most important activity of our day. It is the most important physical means one has of developing one's individuality. Second, it is a social activity. One seldom works alone. In a work team one has the opportunity to express equality, democracy, meaningful relationships, co-operation and solidarity. Third, it is a means of providing the livelihood with which one can attain the means of further self-expression and self-mastery. Running through these 'objective' consequences of labour is a subjective psychological thread. That is the idea of working not for oneself in the egoistic sense, but for the community as a whole and thereby for oneself. One's labour is both a result and a means of expressing one's identification with the community and all that it stands for. In fact this applies to all spheres of community life. One's participation in the decision-making process and one's acceptance of the principle of equality are equally signs of identification with the community.

This goes to show what is already abundantly clear, that the life of the community consists of various processes and activities that imply each other because they are logically subsumed under the fundamental conceptions of human nature and social life. So the way we labour is bound to our other principles. The principles of self-expression and self-mastery lead to the conception of self-labour. This concept has a dual meaning. In regard to self-expression it means that one cannot engage in activities that are not of a creative kind. Simply to engage in commerce or entrepreneurship (which are concerned with creating capital for its own sake or for materialistic ends) is not creative. One may only engage in activities which are an extension of one's true individuality. Similarly, in regard to self-mastery, one may only engage in activities not requiring one to attain mastery over or profit at the expense of others. To hire labour means, by definition, that one cannot relate to the labourer in an intimate, honest, meaningful, solidaric way, as one does with one's fellow community members. One cannot even if one wants to, since the whole purpose of hiring him was to use him as an instrument to attaining one's own goals, however ethical your subjective relationship to him may be. To relate to a person as an instrument and not in terms of his inherent qualities is to debase the nature of our relations with others, hence to debase our own human qualities. And it also means limiting *his* potential for self-mastery, which is unethical.

This helps to highlight a fundamental element of community life. The community can 'hang together' only through the members having an identity of fate. In practice this means two things. Members must identify with the past and (more important) with the future of the community, such that their own future and the community's future are one and the same. We rise and fall together. This is another way of saying we have *unconditional* commitment to our community. We do not say 'if the community does or achieves such and such, then I will stay, otherwise I won't', since this implies that there is an individual identity onto-logically and morally distinct from the community's. No true community could operate successfully or manifest its raison d'être with such limiting conditions or separate identities. Identity of fate also means that members relate to each other in an atmosphere of mutual trust, i.e. they consider their presence to stem from a common desire to express their humanity and recognize that this can only be achieved through mutual effort. Should one person claim that he has an inherent right to gain for himself at the expense of others, the entire fabric collapses. Life in the community presupposes that each will work for the benefit of others as much as for himself, that no-one will be egoistic. The moment this assumption is undermined, mutual suspicion, jeal-ousy and mistrust arise. Not only will people probably consider themselves silly for being self-righteous while others are feathering their own nest, but operationally the community will have to take a different character (primarily through the use of coercion) and the entire moral nature of the community disappears.

It is this which distinguishes the true community from the pseudo-community. In the latter, there may well be a modicum of co-operation, equality, democracy and solidarity. But these are considered only as a means, even as a necessary evil, to achieving 'higher' ends – namely individual 'advancement'. It is morality for the sake of egoism, not for its own sake. In the true community these norms are enjoyed not only for their pragmatic value but in and for themselves: they have an intrinsic value since in them we find our true sociality viz. our true natures, and to find our true natures is the highest goal to which we can aspire.

All this is open to the rest of humanity (apart from our Jewish-national obligations). But most of humanity is too concerned with denying their true natures – hence poverty, misery, crime, suicide. The Kibbutz is a unique institution in that it is not only conscious of what is necessary to lead a morally worthy life – it is actually doing it. (Of course this does not mean that Kibbutz members are perfect or that Kibbutz society achieves all it intends to achieve. On the contrary, shortcomings are many and the threats from outside – political, economic, social – make the Kibbutz's task more difficult, which makes constant effort and vigilance necessary.) The Kibbutz has an obligation to help others come to the same realization. The Kibbutz must be the vanguard of a more righteous society in both the national and universal contexts. The whole world does not have to become a Kibbutz – but unless the level of consciousness and the principles of belief found in the Kibbutz are realized, people will continue to suffer, at best to lead empty and meaningless lives. The Kibbutz is not utopia; it is not a paradigm of justice and perfection, but at least it is conscious of the need to move in that direction and has understood the principles on which to do so. It is this which sets it apart as an example for others and imposes on it obligations towards them.

This raises the last aspect of Kibbutz ideology that we need to consider – the Kibbutz's national context (at which point we break the 'first person narrative'). While the foregoing could be universally argued, the Kibbutz arose in specific historical circumstances, and these are basic to its ideology. The desire to influence the immediate environment and play a role in the national enterprise became strong elements of Kibbutz life. Four different arguments can be put forward here. (1) The Kibbutz is morally obliged to inject its own internal principles into Israeli and, ultimately, world society, since this *is* the right way of life, or at the very least, the right set of principles on which any way of life must be predicated. (2) The Kibbutz is the highest expression of socialism operating in a pseudo-socialist, thinly-disguised capitalist society which, by its nature, will attempt to suppress it (the Kibbutz); hence the

Kibbutz must attempt to influence it first. (3) Practically, the Kibbutz cannot isolate itself from the surrounding framework since the latter is larger, stronger and antithetical to Kibbutz ideas, even if it tolerates the Kibbutz. For the Kibbutz to succeed in such a framework requires it to engage in various activities contrary to its principles (e.g. buying and selling on a capitalist market), and this vitiates the internal moral quality of our lives; hence we need to ensure that this problem does not arise by influencing surrounding society. (4) Whatever its internal principles, and whatever the nature of Israeli society, the Kibbutz has a moral obligation to be a pioneering force in Israeli society, to serve the needs of the state and the entire Jewish nation, to be an example of dedication, selflessness and courage, and was in fact founded for those very reasons.

Whatever the motivation or the rationale the conclusion is the same in each case – the Kibbutz must try to influence Israeli society in the right direction. If it fails in this regard it may still be an island of righteousness – but a very much poorer one.

Personal growth and mental health: a therapeutic philosophy

In the Richmond Fellowship there is no one explanation of the causes of mental illness. No attempt is made to ascribe all mental illness to, say, organic defects or arrested emotional development or the consequences of a capitalist economic system. These may or may not be the causes of illness but arguments about them are not necessary to the Fellowship therapeutic philosophy. What is important is that whatever the causes the residents of Fellowship houses share certain problems, and since it is these which were the direct cause of their emotional breakdown it is these which need to be tackled.

Residents have a few basic problems, all closely related. These are a lack of identity, an inability to communicate fully, an inability to cope with stress or even normal (by average standards) situations, failure to relate constructively to others, failure to be constructively aware of one's own states of mind. As such, the mentally ill person is not a satisfactorily functioning personality, neither in his own eyes nor in the eyes of others. This is precisely the opposite of the healthy individual. The satisfactorily functioning individual is one who is familiar with and can understand his own emotional states and personality traits; can define more or less clearly his goals in life and chooses the best means of attaining them – not as some abstract aim but as an extension of what he knows he is capable and not capable of achieving; is responsible for and to himself; can relate creatively to others; can cope with life generally and with particular problems that arise in it. In short, the healthy person is one who has a general sense of purpose and satisfaction which, even though not fully attained, is somehow progressed towards, and even if obstacles and painful setbacks occur, these are coped with and eventually overcome.

The mentally ill person is far removed from this situation. He cannot articulate his aims; he will not take responsibility for himself (he wishes others to do so for him); he cannot relate creatively to others or cope with many situations; he refuses to come to terms with his own traits or even simply to define them; he has no sense of purpose or satisfaction (though he may wish he had them) and frequently he does not even envisage the possibility of attaining them.

The point of a therapeutic community is to create a framework wherein the individual who is not so sick that he cannot see that he is, can overcome the above difficulties. This is a framework where he can put his past – so confused, mystified and seemingly irrational, and so infused with shame and guilt – into its proper and rational perspective. From this he can place his future into an equally proper and rational perspective. Just as there is no model of the causes of illness so is there no conception that there is only one way to treat it. The values of a therapeutic community are universal but not the means of attaining them. In this case a certain type of milieu is aimed at. It is unrealistic to expect the sick individual to become healthy on his own: without help from others his chances of doing so are slender. But other people are not simply to be seen as a means to a private therapeutic end. One is bound to go through the rest of one's life in a pattern of relations with others, hence learning to relate to them positively is a necessary part of learning to cope with life. At the same time, living in a community can be an exercise in learning responsibility both towards oneself and towards others. This can refer to simple tasks such as learning to cook or keeping oneself looking presentable, or to more complex and demanding tasks such as helping others through difficult situations. Nor is this simply a 'technical' education. From it people can learn that their environment, physical or human, is not something to be feared but something one can relate to constructively and can even, up to a point, control; and if the community in which one lives is set in a neighbourhood and even integrated with it, one has the opportunity to enter the world at large and to learn to cope with it, especially if one finds work, thus learning to gain independence at both the material and emotional levels.

A therapeutic community is necessary to these ends (as opposed to the individual having to manage in the world on his own). If a person has been in a mental hospital for only a short time he is unlikely to have made such a radical and sudden personality change that he can achieve these aims without the assistance of others. On the other hand, a person kept in hospital too long, even if he is progressing, is also in a difficult situation, since he has often been overprotected and isolated from 'real life' and may have become dependent on the institution – a classic phenomenon. In either case, to make a person independent when he is not yet ready for it may well lead to rapid rehospitalization.

One needs to acquire both the desire and the means to be a properly functioning individual. The mental patient usually leaves hospital when the symptoms of breakdown have disappeared. Yet he is a long way from being a healthy individual. Until he sees what health is, manages to define what it means for him personally and acquires the ability to move in that direction, his situation is delicate to say the least. The perception of health and the movement towards it are slowly and frequently painfully acquired; the individual therefore requires an environment which can help him and make demands on him, yet cares for and protects him during such an acquisition.

All this points towards an important consideration, namely that illness is not to be construed simply as the absence of health nor, more important, does health follow simply from the absence of illness. We have contrasted the characteristics of the emotionally ill and healthy but these are not the only possible situations: on the contrary, there is a vast, grey, murky area inbetween into which most of us are born and remain for the rest of our lives. It is an area in which we *do* indeed have goals – but these have been defined for us by others and are geared more to the satisfaction of social conventions than of personal need and identity; we *can* cope with our problems – but more by avoiding them and denying their existence than by confronting them directly; we *are* in touch with our personalities – but not too much lest we discover aspects of it we may not like or may even have to fear; we *are* able to communicate with others – but largely in the direction of expressing our demands on them, without really wanting to know or understand their demands on us; we *do* have feelings – but are afraid to express them too openly lest we be labelled as ill or abnormal; we *do* have fears and anxieties – but hope that we will manage life 'successfully' by refusing to recognize or come to terms with them; we *do* perhaps have a vague sense of satisfaction in our lives – but it is far removed from the depth of satisfaction we are capable of attaining. And perhaps most important of all, not only does this situation exist but we are generally not prepared to admit that it does.

To the extent that the therapeutic philosophy of the Richmond Fellowship is linked to a critique of society, this is it. No attempt is made, even implicitly, to explain why the majority of us grow up in this area of non-illness and non-health. There is no religious, economic, historical, cultural or psychological reduction. It is a fact of life which all of us need to understand – and then contend with. Personal breakdown occurs when people hovering on the fringes of this psychiatric limbo step, or are forced to step, beyond it, so that not only are they not healthy but become ill. So to relate to such people as somehow inferior to the rest of us is absurd, since all of us are in reality not very far removed from their situation.

It follows then that the aim of a therapeutic community cannot simply be to treat emotional illness. Treatment is a negative activity; it aims at the removal of the symptoms of a problem. This is what mental hospital does but, if this is what you aim at, all you are really achieving is the transportation of the individual from a state of illness to a state of non-illness, from which state he became ill in the first place and is only too likely to become ill again. The aim of a therapeutic community must be to help people become healthy, to show people that they have choices in responding to situations, that they need not only respond to them in preconceived or stereotyped ways. They have choices too in life, and by choosing with responsible self-awareness they are attaining emotional freedom. Simply to act as you like is not freedom. To act in terms of your capacities, your relationships and the totality of your needs, and to accept responsibility not only for making choices but for their consequences too – that is freedom. This means that the individual needs to come to terms not only with himself but also with his society, and to find a fruitful interaction between them. To come to terms only with one or the other is destructive; to have a creative tension between the two is intrinsically satisfying and a sign of emotional health. The therapeutic community aims at helping the individual find a private and individual identity *through* a group – not to take on that *of* the group, even that of the therapeutic community, however praiseworthy its aims. If there is a grey area between the extremes of sickness and health, there is a bright and potentially satisfying one between total withdrawal and immersion, since from the viewpoint of emotional health they are both sterile.

There is no assumption here that all you need to do is help people understand why they are ill, from which understanding a process of recovery automatically follows. To attain mental health is quite literally a matter of hard work. We need constantly to make a conscious and determined effort, constantly to strive to understand our relationships with others, our attitude towards them and the way they see us. People may be able to function quite adequately without these but only on this basis can *health* be attained. It follows that this cannot be a purely private process nor, even if we are interacting with others, can it be a purely one-way process. Only in a dynamic community where all share this common aim can the individual, whether he has suffered break-down or is merely in a state of non-illness, attain mental health. It is through constant interaction with others, in which an atmosphere of mutual good faith exists and in which there is ongoing feedback, understanding and sympathy, that one can understand better who and what one is, and how one relates to others. Criticism and anger are also legitimate since this is part of the problem of living with others. The question is whether these are expressed in an atmosphere of good faith and whether they can be used constructively to further the attainment of positive ends.

Frequently, people come to houses with preconceived notions about themselves, e.g. they can only survive with heavy medication, or they are the ill people of society, or they have no worth. They may also hide behind the security of psychiatric labels while simultaneously fearing them; or they may bear the stigma of having been in mental hospital and are imbued with shame, guilt, fear and confusion. To remove all these symptoms at the very least is the aim of the therapeutic community.

There is no guarantee though that the individual will attain good emotional health; at any rate, such a condition is hard to define in concrete terms. All that one can realistically strive for is that the individual should want to be healthy; that he should realize that health must be defined positively and not negatively (it is not a state of non-illness); and that he should begin to work actively in that direction. He must learn to value himself (frequently his biography is one of negative evaluations from others and by himself, hence the need for a community in which he is valued), and he must learn to accept himself for what he is and is not, can be and cannot be. Ultimately (in terms of his life in the community) he will, if he has achieved such awareness and the basic 'tools' of maintaining it, have made this necessary breakthrough. It is this breakthrough that the community aims at. It is not concerned to define for the individual what his private goals should be or how he should relate to others or how he should define a feeling of satisfaction in life or how he should cope with stress. It aims at a situation where, even if the individual is not helped in the sense described above, he has at least learnt to function adequately.

So a therapeutic community is 'merely' concerned with helping the resident arrive at a situation where he can do all this for himself and is able to lead a relatively independent life after his stay in the community – at the very least without suffering a recurring breakdown and hopefully with the desire and ability to explore further personal growth. There is no conception here of 'cure' or 'success'. This is too much of a cut-and-dried approach implying a clinical distinction between sick and healthy and having misleading biological overtones. One could perhaps look for statistical criteria of success, e.g. rates of re-hospitalization, entry into employment and so on, but the real criteria of cure and success are far more intangible. They lie in the individual's ability to look at himself squarely, to understand the nature of his wants and needs, his actions and relations, and to come to grips realistically with his problems as they arise. The question is not whether the individual will have difficulties in life but how he will respond to them as they do arise. Once again, though, the community must be realistic – this situation is only arrived at after a state of basic adequacy has been attained. It is the latter that the community must actually achieve but the attainment of health must be its ultimate goal.

Striving for personal growth is a never-ending process: it is, by definition, unattainable in absolute terms. The individual who declares that he has achieved full emotional health is only likely to be disguising his lack of it. This does not mean that we all need to go around constantly deploring our lack of health, only that we should recognize that there is always room for further growth, for better communication, for deeper understanding, for more creative relationships, for more efficient coping. Unfortunately though, many people are far removed from that situation, and the problem of those living in a therapeutic community is not how to complete the process of growth – but how to begin it.

In all this there is one fundamental assumption without which the whole philosophy collapses, that is, that most human beings (apart from those suffering from brain damage or organic schizophrenia) are basically healthy or are capable of being so, and that good human relations are a sine qua non of this health. We all need good relations; the aim of a therapeutic community is to provide them in a style that some need more than others, but the fact that they need that style is not a sign of some deficiency on their part, rather of their being normal. It is frequently society's refusal to recognize this which has caused mental illness. To this extent mental illness is a sign of a sick society.

From these assumptions it follows that the individual resident is to be treated as an adult, a mature person, one who has rights and needs. He may not feel that way about himself and his society may well reinforce his negative evaluation (personal relations, difficulties in finding employment, family) and both may see him as playing the sick role. It is this entire range of problems which needs to be tackled.

The foregoing can only be attained if a certain type of atmosphere prevails – an atmosphere characterized by open and honest communication; by an attitude of mutual caring, but not to the extent where this creates feelings of dependence on staff or on the community as a whole; in which individuals accept the need to take responsibility for themselves and others; in which they genuinely try to achieve the primary breakthrough mentioned above; and in which there is a feeling that over and above each individual's private need to be in the community, a culture of togetherness and pleasure prevails. Clearly, then, a therapeutic community needs to be something more than an institution in which a number of people happen to be under one roof, each pursuing private ends unrelated to those of the others. Nor can it be a halfway house whose only purpose is to contain mental illness. The community, though, does not aim at becoming a substitute for the world at large, nor for families in it, even though it can and should have a family-like atmosphere. Nor is it trying to convince society to restructure itself on therapeutic community lines – although it very much wants society to adopt its values. In this respect there is a contradiction in its aims. To be therapeutically successful it needs to create the atmosphere and culture of a community – togetherness, sharing, caring, common aims, close friendship – but, unlike other communities which share these qualities as permanent ends in themselves or as a means to attaining supra-individual goals, the community is a self-denying one. It creates a community culture in order that its members can live without such a culture, certainly not on the scale of the therapeutic community. This is not to say that life outside the community is necessarily 'cruel, nasty, brutish and short', only that the values of the community are only marginally expressed in the daily situations the resident is likely to encounter. The successful member of a therapeutic community is paradoxically not one who commits himself to it but one who is able to deny it. Yet this is not as paradoxical as it first appears, since while the resident is expected to be able to live without the specific community he matured in, he can be expected to carry the values and tools he acquired with him into the wider world. These values and tools are the means of sustaining him in that world and helping him to grow in it, and even – though this is a lofty aim – of helping others to acquire them too.

Discussion: the centrality and peripherality of ideology

An intentional community has two conflicting needs: to sustain continuity and to be open to change. Continuity serves to give the community an identity, an historical perspective, a sense of uniqueness and mission. The 'intentionality' of these communities is rooted in the idea that its values and goals are not ad hoc or transient; it is precisely their transcendent nature which gives the existence of the community its validity. Unless the community feels that it is basically the same group as was originally founded, with the same aims, principles and view of the world, and unless the aims are central to the raison d'être of the community, it ceases to be an intentional community. From a sociological perspective there is of course no a priori reason for the community to be intentional; but from the viewpoint of the members concerned such intentionality is fundamental and this requires ideological continuity.

Yet clearly the community could not survive if it did not adapt to changing circumstances – which could be both internally and externally generated. Adaptation and change can be expressed in social structure, economic practices, relation to the environment, mores and the theoretical rationale for them. It follows from this that if the community is to ensure both continuity and change then the ideology must be so structured that its basic premises remain intact, although the specific expression of them may vary quite considerably. This means that the basic premises must be highly generalized conceptions about the nature of man, society and the universe. Certain conclusions 'inevitably' follow; as circumstances change, other conclusions, equally consistent with the basic premises, can 'inevitably' be drawn.

It is significant that members of the community do not themselves see the ideology in such loose and fragmented terms. On the contrary, they tend to see it in holistic terms. While social scientists may argue as to whether there is a distinction between ideology and knowledge,[2] such arguments are superfluous in intentional communities: for their members, ideology *is* knowledge. At any point in time they may well argue that the norms and institutions currently practised are the inevitable and logical consequence of the interplay between basic assumptions and values on the one hand, and social-environmental circumstances on the other. In their view, all elements of the ideology and all aspects of the society form a complete and consistent whole, albeit in inchoate form. Their tendency to think this way is a consequence of the community's intentionality. To speak of the openness of the ideology to various and even contradictory interpretations, and to accept consciously that many aspects of social life are not related in any way to the ideology, is to threaten the continuity and 'inevitability' of the community's aims and purpose. The whole basis to an intentional community is the members' perception that their beliefs and the way of life based on them are morally, logically and historically necessary. It is not an arbitrary intentionality nor one reducible to private need or interpretation. This perception is the basic thrust of a persisting, intentional community.

Let us put the matter another way, since I believe it is crucial to membership of a community and to the community's collective persistence. I explained earlier that the ideological schemes I presented were ideal constructs. Now the point is that in the ideological consciousness of members there is a basic and necessary duality. At the subliminal level the ideology, that is the abstract system I presented, is seen as precisely that – a system. For the member it is a logical pattern, a comprehensive statement about him and his universe. It is not simply an academic intellec-tualization, it is his identity. It is his frame of reference, his criteria for right and wrong, the basis to his thinking about behavioural norms and social structure: it is his perspective on his place in time and space. These are the parameters of his universe and his rationale for what the universe contains. But, and this is the crux of the matter, the vast majority of members have 'taken up' this identity in only a sub-conscious, half-articulate and inchoate way. At the level of consciousness they can only reflect or expound on the rationale of that identity – their ideology – in terms of slogans, clichés, accepted wisdom. They simply *know* that equality is right – why it should be so or what the implications are is only half understood, if that. I do not wish to appear condescending, but the reactions of the majority of members, when presented with the foregoing exposition of their ideologies, range from the mildly curious through to the uninterested, the uncomprehending or the incredulous ('is *that* what I think?!').

In short, for the majority, the ideology, i.e. the explicit rationale of their public identities, is simply given. They do not wish to make it explicit or are simply not capable of doing so. Hence the duality I mentioned earlier and the necessity for it. The member needs to see his identity as a systematic and comprehensive whole: if not, his identity loses its stability. Yet at the level of day-to-day living he needs to be *in*articulate about it. If not he will suffer psychological strain, will need consciously to reflect on the relation of each action and decision to the ideology, and will be severely handicapped in his ability to change, adjust or modify (or, if he did, he would have to go through lengthy intellectual justification for each change). Since for the majority of us such intellectual extravaganzas are beyond our ability or are time-consuming or simply a hindrance to decisive and practical action, it is not worthwhile making the ideology too explicit, comprehensive and articulate.

I suggest therefore that commitment to an intentional community entails an implicit identification of the member with the systematic and comprehensive ideology in which his own identity is anchored, while simultaneously he avoids articulating the assumptions, principles and rationale on which it is built in order to allow for more efficient, relaxed and practical day-to-day living. Cynics may well see this situation as hypocrisy, loss of idealism, weakness or whatever: *I suggest though that without this duality community persistence would be impossible.* The communities we are studying have changed, in some respects quite considerably, over time. Whatever members may themselves implicitly believe, the ideology in fact *is* in most respects arbitrary and ad hoc, is open to change, and has nothing at all to say about many aspects of daily life. The strength of an intentional community lies largely in the *fact* that this *is* the case, together with the *belief* that it is *not* the case.

I should emphasize that it is not a condition for an intentional society to be founded that it must have transcendental aims and values. But if it is to persist beyond the life-span of any individual member it needs to have goals and values which, in the eyes of members, transcend their own lives; furthermore, the goals and values must be of such importance that they are worth trying to attain and sustain beyond their own lives. For the members the goals and values of their communities do not derive their worth from the fact that they happen to have been understood by themselves (the members), even less because they meet members' private needs. The worth of the values and goals is autonomous and transcendent; the community's members are those who, having perceived this worth, need to ensure their continuity. Because it is they who have understood them it is they who need to fight for their preservation. This is what makes the communities unique and invests them with historical mission. I must emphasize that the communities we are studying have not always held closely to this position – and it is precisely in such circumstances that the community enters a period of crisis. The perception of worth over and beyond the immediate life of the community and its members' lives has been a powerful factor in community persistence; the weakening of this perception has frequently coincided with internal struggles, economic weakness, overemphasis on material success and inability to attract and hold members. (I say 'coincide' since the symptoms of crisis may be both cause and effect regarding the weakening of universal beliefs.)

Having emphasized the importance of supra-community and supra-individual beliefs to the ideology, I now wish to stress the equal importance of the opposite. The two are not necessarily contradictory. Just as an ideology rooted entirely in the here-and-now lessens the probability of persistence, at least on the scale we are here examining, so too does an ideology rooted exclusively in the transcendental. At the initial stages of community development the emphasis is usually on sacrifice, collective effort, working for the greater good. However, this cannot continue indefinitely if the community is to expand or persist over a lengthy period. I suggest that the strain placed on individual members would be too great – that unless place were made for the satisfaction of the individual in *this* world the community could not retain or attract members.

There are three areas in which the individual can be highly valued. The ideology can see all his collective efforts as ultimately being reducible to the private welfare of the individual; the community can provide complete social and material security for the individual; the community can provide him with opportunities for individual satisfaction, e.g. in work. Of course the fact that the ideology contains assumptions in favour of the individual does not mean that these are always expressed in practice. We will return to this later. Here we note that the ideology of our communities recognizes the individual at all three levels, albeit in different ways and in differing degrees. They provide for individual salvation and individual self-realization; they provide for collectivism as an ethical end in itself and thereby provide individual security; and (in varying degrees) they allow for individuals to gain private satisfaction. The crux of the matter here is that the ideology argues that while on the one hand the individual is to be valued and supported in his own right, he can achieve this only in the context of the community way of life and the transcendental principles it expresses. This is not the same as saying that the individual must find himself by giving himself up to the greater good. In that case the individual is valued only as an instrument. I am arguing that he is valued as an end in himself but *only* in a particular and supra-individual context. In none of our communities do individuals exist *for* the greater good (Christ, the Jewish nation, the healthy society). They exist and have value entirely in their own right – but to be full individuals they need to live in a particular kind of community and to act in certain ways. (There are different degrees of emphasis in our three groups of communities on the relationship between the individual and the community. Amongst the Hutterites one detects that the idea of giving oneself up for the greater good is strongest, although recognition of the individual is extremely important. Tending in the opposite direction, the therapeutic community emphasizes the need of the individual to 'cure' and 'rehabilitate' himself, or to 'grow' as a person via community therapy, and the intrinsic value of community living is secondary. The Kibbutz lies between the two.)

This balance of the transcendental and the individual is relevant not only to the content of the ideology but also to the individual's legitimation of it. The member feels that the assumptions, goals and values of the ideology exist independently of his volition, yet he still feels very much that it is *his* ideology and *his* own creation – because *he* has seen its transcendence and has translated this into reality. The very fact of having seen it gives him a special obligation to work towards the ideology's implementation. The situation is analogous to the sculptor who 'sees' his future creation in a formless lump of wood or stone. The final product is unquestionably his own creation – and he sees it as such – but he may well argue that that was only possible 'because it was there all the time'.

A further aspect of the content of the ideology lies in its ethos of human relations and its emphasis on brotherly love, caring and non-competition. Once again, I am definitely not arguing that the communities studied always show these characteristics: their failure to provide them is another index of crisis in the community. But the fact that they do exist as values is in itself a source of security for the individual and a contribution to his sense of worth. Furthermore, the individualistic goals of the community are not mutually exclusive[3] – whatever it is that the individual must attain in life and in whatever way he is valued, there is no element or need for competition. In each case the goals are non-material and can be attained by everyone (salvation, self-realization, personal health). In fact, not only is competition unethical and unnecessary but active co-operation is mandatory since the greater the co-operation, the greater the possibility of attaining one's goals.

Another element worth noting is the principle of effort. Each of the ideologies emphasizes that individual and collective goals will not be attained unless one actively strives for them. Both the individual in regard to his own goals and the community in regard to its collective goals need to invest goal attainment with maximum energy. This serves as a motivation to the individual and as a rallying-call whenever crisis is faced. It also relates to the principle of voluntarism, which is found in each of the ideologies. Only a person who is conscious of the values of the community, who *actively* internalizes them and who commits himself to their realization, is going to attain the prescribed goals. A consequence of this has been the communities' emphasis on consciousness of goals, selectivity, education and constant appeals to greater determination – all of which have contributed to their persistence. (However, see my comments in Chapter 8 which argues that the converse of effort – play – is an equally important element of intentional community life.)

Another aspect of ideology is its anti-intellectualism. By this I do not mean that there is opposition to discussing matters intellectually. But there is a definite suspicion of too much theorizing (and in fact this is one of the reasons for the communities being founded); with this goes the perception that it is action that counts, not talking ('while others are talking, we are doing'). This applies both to the community in its overall relation to the world and to the member who wishes to divorce himself from active work. The very fact of their community's persistence is for the community members sufficient proof of the correctness of this view.

This phenomenon gives us a further clue as to the function of ideology in intentional communities. We generally understand intellectual (as opposed to intelligent) thought as a questioning of fundamentals, a process of subjecting all belief to critical analysis, a refusal to take value-systems for granted. Now, in intentional communities the intellectual does not fulfil this free-floating, Mannheimian[4] function of the intellectual. This does not mean that there are not intelligent members of intentional communities who can articulate and rationalize the purposes and processes of their life-style. But in this case their function is to expound the given ideology in clearer fashion and to use their analysis to help structure the community in accordance with fundamental

principles. It is not their function to question the principles themselves. There is, of course, some clear logic to this: if anyone
questions the principles of the community it is open to him to
leave; in short, there is no place for the intellectual deviant. This
also stems from the fact that in intentional communities ideologies
are comprehensive belief-systems; they are not ad hoc problem-
solving mechanisms. The latter can be questioned, but not the
paradigm itself. And further, as we shall see in our discussion on
the individual in intentional communities, there is no place for
anyone who wishes to be half in and half out, as is the detached
intellectual. This anti-intellectualism therefore demonstrates four
aspects of intentional communities: praxis (the process by which
thought and action stand in an integrated, dialectical relationship);
voluntarism; involvement; and the totality of ideological belief.

We should also mention the pragmatic and non-utopian nature
of the ideologies. On the one hand they are optimistic and futuristic – without these qualities there would be little point to having
an intentional community. These serve as motivation to members:
'We *will* eventually succeed.' Admittedly, in the initial stages of
the community there is great excitement and energy, but this tends
to be dissipated over the years as routinization sets in. In all three
cases studied here there was an element of pragmatism which
strongly tempered the initial utopianism. The Hutterites were far
less millenarial than the other Anabaptist groups and in fact saw
the negative consequences of millenarianism for others (e.g. the
Peasants' Commune). The Kibbutzim had high hopes but did not
see their task as revolutionizing Jewish national life (at least not
overnight). The Gedudei Ha-avodah eventually gave up on that
aim, while the Marxist-orientated groups believed in an involvement with the wider community and evolutionary change. In the
therapeutic communities their external aims only developed at a
later stage; in fact, they did not even have long-term aims initially.
The communities have not felt that they will usher in the End of
Days – neither for the world as a whole nor for the communities'
individual members. The community has moral, social or political
obligations and even a degree of influence on the world, but does
not expect total success. The implications of this for the individual
are discussed in the conclusion to Chapter 8. What concerns us
here is that this non-utopianism has meant that the communities
have not had unrealistic expectations about their ability to
influence the world or to attain their internal goals. They expect

their task to be difficult, but they derive confidence from their knowledge that they are on the right path. This has led to a balance between determined idealism on the one hand and a calculating, business-like pragmatism on the other.

At the same time the community exists so that members can attain some higher aims – but only if the individual actively and consciously strives for this. Thus the individual on joining the community should not expect the world to change of its own accord, nor should he expect to attain his goals in some mechanical manner. The community as a whole has to struggle in the world at large; and the individual must make a determined effort within the framework of his own community. While individuals may hope and pray for a perfect world there is nothing in the ideology to indicate that it will be found – and if found, that the path to it will be easy. The best they can aim at is a better world, but even that attainment is a matter for individual dedication, effort, persistence and struggle within the community. The same applies to the community *vis-à-vis* its environment. In other words, the individual can only attain his aims through his *own* efforts; the community as a whole can only attain its aims through *its* own efforts. So, by emphasizing the need for individual effort (it is not enough just to be a formal member of the community) and for collective effort (the world will not change easily, and may even be hostile) the individual's level of commitment is raised. Yet, we should note, despite the futuristic orientation there is no denigration of the here-and-now. Life must not be hedonistic, but that does not mean that all pleasure must be deferred until some distant future arrives.

In conclusion, I suggest that the ideologies of each of our communities contain a number of apparently contradictory themes: a systematic, comprehensive, articulated ideology – a loose, partial, 'taken-for-granted' ideology; the collective good – individual good; satisfaction in achievement – consciousness of imperfection; future orientation – daily gratification; the right way of life – the need for greater effort; idealism and lack of compromise – pragmatism and adaptation. It is by living with, or rather by subtly balancing these opposite themes both in theory and practice, that the communities have managed to persist.

Chapter 6
Ideology, structure and change

We can now illustrate our arguments about ideological and social change in the communities we have studied.

Changes in social practice

If we compare Hutterite colonies and Kibbutzim as they originally were and as they exist today, we can see great differences. Yet as far as contemporary members are concerned they are acting within the same ideological framework as their predecessors, i.e. in essence they are the same group as before.

The Hutterites

(1) Missionary work, which was once fundamental to the ideology and to the community's very existence, is now non-existent. Missionary work was never taken up in America or Canada because the Hutterites knew how vulnerable their situation was and that proselytizing would only evoke further negative response. They frankly admit that they were concerned only to settle down peacefully and not have to face further persecution.[1] Today, however, other groups are seeking them out for assistance in setting up Christian-based communes and the Hutterites are only too glad to help.

(2) In Moravia they were, relative to the times, technologically advanced. On arriving in America they insisted on being technologically primitive; now they accept the need for technological progress.

(3)   There is a constant grass-roots push to liberalize rules about dress (more individuality, more colour). Changes are slowly occurring here.

(4)   The ideology proscribes involvement in public affairs. This is by and large adhered to but where Hutterite interests are affected involvement is seen as legitimate. While Hutterites will in principle not vote in elections, they will do so on issues directly affecting them. They are also prepared to sit on provincial committees for agricultural marketing and one member in Manitoba belongs to a provincial education committee dealing with teaching English as a second language.

(5)   The Hutterites have been staunch in their pacifism. In the First World War they steadfastly refused to be conscripted in America and were persecuted as a result (hence their move to Canada). In the Second World War they did forestry service or worked on neighbouring farms as an alternative to conscription; instead of buying War Bonds they contributed to the Red Cross.

(6)   The principle of giving people money only if they need it, and to the extent that they need it, has given way to personal allocations. To counteract charges of favouritism for those who make more frequent trips to town, allocations of barely more than one dollar monthly are made.

(7)   Living standards have been kept low in line with the principle of simplicity. Yet there have been improvements over the past few years.

(8)   English school has been introduced. While the Hutterites have always attempted to maintain an autonomous education system, they have been forced by the provincial governments to introduce 'English School' (provincial curriculum), to keep their children in school until the minimum school leaving age (Hutterite attempts to leave school at the age of 15 when the minimum age was raised to 16 failed) and to be taught by qualified teachers.

The Kibbutz

(1)   While ultimate authority resides in the general meeting there has been a shift to decision-making in committees or by specialists.

(2) A variety of means exists of allocating personal goods: the 'help yourself' system (as in the early days when there was little to help yourself to anyway); the point system (where goods are given a point value and the individual can acquire goods to a certain total point value); the personal budget system (the individual gets cash to a certain value in each sphere – clothes, furniture, etc. – but cannot transfer cash from sphere to sphere); the combined system (the individual is given one lump sum to do with as he likes).

(3) Most children sleep in children's houses; some sleep in their parents' home and there is a trend in this direction.

(4) Some Kibbutzim emphasize smallness, others favour large numbers.

(5) The different Kibbutz movements have different conceptions about the degree and kind of centralized control that should exist. At one extreme (Kibbutz Artzi-Mapam) members automatically receive membership of the political party to which their movement is affiliated, and while political debate is entirely open and democratic, ultimate decisions are binding on all. At the other extreme party membership is a matter of personal conscience and there is no overall political decision-making.

(6) The Kibbutzim have used and do use hired labour. (This is now virtually non-existent in services and agriculture and will probably decline but not disappear altogether in industry.)

(7) Industry has taken a central economic role in what was originally conceived as an agricultural undertaking.

(8) There is a continuing trend to improving living standards. (While the Kibbutz never believed in austerity for its own sake, there was much emphasis on simplicity; high living standards were associated with bourgeois decadence. Today there are fewer guilt feelings about living standards.)

(9) Work is seen more as a means of personal satisfaction and economic contribution than as a quasi-mystical and cathartic activity (as was the case in the early days).

(10) The Kibbutz engages in entrepreneurship (e.g. guest houses).

Tables 6.1 and 6.2 show some changes in Hutterite and Kibbutz society between the early days and today.

Table 6.1:   *Changes in Hutterite society*

Sixteenth Century	Twentieth Century
1 Agriculture	Agriculture
2 Crafts (for sale)	–
3 Service (for sale)	–
4 Technologically progressive*	Technologically progressive*
5 Autonomous education system	Quasi-autonomous education system
6 Educationally progressive*	Educationally conservative*
7 Total rejection of state	Rejection of state (but less than total)
8 Very limited personal independence	Limited personal independence
9 Austerity seen as end in itself	Advances in living standards (but limited and controlled)
10 Inter-colony co-ordination, centralized control	Inter-colony co-operation, limited centralized authority, confined mainly to Leut
11 Deviance not tolerated	Limited (if covert) deviance tolerated (unbaptized only)
12 Pacifism absolute	Alternative service
13 Missionary activity	None (but ready to help others if asked)

* Relative to the times.

Some things have not changed at all in both cases. Chiefly, this refers to the collectivist nature of the communities – that the community is totally responsible to its members and that members are totally responsible to and for the community and are, ideally, totally dependent on it. Nor have the principles of voluntarism and of equality irrespective of effort been changed. Nor do members feel that other principles have been vitiated. Where a principle has been abandoned, this has been justified by appealing to a higher principle, such as survival itself. This was the case with the Hutterite abandonment of missionary work, but the Hutterites in no way feel they have 'failed' in this regard (they are simply waiting for better days). The same applies to their partial compromises on the subjects of public involvement, alternative service

Table 6.2: *Changes in Kibbutz society*

Early Days*	Today
1 Agriculture	Agriculture
2 –	Industry
3 –	Hired labour
4 –	Commercial practices
5 Work as catharsis	Work as self-realization
6 Kibbutz as autonomous economic unit	Regional economic planning
7 'To everybody according to his needs'	More mechanical distribution of consumer goods
8 Informal education system (no exams or degrees)	Formal education, university
9 Atheism	Rejection of orthodoxy, search for relevant tradition
10 Low status for family	Family plays stronger role
11 Unspecialized decision-making	Specialization

* I have not put dates here even though I am referring mainly to the 1910s, 1920s and 1930s. Some Kibbutzim though were already moving out of the early phase while others were only entering it. 'Early days' refers therefore more to each Kibbutz than to the Kibbutz movement as a whole.[2]

and English school. *In each case they have made just enough compromise to protect their interests or prevent undue confrontation with their environment, but not so much compromise that they feel they have abandoned their principles.*

The need for change: ideological inconsistency

The point is that if the community is to survive, it frequently cannot put its pure ideology into practice. If the Hutterites had insisted on using the horse and cart to this day then they would be economically backward to an extent to which many members would find unacceptable, and the opportunities they (chiefly males) find for personal satisfaction would be lost. Also their strength *vis-à-vis* the surrounding society would be grossly weakened. This particular observation helps us to understand a basic consideration. The Hutterites and Kibbutzim have always recognized, even if only implicitly, that in order to survive in a hostile environment, to be a source of strength and appeal in that environment, to implement fundamental social and moral beliefs and to provide individual satisfaction, *they need to start from a position of economic strength.*[3] So if compromises have to be made in the name of economic considerations, they can be justified on the grounds that without such compromises the chief purposes of the community, and even its very existence, will be threatened. Furthermore, economic strength means economic contribution to the host society, hence less chance of rejection (although it can and does arouse considerable resentment – both the Hutterites and the Kibbutzim have suffered a 'backlash' of economic acceptance).[4] Similarly, economic strength means not only economic but social and political independence, a freedom from external coercion, the absence of which would not only mean undue ideological influence from outside but also a loss of faith on the part of members in their ability to control their own lives. Economic strength also allows for a wide range of economic activities and for a labour surplus – both crucial to providing members with wider opportunities for job and personal satisfaction. Finally, both the Hutterites and Kibbutzim use their economic strength for expansion – the Hutterites by acquiring land for splitting, the Kibbutzim by subsidising the development of new settlements when the government was withdrawing subsidies. It is almost superfluous to emphasize the need for economic viability to ensure communal persistence; however, the Hutterites and Kibbutzim have gone beyond this and have become economically successful.

We should also note that, while the ideology is rooted in an abstract morality, many of its details are in fact geared up to sustaining social solidarity. The value of simplicity in living standards is not only an intrinsic moral principle, it is also a means of social control and a basis for social cohesion. But if cohesion is threatened by taking simplicity to exaggerated extremes (as members see it) then adjustments are easily made. Simplicity is such a flexible term that the Hutterites, for example, can improve living standards a little to satisfy members' needs and still claim that they are keeping to the principle of simplicity. We can also note then an 'over-explicit' definition of simplicity would not have allowed for this accommodation.

At this point let us digress for a moment, because the question of economic strength can be complex. Almost every commentator on communal societies, whether acknowledging the importance of a secure economic base or not, will argue that 'too much' economic success can be a danger to the community. While there is a grain of truth in this argument, it is in fact simplistic and does not deal with the real issues at stake.

The significance of economic success can tell us much about the nature of intentional communities. In Chapters 8 and 10 I discuss some of the defining qualities of intentional communities, such as *authority, sharing* and *dependence*. At this stage let us say that these are qualities which make intentional communities precisely that rather than, say, co-operative societies. In addition, intentional communities usually attempt to generate a feeling of 'we-ness', a group spirit, a sense of community. However, the latter are socially desirable characteristics of intentional communities, *not* defining qualities. The argument 'against' economic success fails to perceive this difference. Apart from the fact that it is difficult to define how much economic success is success (i.e. at precisely what point economic success becomes a threat to the community) it fails to realize that a high standard of living need not upset the defining characteristics or conditions of communality or intentionality. What is true is that where there is much disposable income individuals in intentional communities may concentrate on their private lives and on raising their living standards rather than on the social life of the community. The result is that the 'we-feeling' can decline, the individual becomes self-absorbed and less community-oriented. Observers (and many insiders) see this as a 'decline' in the collective nature of the community. In fact, though, this need not in any way detract from the defining qualities of the community. Whether the community is rich or poor, whether individuals are totally community-oriented or more self-indulgent, need not affect in any way the essential components of communality: authority (the community is the ultimate source of authority – of deciding which areas of life are 'communal property' and which not); sharing (that certain areas of life – as decided by the community – *must* be shared by all members); and dependence (that the individual requires the community to satisfy essential needs). (These definitions require qualification and amplification – see our discussions on the individual (Chapter 8) and on exclusive relations (Chapter 10).) The point is that these defining qualities of intentional communities are quite independent of standards of living: they can exist and operate quite adequately, irrespective of the degree of economic success achieved. For this reason one should not necessarily equate economic success with communal failure, even if greater individualism is evinced.

However, this matter does not end here, because there is one essential dimension of community life which can be affected by high living standards. In intentional communities there is no such thing as unemployment. Apart from the fact that a work ethic prevails and that the notion of some people working while others do not would be considered unfair (and, interestingly, the unfairness would be thought to be against those *not* working – even if their living standards remain – because of their being denied the creative, social and moral value of work), unemployment would be a form of withdrawal (another theme developed below). Now, when there is economic success, various things can happen. The community can use its available capital for investment, expansion and growth, thus providing a wider range of occupational opportunities while still *demanding* of individuals that they work and work hard (which, apart from being an economic consideration, also means that the individual is engaged in the overall life of the community). This is what the Kibbutz has done and partially explains the Kibbutz's industrialization trend. Or the community can save money, i.e. deliberately hold down living standards and deliberately not re-invest, and then use the money for extra-community purposes. This is what the Hutterites have done and partially explains the phenomenon of splitting (for which considerable sums are required).[5]

The danger arises when, as a result of economic success, individuals become superfluous to the economic functioning of the community, so that both their sense of dependence on the community and their sense of involvement in it are attenuated. This is not so much a question of them saying 'I don't need the community' as of the community saying 'we don't need you', and the consequences this has for individual identification with his community. This can happen with any individuals in an intentional community, i.e. to any person whose labour is not integral to the economic structure of the community or does not labour at all, a situation more likely to arise with economic success, but which could equally apply to others, e.g. members who are too old or sick to work. And it affects one group in particular, namely, the younger generation, a point discussed more fully in our comments on collective education (Chapter 7).

To return to the issue of ideology and change. The Kibbutz has had less authoritative sources for its ideology than have the Hutterites. Hence it has tended to seek a variety of forms according to personal inclination and outlook, yet all within the broad framework of the ideology. So there have never been arguments in the Kibbutz as to whether there should be democracy or equality. Yet what these substantively consist of is highly unclear. Democracy means that the general meeting has ultimate authority and control, but this has also meant that committees or specialists have been able to take much control. The principle of equality has always meant 'to each according to his need' but various ways of meeting need have all seemed to their protagonists to be consistent or, in fact, to be *the most* consistent with the principle.

This helps us to understand one of our theoretical points – that members sometimes see the Kibbutz's institutions (e.g. personal budgets) as *nothing more than a means* of implementing equality, whereas others may define equality *in terms of its taking a particular form*. Much argument within the Kibbutz movement has stemmed from this contradiction. The matter of children's sleeping arrangements is a good example of this. Some have argued that children sleeping in children's houses *is the definition* of collective education. Others have argued that it is *an educational technique only* and that if children sleep in their parents' home there is no reason to assume that they (the children) will fail to learn collective values.

We can note further that the idea of having a society based on self-realization, equality and democracy has in fact no inherent connection to how the Kibbutz should relate to its environment or even whether it should do so at all. I suggest that in communal societies members tacitly see various aspects of the ideology in terms of causal connections, but while each area (such as the ones just mentioned) can no doubt be legitimated in its own right, I cannot see that one necessarily and inevitably flows from the other. This explains why different groups are so insistent on their's being the correct interpretation of the proper Kibbutz-environment relationship, but why, too, different interpretations are possible.

Much the same applies to the size of the community. A case can be made for relating size to democracy. Yet by considering a system of, say, council-rule (where in a large Kibbutz the general assembly only meets from time to time and is replaced by a council of twenty to thirty members) to be equally compatible with the principle of democracy as is everyone meeting informally every evening (as happened in the early days) one can say that in a large Kibbutz there is as much democracy as in a small one. Only when people *define* democracy *as* 'everyone-meeting-informally-every-evening' does dispute arise.

The question of hired labour shows us a further aspect of ideology at work. There is hardly a voice in the Kibbutz movement which justifies hired labour, [6] yet it exists, and at times in no small measure. Its emergence showed two contradictions in Kibbutz philosophy. One was the need to keep abreast of the environment regarding living standards, the other was to serve the needs of the nation. Both meant industrialization – hence hired labour. But this was against Kibbutz principles. However, the Kibbutz has solved the problem simply by saying: 'This *is* a problem, but slowly we are overcoming it and then everything will be satisfactory.' It is a contradiction which is simply lived with until better days. The ideologically sensitive members see this as internal weakness or as a succumbing to external forces but not as a sign of basic failure; rather it alerts them to the need for greater vigilance and more determined effort to attain Kibbutz goals.

Finally, in connection with therapeutic communities, we can compare Richmond Fellowship houses with other therapeutic communities. All adhere to the same basic principles of personal growth, communication, honesty, respect for the individual. They all agree, too, that as an operational principle, your entire life is relevant to therapy. Given those broad ideas we can see how different communities have applied them in different spheres.

The size of the community, its structure, its policy on medication and its conception as to whether to be involved in the environment or not, are all matters it has to take a stand on. In each case the policy has to be related to the basic goals of the community. Yet from Table 6.3 we see clearly how different policies can operate in each sphere and how different permutations are possible. What I am saying is that given the overall goals of the community it can be either small or large, and whether it is small or large tells us nothing about whether to use medication or not, to be or not to be involved with the environment, to be democratic or authoritarian.

Table 6.3:   *Comparison of therapeutic policies*

	Size	Structure	Medication	Relation to Environment
Richmond Fellowship	Small (15–20)	Democratic*	Quasi-	Involved*
Henderson[a] *Hospital*	Large (40–60)	Democratic	Non-	Withdrawn*
Phoenix[b] *Houses*	Small	Authoritarian*	Non-	Withdrawn

a A therapeutic community in a hospital setting.
b A drug-rehabilitation community; this model is widely used in drug rehabilitation.
* I use these terms loosely and relative to each other.

There are certain considerations and qualifications we should note regarding all three groups of communities. The first is that because of the possibility of incorporating different structures within a single conceptual framework, the communities have been able to adapt to changing circumstances without feeling they have in any way abandoned their basic meanings, frame of reference, concepts, goals or principles. In this way the community has sustained its sense of purpose and identity while simultaneously being able to accommodate to changing needs. Along these lines we can also argue that given the basic outlines of the ideology, a variety of communal structures have emerged. There are over 230 Bruderhof, over 260 Kibbutzim and sixty Richmond Fellowship houses; the Hutterites were one of six Anabaptist groups and there are three Hutterite streams; the Kibbutzim exist alongside the Moshav Ovdim and the Moshav Shitufi[7] and there are three (until recently four) Kibbutz streams; the Richmond Fellowship houses are one kind of therapeutic community and one kind of halfway house among literally hundreds, and represent only one stage in a 'continuum of care'.[8]

This has a number of consequences. For one thing, a person identifying with the ideology can choose from quite a variety the particular institutional forms appropriate to his needs and personality. He may see his choice as being ideologically necessary and objectively 'the best' and this will add to his feeling of well-being in the community. Furthermore, the existence of a number of communities which are all variations on the same theme also means that each can be relatively homogeneous. A person not satisfied with the forms of his actual or potential community need not subvert it from within – he can simply go elsewhere. 'Elsewhere' refers to another community within the same network and having a rather different structure, albeit within the same frame of reference. Hence there is less threat to that community's interpretation of the ideology than there would have been if it were the only existing interpretation.

The need for cohesion: ideological consistency

If I have gone to some pains to show that change and adaptation are possible because of both the loose structure of the ideology and the lack of causal connections between its elements, I now wish to redress the balance. A large degree of flexibility and even contradiction is possible – but this is not infinite. As a general assertion we can say that if the community is to persist it needs to recognize that the acceptance of any one element of the ideology *constrains* the degree of variation in the others. For example, we have seen that the basic premises of social therapy do not tell us in any way whether therapeutic communities should be involved with the environment or not, but if we *do* choose to be involved with the environment, or to present a certain image to it, then we are automatically limited in the therapeutic techniques we can use – for example, primal screams or infantile regression will be out simply because this will lead to conflict with the environment. Similarly, there is no inherent connection between democracy, equality and using or not using medication, but if one does choose to use medication then a complete medical model cannot be adopted because this makes all the arguments about honest communication superfluous; nor, if the community believes in democracy, equality and personal responsibility, can staff prescribe and administer drugs. Such a setup negates the foregoing principles of the community. Hence, a *non*-medication system or a *quasi*-medication system is logically possible and functionally efficient in terms of social therapy, but not a *full* medical model.

We can apply the same kind of argument when we compare the Hutterites and Kibbutzim regarding social control. My argument is that there is no priori reason to say that for an intentional community to persist there should or should not be formal sanctions. The Hutterites have formal sanctions for deviant behaviour, the Kibbutzim have none (Chapter 9). What does need to exist though is compatibility between the policy on sanctions and other elements of the community's life – its ideology, its structure, personal needs and so on.

Among the Hutterites the individual is considered inherently weak; there is only one source of authority (the New Testament as interpreted by the Founding Fathers); there is a quasi-authoritarian structure. So the imposition of formal sanctions is not only not contradictory to these elements of Hutterite life, it is virtually a necessity. Not to have such sanctions would be to undermine the authority structure or to suggest that the individual is totally responsible for and to himself. In the Kibbutz the individual is seen as being inherently good; he is responsible for and to himself, for and to the community; the structure of the community is a means of enhancing the here-and-now value of the individual. So to impose formal sanctions here would be to deny the individual his fundamental status of being equal to others and would deny the conception that the community is its own source of authority, and that the community is constituted of its members, and them only, at any particular time. So, for the Hutterites to abandon sanctions or for the Kibbutzim to impose them, would be equally incongruous and ultimately disruptive.

However, I do not want to go to the other extreme. One cannot work out with pen and paper that if the community is characterized by a, b and c, then it must or must not have qualities x, y and z. The reason is that compatibility between elements is not simply a matter of logic but also of the perceptions of members. To some extent the argument I used in the preceding two paragraphs regarding sanctions was a matter of post hoc reasoning on my part. We can perhaps generalize and associate on the one hand an authoritarian structure and formal sanctions, and on the other hand a democratic structure and no *formal* sanctions. (In the case of therapeutic communities, the contrast is clear between Fellowship Houses and Phoenix Houses.)

The problem is that we cannot state precisely how authoritarian is authoritarian or how democratic is democratic. The Hutterites *see themselves* as being democratic and that is the heart of the matter. Nor do they see their rules as being authoritarian, restrictive or repressive – on the contrary, for them the rules of the community are natural and morally necessary. The good Hutterite in their thinking *wants* to live by the rules; he has no need or desire to subvert the authority structure. Since it is what he wants anyway, the system is not authoritarian as far as they are concerned.

So, to a large extent, what is compatible with what depends on the perceptions of members themselves, and the observer needs to impose not his own logic on them but the logic of those involved. In this way permutations of institutional forms are possible which to others acting within the same frame of reference may seem downright treacherous. Arguments within the Kibbutz movement about children's sleeping arrangements have seemed to some as being fundamentally in opposition to Kibbutz collectivism and to others as being compatible with it. To some therapeutic communities, personal growth and the concept of a democratic community are opposite sides of the same coin; to others they have no connection at all.

I am therefore arguing (1) that a single ideology (or single element within an ideology) can be concretely expressed in a variety of ways; (2) that these ways need to be compatible in terms of the subjective perceptions of the members themselves, however incompatible they may seem to others; yet (3) that there are, nevertheless, objective limitations to these variations, and that a community's functional efficiency is subverted to the extent that such limitations are ignored. As a further example of (3) let us look at occurrences in each of our communities.

When reparations money began arriving in Israel from Germany after the Second World War, the Kibbutzim had to do much soul-searching as to how to handle it, since some members received substantial payments. The principle was unequivocal – members must hand the money unconditionally to the Kibbutz. But many did not do so through fear that if they left the Kibbutz one day they would have nothing to fall back on; others left rather than hand the money in. As a result of this some Kibbutzim even collapsed. Now the point is not whether it was inherently logical or moral to handle the matter one way or another. (In fact, the way in which it was eventually handled was a classic case of an intentional community compromising on its 'pure' ideology so as to sustain individual feelings of well-being on the Kibbutz, thus keeping both the ideology and the Kibbutz membership fairly intact. Members were required to hand money in, but received it back if they eventually left; even as members they could use some of the money for special *Kibbutz-authorized* purposes, e.g. an overseas trip.) For the Kibbutz to have said that members could keep reparations money and do what they liked with it would have grossly contradicted Kibbutz ideology and its existing application. From the viewpoint of functioning it could only have embarked on that policy if there had been an accompanying change in ideology and in the other institutional forms. From the viewpoint of operational efficiency only, there is nothing to choose between a Kibbutz and a Moshav. But if the Kibbutz had chosen to ignore reparations entirely it could only have continued persisting by becoming something like a Moshav (with greater contractual relations) – as a Kibbutz it would have broken down since bad feeling at a subjective level and institutional contradiction at an operational level would have developed *and did develop* until a solution which was ideologically acceptable *and* personally acceptable *and* ideologically-personally compatible was found.

If we turn to the Hutterites we can follow the same lines. The Hutterites believe in pacifism, missionary work, uniform dress, withdrawal, an agricultural economy, collectivism, adult baptism, non-contraception, a certain social hierarchy and so on. It is difficult to define 'the Hutterite way of life' – it is simply all these elements in their concrete application together. One element can be abandoned totally with little or no effect on the others – this is precisely what happened in the case of missionary work – but to what extent is this possible?

The common thread running through all these aspects of Hutterite life is that they are said to have a common source, and that the collectivity of Elders *and it alone* decides on matters of policy. So whether the Elders decide to be pacifists or not or to change dress styles may be unconnected, but the idea that only the Elders can decide is fundamental; any change in this must lead to changes in the overall status structure of the community – male over female, married over unmarried, baptized over unbaptized. The splits and excommunications that took place at Big Bend, Interlake and Forest River colony[9] were not so much because they adopted another religion or new social practices (drastic as that was) but because their so doing subverted the entire authority structure of the sect. Similarly, there is no inherent reason why there should or should not be light industry, but to sustain it would require a different educational system, a different occupational hierarchy and possibly a different kind of involvement with the outside world. Finally, there is no inherent connection between missionary work, the principle of non-contraception and an agri-cultural economy. But if there were to be missionary work the population would presumably be greater than it is now. Yet with an agricultural economy living standards are then going to be limited and especially if the possibilities of acquiring land are restricted.[10] So if the population is going to grow living standards might have to drop *or* a non-agricultural economy (in part) would have to be developed; if it is not going to grow more than at its present rate then either contraception will have to be introduced *or* missionary work abandoned. The last was the solution accepted (albeit for very different reasons). So while each element of Hutt-erite life can be changed within the ideology, the way such changes take place will affect the way other elements operate; cumulatively these changes can lead to a Hutterite way of life somewhat different from that we now see (just as modern Hutterite colonies are rather different to their Moravian predecessors), and if a certain congruence is not kept between elements, destructive conflicts can develop.

We should also note that both the Kibbutzim and the Hutterites have recognized the interaction between living standards and involvement with the outside world. Such involvement inevitably leads members to demand higher living standards, just as a desire for higher living standards necessitates externally-directed econ-omic activity. In both cases leaders have attempted to control the rise in living standards but never to the point of withdrawing totally from the environment, since this would be economic and social suicide. Nevertheless control is necessary in this sphere for economic, ideological and social reasons (the virtues of simplicity and social control). Regarding therapeutic communities I have already made the point that there is no inherent connection between the constituent elements of the ideology, but once a practice is adopted (e.g. medication) there must be limits to the extent of its implementation otherwise other principles may be undermined (e.g. democracy).

Ideology as a force for integration and change

To summarize then, the ideology as it is structured and the various aspects of communal life are, up to a point, a system (as we defined the concept earlier). Therefore they cannot slip apart too much. Yet they are sufficiently unintegrated for change to be introduced in one aspect, or even dropped altogether, without necessarily affecting the other aspects – so the community need not feel it has violated its basic identity. The communities we have studied here have persisted in large part precisely because, as we have shown, they have generally acted within the basic framework of the ideology and kept the community as a fairly integrated system, yet have been sufficiently pragmatic to take advantage of the possibilities its lack of integration has left open for change and adaptation. By balancing the need for system-integration and identity on the one hand, and the need for flexibility and adaptability on the other, they have sustained their sense of meaning and purpose and have related it successfully to the demands of the real world.

Finally, we should note the nature of ideological debate in intentional communities. Sometimes there are debates about fundamentals, that is, whether the basic propositions of the ideology are correct or not. This has led to splits in the community (the three colonies mentioned among the Hutterites, the early 1950s in the Kibbutzim). More frequently, though, debate takes place at the lower levels of the ideology. Here the basic premises, goals and norms of the community are taken for granted. Debate is, however, often conducted *as if* it were about fundamentals. Seldom does it happen that people propose arguments on the basis of 'it suits me personally' but rather that 'this is what our ideology is *really* about'. This is inevitable precisely because ideology permeates and transcends so much of community life. It is the inviolable source of authority: arguments in terms of ideology are 'moral' and 'objective'; all else is 'partial', 'relative', 'egoistic'.

Despite all this the observer cannot help noticing how much debate, despite its ideological overtones, is rooted in personal traits, outlook, experiences and day-to-day situations. The individual himself may not recognize this. He may insist that he is only concerned with realization of the ideology and the community's good (though he may be very quick to point to the personal nature of the opposition's argument). I am not suggesting that this is rationalization or self-delusion or hypocrisy. On the contrary, if all that I said earlier about identity is true then this situation is necessary and inevitable. One does not live by ideology abstractly. One's adherence to it is rooted in all aspects of one's identity. Hence one's interpretation of facts is not simply a matter of metaphysical logic but of incorporating those facts, manipulating them and adjusting to them in terms of one's needs, experiences, perceptions and so on. Only in this way is identification with a community possible. The moment the interpretation and application of the ideology begin to disrupt one's identity one is likely either to leave the community or to become deviant within it or to attempt to change the ideology. So debates about change take place at two levels simultaneously: the 'pure' ideological level (this is necessary to community cohesion) and the personal level (this is necessary to personal identification and commitment), although the distinction between the two is usually not explicitly set out.

All this may help to explain a phenomenon which has frequently been noted in the literature on social movements and sects. This is the intensity of debate about what to the outsider appear to be trivial matters. Why is it so important what colour one's buttons should be or whether one should use buttons or press studs (Hutterites) or whether one gives a person points for three shirts or the cash equivalent (Kibbutz)? There are a number of reasons for this. One is that the small debate is often a reflection of a more fundamental debate. It is a vehicle by which the basic questions of the community are debated without having to spell out the fact that it is fundamentals which are being debated. To open fundamentals to debate is, in an intentional community, potentially to raise doubts about the community's very right to exist. The problem is overcome by arguing fiercely about apparently trivial matters which in their triviality encapsulate the fundamental issues.

This phenomen is also rooted in a basic aspect of communal life. I have stressed earlier that the individual's identification with his community is his means of sustaining and strengthening his identity. Yet I also show later that communal life has many strains and tensions for the individual. At a more generalized level we may argue as follows. The individual member seeks to establish *and assert* his identity. He does this by identifying with a particular social group. This means, though, that he is achieving his goals by submerging himself in the group. Therefore he is paying a price for sustaining his identity, since identity implies a degree, however minimal, of uniqueness. He has an identity, but this identity has lost some of its individuality. He needs to correct the balance. This is partly achieved by giving him various means of personal satisfaction in the community: the ideology specifically enshrines his personal value, there is an ethos of caring, and there are specific mechanisms of personal satisfaction – positions of responsibility, status, occupational opportunities.

I would now like to suggest that debates about trivia serve the same purpose. The individual seldom opens up fundamentals to debate; it is difficult to do so nor perhaps does he very much want to. Precisely for that reason he can assert himself by debating or questioning the concrete and day-to-day applications of fundamentals. Fundamentals may be holy writ: their applications are not. The latter can be legitimately questioned, and by questioning them the individual is asserting his 'control' over the fundamentals and his private variation of them. In so doing he is gaining for himself a degree of individuality; he is, in a sense, 'conspiring' against his society (cf. our discussion of alienation). On a larger scale the same argument applies to debates between groups acting within the same ideological framework. By asserting different views of small matters they are asserting their uniqueness, their moral superiority (*'we* know what the ideology *really* means') and are thereby strengthening their group cohesion.

In practice this has been reflected in the various attempts to unify the separate trends. Both major communities have been very wary in this regard. In the sixteenth century there was a degree of co-operation between Anabaptist groups but at times there was intense antagonism. The Hutterites would only join up with others if the latter did all the compromising (which never happened). In this century other groups have joined them – and have then been excommunicated for not accepting Hutterite practices fully. I refer here to Julius Kubassek's group[11] and Eberhard Arnold's Bruderhof.[12] But even within the Hutterites there is little desire for unity of the three Leute. There is even a degree of tension between them as in the recent court cases on taxation.[13] The Kibbutz movements too are most wary of unifying: they are prepared to co-operate in technical or external matters but less on ideologically relevant affairs, e.g. having a homogeneous education system, and there is little contact between the Kibbutzim and the Moshav movements. (Recently, though, the Ichud and Meuchad movements united; it remains to be seen how integrated they become.) We should note, however, one significant aspect of this – the groups which have most favoured internal unity and outward-looking co-operation (the Schmiede-leut and the Ichud movement respectively) are also those which internally are the least conservative and are considered by the others as 'too liberal'.

For intentional communities, where ideological saturation is basic, others of a similar persuasion can do no right and vice versa. If they are too ecumenical (internally or externally) then they are traitors to the faith, or at best have watered the ideology down to meaninglessness which is a curse to themselves and a threat to the really faithful; if they are uncompromising then they are gratuitously narrow, rigid, exclusive, self-righteous, behind the times, and the oppressors of personal freedom.

Chapter 7
Socialization

Commitment to faith and community: the Hutterite
education system

Essential to the persistence of Hutterite society in relatively
unchanged form is of course the socialization system. The relation
between sexes, the age hierarchy, economic activity, attitudes to
the outside world – all these depend on having members with
a particular set of values and skills and certain perceptions of
themselves, their society, their environment. The education
system is geared up to having precisely such members, yet it is
not simply the education system in its own right which achieves
this. Like most other aspects of Hutterite society the education
system is integral to the wider life of the colony. Put otherwise,
we may say that the very fact of living on the colony is in itself
an education; the system of child-rearing is one element in the
continuity of theory and practice and of specific colony practices.
Just as much as education (in the formal sense) props up 'the
system' so does 'the system' prop up education. A child growing
up on a colony is meant to *learn* formally and to *experience*
informally what it is to be a Hutterite. The two are meant to
complement and reinforce one another, thus providing a system
which is self-perpetuating because it is internally consistent. The
aim of child-rearing is to make the child understand, accept and
practise that consistency.

Let us first note briefly the process of growing up in a colony.
The stages are as follows:

(1) 0 to 2 years: looked after by the mother and other family
     females.

(2)   3 to 5 years: Kindergarten.
(3)   6 to 16 years: German school and English school.
(4)   16 years to baptism (about 20–22 years).
(5)   Baptism to marriage.

Although each stage is accompanied by its own expectations, practices and discipline, their aims, educational principles and assumptions are the same. The basic assumption is that human beings are inherently sinful, that their carnal and egoistic natures will, if not contained, inevitably come to the fore. If left to themselves, to their natural tendencies, children will have no sense of justice, co-operation or communality; they will be jealous of others, ambitious and lustful. Hutterite society is predicated on the opposite of these traits: therefore children must be taught to accept what they cannot and will not accept of their own accord. Nor are these virtues to be inculcated through a 'rational' education in the sense of persuading them through reason or even through appeals to their advantage. They (the virtues) must – can only – be inculcated through a particular set of educational practices and through having a colony life-style consistent with them.

One can say that the aims of the education system are to teach the child not to be self-willed or to have individual ambition; that the group is superior to the individual, so that colony needs and daily organization take precedence over private matters; that he must accept discipline as determined by his superiors, and that this discipline is the consequence of his own actions, for which he is himself responsible; that he must know that the colony has a right structure in terms of age, sex and authority and that he must be obedient to those who have authority over him; that co-operation is a virtue and may involve self-denial, which is both a virtue in its own right and the means to enhancing co-operative life and the general welfare of the colony; that there are no material or social rewards for correct behaviour, such behaviour being its own satisfaction and being the key to life after death; that everything he learns is not the creation of man but of God, whose law is not to be questioned nor doubted.

There is in the Hutterite system no place for the concept of self-realization. A child who has learnt the above has gone through a process of 'growth and achievement'. In Hutterite thinking the child is incapable of attaining this by himself. Since all colony beliefs are derived from God, achievement means accepting these beliefs: since the child needs help in so doing and since the colony as a whole is responsible for and to the child, educational practice must ensure that he learns what he ought to learn. Hence there is no attempt at teaching the child self-discipline. He is expected to internalize the values and to act according to accepted practice automatically. Self-discipline would imply a code of behaviour deliberately and consciously arrived at, one which you act by because *you* have concluded it is good. This has no place in Hutterite thinking. The individual must accept them (Hutterite belief and practice) because they *are* good; and since it is not possible and is at any rate undesirable that children accept them of their own accord, they (the children) must be taught the values in unequivocal fashion.

Education begins virtually from the day the child is born. From an early age he is toilet-trained; this is both a discipline in itself and a means of making him adjust his daily schedule to the needs of the colony. After a short break the mother begins to work; her work-schedule has to take precedence, like other activities such as church-going, over the baby's private needs. This serves as a further educational lesson – that the child does not control his environment. (It would not be correct to argue that the mother leaves the baby for church because of the status of religious services. For the Hutterites the services can be ignored when there is a pressure of work. Religious *ritual* is not central to the Hutterite way of life.) We should not get the impression that attitudes to babies, or any children for that matter, are cold or mechanical or harsh. Within the framework of the accepted rules, and without seeing any contradiction between discipline and warmth, the latter is displayed to the children at the same time as the former is demanded of them. The baby is frequently looked after by grandmother or older sisters (the work of young girls frequently entails childminding) in order to allow the mother to perform her colony duties.

This sense of subordination is extended to the kindergarten. The children here are often given poorer food; in two of the Leute their facilities are poor; they have few toys or amenities. The children are taught hymns and prayers and anything else of a ritualistic nature they can absorb, but there is no institutionalized play nor is there any emphasis at this or any other stage on creativity or personal development. Decorations, too, are virtually non-existent (paintings and photographs are considered idolatrous, although they are appearing in homes) and are seen as frivolous. At all stages too, the child is not praised for being good or successful at something. Such praise would lead to jealousy and competition. For this reason the children are taught to reject competition or ambition – these imply self-assertion, individuality, egoism and superiority, all of which are against the Hutterite ethos.

The communal principle, too, is asserted at this stage. The child may not bring anything from home since this would be a sign of private property. At any rate, it would encourage possessiveness and jealousy. Generally parents are discouraged even from giving their children presents – this would have the same effect and worse since it would lead to pampering (although this too is slowly changing).

For this reason, then, there is in the German school definitely no emphasis on academic excellence, and as far as possible this is discouraged in the English school too. The difference between the two should be clarified. The German school is run by the German teacher who is a member of the colony (a senior one, too, by virtue of his post). Its purpose is to teach the child Hutterite belief and practice, meaning an education in Bible, German, Hutterite history and liturgy. Originally other educational rudiments such as writing and arithmetic were taught, but this function has now been taken over by the English school. In the latter the children are taught the main elements of the provincial educational syllabus. The teacher here is invariably an outsider (attempts to train Hutterites themselves have proved largely unsuccessful) who frequently lives on the colony. He does not have an entirely free hand however. The Elders will only accept someone as the English teacher whom they feel will not attempt to usurp colony practices or beliefs. Although he is required to cover a particular syllabus he is discouraged by the Elders from teaching things they feel threatening, nor may he use any means he likes. Clearly conflicts can arise – the provincial syllabus provides for sex education, the theory of evolution and use of audio-visual aids, and these are contrary to Hutterite belief. The colony attempts to minimize these either by direct interference or by denying them in German school.

While the English teacher must be acceptable to the local School Board, the German teacher is usually not a professional: his own adherence to belief and his ability to communicate it and to impose

discipline are more important to the Hutterites than formal peda-
gogic skills. He works independently. Parents seldom intervene
(unless they want him to administer special punishment to their
child) nor does he especially get involved (regarding education)
with the parents (unless he feels that they are too lax in their
upbringing).

German school takes place in the morning and afternoon,
English school between. (Symbolically perhaps, this is a statement
of the priority and finality of the German school. This is emphasized by the fact that the English school may not encroach on any
colony activity: the child may not be kept behind after school,
for example.) The child is taught by rote – this emphasizes the
'givenness' of his belief system. His individuality is once again de-
emphasized. He is taught not to be too curious about the outside
world and, should he deviate from the rules given him, he is
admonished and even given corporal punishment. The child is
expected to identify with his peer-group since each age-group has
its own expectations and deviations. When a child acts according
to what is expected of his age-group his behaviour is considered
natural, whether what he did was good or bad. Punishment is
therefore meted out in accordance with what is expected of, say,
a 9- or 14-year-old. On the other hand, the child is not praised
for doing something especially good. This is as much a deviation
as doing something marginally bad. The individual is meant to
prove himself not by outstanding behaviour but by undemonstra-
tive adherence to the rules. He also continues to learn what he
has been taught from an early age – rejection. Since he is inferior
to those above him, he must accept that they will, at times, reject
him, or simply emphasize to him his inferiority (e.g. keeping
children waiting for long periods to have their needs met).

This is not to say that the child is not loved, only that he has
to know his place. He must learn not to assert himself too much,
nor to be too individualistic, nor to be over-imaginative. The
danger of these qualities is that he may feel himself independent
of the colony or unable to abide by colony norms (which are
predicated on the individual subordinating himself to authority
and to the colony as a whole). In short, the individual must not
want to leave the colony, and should he nevertheless want to,
should not have the confidence to do so. For these reasons, too,
children are not to be pampered or shown favouritism (by parents
or teachers).

Herein lies the danger of the English school and the need for its containment. The teacher may invoke alien values or a corrupting life-style: if he smokes in front of the children or invites them to watch TV or helps them to buy forbidden goods he could pose a real threat to colony values and even to the likelihood of the child staying in the colony. He is able to divert the child away from the two most important stages to come in his life – baptism and life after death. Anything that subverts the child's concentration in attaining these ends must be counteracted.

At 16 the child enters the adult world. He leaves school, begins to work alongside the adults and eats in the adult dining hall. If until now he has been taught to identify with the adult world, to see it as his model, now he can actually become part of it. By this age he has learnt all he needs to know to be a full colony member. His actual behaviour will still be suspect and his work capacity will have to develop, but basically he is ready to enter the last stage before becoming a full member. There is no need for him to continue with formal studies: he needs a trade and for this practical experience is worth more than anything else. Too much education is likely to turn the child away from physical labour, especially farming, and will encourage him to want to travel, question, doubt.

There is a long build-up to the actual act of baptism.[1] In this period the individual is expected to act with far greater responsibility than he has until now, although deviation within the prescribed limits is expected. In this period he may also try out the outside world. The process of baptism involves lengthy sessions with the preacher: the colony must be certain that the prospective member fully understands the responsibility he is taking upon himself and expects him to prove himself in both word and deed. He must declare both his understanding of and readiness to abide by colony belief, practice and discipline, and must have shown in his behaviour that he is the sort of person who will in fact do so. He must also display the kind of personality an ideal Hutterite is expected to be – humble, devoid of self-assertion, obedient to God and colony. With baptism one's formal colony education is complete, but informally life in the colony is meant to be a process of perpetual education, even until death.

Two observations indicate the success of this education philosophy. One is the low defection rate (see Chapter 9 for further discussion; it is also due to other factors, e.g. close family ties).

The other is the natural ability the younger generation have for taking on adult tasks. Hutterite children do 'adult' work from the age of about 10 – boys will drive small tractors, girls will look after babies. By the time they are 17–18 any Hutterite child can do almost any colony job. The boys, even if not very professionally, can operate all the agricultural equipment and can work as mechanics, carpenters, welders and builders. The girls can sew, cook, bake, look after the children, do housework. So they have not only been taught that the colony is their right and proper home, they have grown up to see the various roles in it as natural and inevitable and entirely within their competence. This is perhaps the crux of the matter. The Hutterite wishes to stay on his colony not because he is dependent on it nor because he is so isolated that he cannot adapt to or even conceive alternatives, nor because he is weak or unimaginative or educationally limited. Even if these are true (I have my doubts though) they are not in themselves the explanation of the Hutterite remaining in the fold. The Hutterite today sees the outside world and knows its attractions and its values. Yet his identity is rooted in certain fundamental conceptions, especially the need to live a life according to Jesus and to practise 'all things in common'. He has been strongly socialized into accepting the authority structure. At the same time *he definitely sees himself as an individual. The Hutterite himself does not see his life as being narrow and repressive.* The frame of reference he has 'adopted' as a result of intense socialization is for him natural: the parameters of it are the parameters of Hutterite life. We need to put all these elements together – the 'naturalness' of Hutterite belief, the 'naturalness' of the way of life, the ease with which the individual finds his place in that way of life, and his feeling that he is developing and asserting his individuality in it. Cumulatively these factors make the Hutterite feel that colony life is preferable to any alternative.

The quest for communal awareness: the Kibbutz education system

The Kibbutz spends a substantial amount of its income on educating its children.[2] Jewish tradition, not so much in its content but in its emphasis on learning, has no doubt also played a part in this. The founders, we remember, grew up in that tradition, and although they rejected the ghetto concept of education (in terms of its content, its goals and its place in the social structure), they never rejected the importance of education. Here they were also influenced by socialist thinking. The individual, as they saw it, was a product of his society. Potentially, society could shape an individual any way it wanted. Education was an extension of the general principles on which society was based. Hence one of the primary aims was to create an education system which managed to reflect the principles of Kibbutz, thus creating in turn a 'new person'[3] and ensuring Kibbutz continuity. As with other Kibbutz institutions the education system took some time to take definite shape since the founders had simply not given any serious thought to the fact that one day they might need one. Yet with the establishment of families and the appearance of children, something specific had to be decided as to how to raise them.

At first, most members, male and female, felt it was only natural that the mother should stay at home and look after the child. Yet if she did this she had no possibility of herself going out to work. She would be recreating the very situation she had rebelled against – the woman faithfully raising the children at home while the husband went out to work and supported the family. Some women took their children to work with them, yet still with the assumption that the mother was privately responsible for her children. In 1918 they decided that the child's education was the responsibility of the entire community. The males were somewhat hesitant about this and the women themselves continued to be confused. At any rate, though, the idea developed that children must be cared for as a group so that the mothers could be free to work elsewhere; all the adults as a community were now responsible for all the children, irrespective of one's own 'biological situation'.

At the same time, thoughts were turning to the content of that education. The founders were imbued with the idea that through education a new type of individual could be created to whom the ideals of a communal society and of national enterprise would be natural and not an act of rebellion as was the case of the parents. The best way to achieve this, it seemed, was by removing education from direct parental control. This meant that specialists would raise the children, leading in turn to healthy parent-child relationships. At first, influenced partly by Freud, there was much emphasis on non-coercion (since children were 'naturally good'). But the extremism of this view and the attempts to separate parents and children were soon abandoned. The situation needed to be reassessed, especially since this was becoming a cause of families leaving the Kibbutzim. (Already, in 1920, one of the founders said explicitly that the Kibbutz would survive or fail depending on its ability to keep the family.)

From this reassessment, the 'classical' form of Kibbutz education developed. Here the children are brought up from birth in groups of four to six; from 4 to 7 years old they are in kindergarten; until the age of 13 they are at the local Kibbutz school and then go to regional Kibbutz High School (which is sometimes a boarding school). From the ages of 8 to 9 they begin to do physical work in their own little farm; at 13 they begin working a few hours weekly with the adults. They also have their own committees dealing with social problems, entertainment and so on. After school and the army the children do a year of 'national service', e.g. teaching new immigrants or helping weaker settlements. They frequently take a year's leave to see the world; when they return to the Kibbutz they can apply for membership on the same basis as anyone else (that is, there is no automatic membership for Kibbutz children).

What is Kibbutz education trying to achieve and what means are used to achieve it? Kibbutz members themselves like to distinguish between education *in* the Kibbutz and education *to* Kibbutz. This means that the aim of Kibbutz education is to raise an individual who, while being given due recognition of his individuality, will accept the value of Kibbutz life, will wish to live according to Kibbutz values, and will see such a life as being natural and inherently satisfying. The means to achieving this is to provide the child with a learning experience, i.e. an education which combines formal knowledge and personal experience as the basis of growth. Knowledge and experience can only combine properly in the child and he will only relate them to Kibbutz life if the education process takes place in an environment which the child can perceive as an extension of the process he is himself undergoing. So the life of the child must be in itself a recreation of Kibbutz values and his immediate education environment must interact fully, coherently and consistently with its wider Kibbutz environment.

This explains the emphasis placed on the role of the educator.[4] He must not simply be one who transmits knowledge; rather his relationship to the children must be the living expression of the type of relation ideally governing adult members. The children must see him primarily as a member of the Kibbutz (hence the idea that he should have sabbaticals to work in other Kibbutz activities) and not simply as a white-collar functionary.

If it is good for the educator to be involved in physical work, so is it good for the child himself. The child must learn that there is no disjunction between mental and physical activity. In Kibbutz thinking, doing physical work gives the child a feeling of involvement in his own community; it creates a feeling of belonging; it gives him roots in the land and the physical location of the Kibbutz; and it provides a feeling of home. It teaches him that all types of work are equal; he has an opportunity to learn responsibility and other Kibbutz values; and it gives him the possibility of developing his talents in non-academic spheres. The same applies to the 'children's society' wherein the children run their own semi-autonomous institutions modelled on the Kibbutz itself.

This highlights the importance of the education system being an integral part of the environment. Clearly, with the teacher being seen as a member of the community qua member, and with the child himself being involved in both the adult community's work and his own mini-community social life, added to which is the generally intimate atmosphere of the Kibbutz – all these considerations require that one cannot educate 'to' Kibbutz if the Kibbutz itself is deficient in implementing its own values. To educate the child to appreciate certain values in an abstract way only is poor education, but at least it is harmless; to educate him to those values and then to place him in a situation where those he respects and admires practise the opposite can only lead to cynicism and disillusionment on the part of the child, with the chances of his remaining on the Kibbutz as an adult seriously jeopardized. Therefore Kibbutz education is not confined to the classroom nor even to the education system: the child's very life on the Kibbutz is in itself the best education he can get, provided the Kibbutz itself (including the child's parents) acts according to what it teaches its children to believe in.

This, however, does not mean that Kibbutz children should become 'mechanical communitarians', nor does it mean that their entire lives should be centred on the question of values. The child needs to enjoy life – *joie de vivre* is as important to his happiness as any moral principle. And needless to say the child must be treated as an individual – all his special needs and talents must be respected, satisfied and developed. Ideologically speaking this is a moral obligation; at any rate, parents will not remain on Kibbutz unless their children's needs are met. There is, however, a limit to this, namely, the values of the Kibbutz. The child cannot be totally free: he has to consider the principles of responsibility, equality, democracy and co-operation, and he must accept these as necessary constraints on his private life and desires. If he does not, the whole system will break down since a war of all against all will develop. Individual development is positive except when it develops into egoism. The child has to learn to balance his own development and needs to those of all the people in his community. In so doing he will become a richer individual *all round*.

Given that these are the principles of Kibbutz education what in practice have been the results? One way of judging the Kibbutz 'success rate' is by simple statistics, i.e. how many remain within the Kibbutz movement and how many leave. It seems that 50 per cent of Kibbutz-born children stay on Kibbutz; in all, they represent some 30 per cent of total Kibbutz membership. About 30 per cent of adults joining Kibbutzim are Kibbutz-born children.[5]

More important perhaps is the type of individual who remains on the Kibbutz.[6] Whether what has been achieved is a sign of success or failure is once again a matter of perspective but among observers there is a large degree of consensus as to the effects of Kibbutz education on the children. While the idea has long since been abandoned of creating 'the new person', the primary immediate goal has been achieved – to raise a generation to whom the values, goals and way of life are natural and intrinsically satisfying. To the first generation (by which I mean not only the founders of the Kibbutz movement or of particular Kibbutzim, but all those who joined the Kibbutz as adults from other environments) physical labour and communal life were alien ideas. To take them up was an act of rebellion, a personal revolution. To the second generation there is nothing to rebel against, no personal revolution to indulge in. It has become commonplace in the Kibbutz to say that Kibbutz children stay on the Kibbutz not because of ideology but simply because it is 'home'. While there is much truth in this it seems to me that the wrong implications are frequently drawn. Let me emphasize what I regard as one of the most fundamental conditions to the persistence of intentional communities. *No one stays in an intentional community because of ideology only; the ideology will only be adhered to if the community gives one a feeling of home. Conversely, the stresses of living in a community would be intolerable if there were no ideological backing to one's life in it.* Hence the difference between generations in the Kibbutz is not as great as the 'home-ideology' distinction seems to indicate. Further, while the second generation has not arrived at its acceptance of Kibbutz values through a rebellion against an existing environment (for them), they are sufficiently aware of alien values, sufficiently self-conscious regarding their own values, and sufficiently experienced in having to live, contend and even doubt them (their own values) to accept them in fairly critical fashion. In short, there is nothing to indicate that the second generation consists of 'mechanical communards'.

The difference between the generations lies not in their reasons for living on Kibbutz but in the balance between the various reasons and the way in which these have been arrived at. In general it seems as if the second generation has fewer internal conflicts than their parents. The former see Kibbutz life in terms of principles and are committed to its collectivism no less than the first generation, yet are more pragmatic in the application of those principles to daily life. It seems to me that at times the parents' uncompromising adherence to ideology is sometimes a guise for their self-doubts and their guilt-feelings about them. The parents feel a need – because of the fact that joining the Kibbutz was a deliberate ideological act – to assess everything in terms of principle. Their children have fewer doubts and guilt-feelings, not because they think differently but because their life-experience allows them to express openly the same thoughts as their parents, e.g. a desire for higher living standards or more education or changes in children's sleeping arrangements. In other words, both generations see Kibbutz as the locus of their ideology and as their home, and no intentional community could persist unless this was the case, even though different generations may balance the two in different ways.[7]

Creating communal adherence: comments on collective education

The education system today is different, in some ways substantially so, to what it once was. The overall aim of education – to create a person to whom life in the community is morally right and personally satisfying – has remained constant but the ways of achieving this have changed. To a large extent outside influences have been significant here. The communities have accepted outside pressures (the Hutterites) and outside example (the Kibbutz) in raising education standards and in the content of their education. But they have both managed to retain a degree of autonomy (in both cases legally recognized by the state, this recognition coming partially through the readiness of the communities to accept a degree of state control over their education), and this autonomy has helped them to inculcate their own values in their children.

Education is seen as both a personal and a collective end. The Kibbutz emphasizes the former, the Hutterites the latter – but each contains both ends. The child growing up in the Kibbutz is thought of as an individual – but only within a particular social-ideological context. The Hutterite child is taught the supremacy of his social-ideological framework – but he can find much individuality within it provided he does not cross the boundaries of that context. At the risk of repeating myself, I wish to emphasize that *life in a community is equally a matter of ideological adherence and a feeling of home. The success of the socialization process depends on whether both can be inculcated.* The satisfied and committed member is the one who remains despite crises, the one who sees life in the community as more than just a convenience, the one who sees his own life and that of others in both transcendental and here-and-now terms. For him the community is both a repository of his beliefs and a source of private satisfaction. The education system in both cases leads to this situation. (Work is a crucial factor here for both groups of communities.) This is strengthened by the continuity between the education system and the overall life and values of the community. There is no disjunction between the two. In both cases the child is taught to see the colony as a wide-ranging integrated system, of which his education is one aspect. It is both a microcosm of community life and values and the logical extension to them.

The emphasis on education stems from the transcendent beliefs of the community. We have seen that basic to the ideology is a belief that certain goals and values are autonomous of the community and its individual members, *and* that these are worth passing on to others. It follows that strong emphasis on education is necessary to achieve this end. This emphasis in turn leads to biological continuity of the community. The education system is founded on an atmosphere of moral certainty. If and when a degree of critical analysis enters (as in the Kibbutz) the parameters are quite clear. Among the Hutterites there is officially no room for doubt, but the individual Hutterite sees himself as one who has independently, critically and rationally arrived at certain conclusions. We should not then infer from this that the younger generation have become 'mechanical communards'. On the one hand they have moral certainty, but on the other they feel it is a private and individualistic conclusion.

This leads us to a fundamental fact of community life. We can see that in terms of individual expression, e.g. in occupations, clothing or critical thought, the Kibbutz is far more open and wide-ranging than the Hutterites. (This leaves the Kibbutz more open to change and to a lessened ability to indoctrinate the younger generation.) But, regarding the problem of persistence, the *extent* of the range is unimportant. A community can persist equally well if the range exists to the nth or to the xth degree. What is crucial is our earlier discussion on open and closed universes. *In each case the member perceives himself as living in a closed universe, yet within it he sees himself as having a wide range of variations and free choice, and thus defines himself as an individual.* The 'degree of closure' is not important, only that closure should exist and that the parameters should be explicitly defined.

The Kibbutz member and the Hutterite each feel that they have established clear boundaries of moral certainty and social behaviour. They do not (usually) feel that these are restrictive or narrow. To the Kibbutz observer Hutterite life is very restricted and he sees Hutterites themselves as uncritical and unindividualistic, but that is only by his standards. To the Hutterite himself, this is not the case at all, just as the Kibbutz member does not see his own life as narrow and restrictive. The Hutterite sees his life and belief as having certain boundaries, these being for him both moral imperatives and personally satisfying. He is prepared to discuss, debate and question within that framework. He therefore sees himself as being critical, as being a Hutterite through rational choice. The Kibbutz member sees his life in the same way, even though outsiders often conceive of Kibbutz life as narrow, restrictive and unindividualistic. The same applies to occupation and dress. Given the outer boundaries, there is room for variation and in fact variation is even at times encouraged provided the limits are adhered to. Crisis arises when the individual cannot accept the limits of belief or social practice, and each individual member from time to time goes through such a crisis. So on the one hand the limits are accepted – hence the cohesion, identity and sense of purpose of the community; yet on the other hand, variation within the limit is encouraged or is at least permissible – hence the possibilities for the individual to find satisfaction, to feel that he is an individual and a member of the community by voluntary and rational choice.

However, the goal of integrating the education system (indeed the entire socialization process) with the wider social system can have its complications. In our discussion on economic 'success' we mentioned that one possible area of threat is that of the younger generation. This point should now be clearer. We have seen that both the Hutterites and the Kibbutzim view their education system as an extension of the community, as a place for communicating community values, as a reflection, a praxis, of those values. Now, though, we can see the wider socialization process as more than that. That process, if it is to be effective, needs to be structured in such a way that it is quite literally essential to the functioning of the entire system. In other words, the social and economic structures of the community are in some ways dependent on the younger generation, and the socialization system is designed to bolster the community as a going concern. More specifically, this means that the labour of young people in particular becomes an integral part of the overall labour structure. Labour now is not simply a matter of learning the joys of work and acquiring at an early stage the skills to perform adult functions: young labour means that they *are* performing adult functions.

But when the community is economically successful what does it do with the labour surplus that young people represent? As we have seen, the Hutterites do not allow this to happen, i.e. they ensure that the existing economic network does not contract, hence there is no labour surplus – but nor do they allow it to expand in ways which would eventually lead to even greater economic success (e.g. with industrialization) and hence create a labour surplus at a later stage. The Hutterite economy is confined to a few branches which require the contribution of all young people.

The oldtimers retire early, thus creating not only the satisfaction for young people of taking on responsibility but the *need* for them to do so. (The older people then become in some ways economically superfluous, and this is catered for by co-opting them to leadership positions in the *social* system.) So, apart from all the other factors mentioned above – powerful indoctrination, family ties, job satisfaction, sense of home – the integration of the younger generation into the economic life of Hutterite communities is essentially a system-maintaining mechanism leading to a low defection rate.

The case of the Kibbutz is more complex. For reasons not entirely of its own making Kibbutz-born children are surplus to the Kibbutz's labour requirements. Children, we have seen, work in Kibbutz branches from about the age of 13, but this serves more as an initiation into the ways of adult society than as an integral part of the Kibbutz's economic system. There is not much point to integrating them into the system because at the age of 18 they will be conscripted for two-to-three years, during which time they are out of the system. On their return many want a year's leave to travel the world and most do a year of national service off the Kibbutz. At that stage the Kibbutz could attempt to re-integrate them, and in many cases it succeeds. Some however, go to study for a few years, meaning that for about six to eight years in all they are, in effect, not part of the Kibbutz and certainly not essential to its economic functioning. This means that they have no relation to the processes of production and to some extent not even of the processes of consumption. It is true that they are still subject to Kibbutz authority, that their studies and travel are dependent on Kibbutz agreement and often finance; but a situation is created which means that in the young member's formative intellectual years he is detached from the system and can look at it with more critical eyes. The integration of values, experience, perceptions, social attachments and sense of mutual dependency between the young member and his Kibbutz is undermined to the extent that the young member has only a quasi-function within the community. He has no sense of obligation (except as his conscience dictates) nor indeed does he necessarily feel that the Kibbutz has an obligation towards him. The Kibbutz is indeed his home but he can enjoy a marginality to it as regards the *functioning* of that home.

In short, since the Kibbutz wants to enhance the individual's sense of well-being, it needs to promote both living standards and a wide range of occupational opportunities, and for this it needs economic expansion. But this expansion has produced its own labour surplus and in so doing has put the Kibbutz in the paradoxical situation of creating a group of people who feel that they are not dependent on the Kibbutz nor the Kibbutz on them. The net effect is a weakening of psychological-ideological ties and, as compared to the Hutterites, a higher rate of defection. However, this point should be treated in context. Many Kibbutz children do stay within the Kibbutz movement because the reasons for leaving and staying are more complex than the negative social and psychological consequences of labour surplus. Labour surplus has its positive aspects too (as the Kibbutz intends), not to mention the success of 'education to values', family ties and so on, all of which constrain the defection rate. The point, though, is that the greater the degree of individual marginality in an intentional community, the greater the chances of non-identification with it and thus the greater the chances of defection.

Chapter 8
The individual

In Hutterite society

We have seen that the socialization process is intended to create a certain type of individual. This is not to say that among Hutterites automatons are considered desirable or that there should be no difference between individuals. In their thinking this is both impossible and undesirable. What is meant is that all individuals share the same perceptions of the world, past and present, strive towards the same ends, share the same values and adhere willingly to the same norms. This means that the frame of reference for the individual, the responses to like situations and the assumptions under which decisions are made, are shared among and are similar to all colony members. There is no contradiction between this and having individuals of different personalities and skills. It means though that, ideally, despite having individual variations, there will be congruence between colony norms and individual practice, with the norms remaining stable.

Hutterite society has a number of expectations regarding the individual:

(1) The group always comes before the individual.
(2) Each person must know and accept his place in the social-economic-religious hierarchy.
(3) Individuals may not engage in many activities unless specifically authorized to do so.
(4) Each individual is subject to scrutiny by all other members of the community.
(5) No individual may engage in anti-social behaviour (e.g. gossiping, violence, aggression).

(6) No individual may entertain private ambitions (an individual may become a work boss but for the sake of the community only, not for any private motive).

(7) Each individual is expected to act according to the principles of Hutterite tradition and the *Ordnungen* (collective decisions) of the Elders.

What kind of individual then is the Hutterite and how does he relate to his fellow Hutterites? What are his sources of satisfaction and dissatisfaction?

The Hutterite knows that he belongs to the only True Church and that ultimately he will go to Heaven. This gives him a certainty which leaves him free of the fear of death (in fact, his attitude towards death borders on the blasé and even light-hearted, and this can be quite disconcerting to the outsider). Yet he does not assume that he has been born saved or born again, nor does he believe that merely being a member of the Hutterite Church is a guarantee of salvation. He knows that salvation is only assured if he acts according to the ways laid down by Christ and dedicates himself to Christ's community. Salvation is thus an individual goal but only if the individual acts in and through the group. The life of the group, then, is designed to enable the individual to attain his personal salvation. 'All' he has to do is live according to the norms on which the group's existence is based. This may be onerous but is worth the effort. The individual must therefore act in ways which support the group and allow it to materialize and perpetuate its norms. To this end certain personal traits and certain behavioural patterns are necessary.

The individual must be conformist, obedient, humble and responsible to and for himself and others. He must not be self-assertive, since this will threaten the stability of the community. From a doctrinal point of view this must be taken even further: even if threatened physically, he must not attempt to defend himself physically (although he may flee danger). Nor is there room for egoistic individuality in responding to or assessing situations. This means that should the individual have an idea of his own he must present it as an idea for the sake of the colony. There is a right way to act in given situations; it is not up to the individual to determine a way for himself.

The Hutterite therefore wishes his social norms to be explicit and unambiguous. Having been taught that there is a clear order to the world, in terms of its history and structure, he expects to find order in it. Hence clear-cut rules exist: the Hutterite believes not only that they are right but that they will guide him in daily life. For the Hutterite the hierarchy, the divisions of age and sex, the ways of acting and responding, are all given facts of life. They are because they are good, and they are good because they are. This creates in the Hutterite mind a consistency and certainty in life – consistency of belief, practice and emotional need, certainty of belief and of how others in the colony will act. There is in the mind of the Hutterite individual not only no room for doubt but also no doubt that the others too are not doubting. This creates consistency between his own perceptions and expectations and those of others, and means that he is free from tension and uncertainty. The individual not only knows how he is supposed to behave but also that others expect him to behave in that way. Since the community is based on this mutuality of expectation he knows that his status is dependent on his acting according to other people's expectations. He acts in particular ways because he knows his actions to be intrinsically good and because he knows his status in the community depends on it.

The colony in which the individual lives is not simply a home or a means of ultimate salvation. One's life in the colony is quite literally one's being. Not to be on the colony is to fragment one's being. There are two reasons for this. One's existence as a physical being cannot be divorced from one's place in the divine scheme of things. Not to be on the colony is to rob one's material existence of its purpose and meaning. This is true even when one fully identifies with the colony but leaves it for only a short while. To be on the colony is to be in one's proper place in the universe, in Grace, as it were. To die out of the colony implies almost a betrayal of the colony, of oneself, of Christ. The other reason is that other members of the colony are one's family, biologically or morally (Hutterites call each other brother and sister). One has invariably grown up with the other members; one shares with them experiences, either of the immediate past or of the collective heritage of the sect. One's immediate biological family is a fundamental part of one's emotional make-up: its intimacy and intensity of relations leads it to be an extension of oneself. To a lesser extent this is true of the entire colony; one is dependent on them both.

All this is not to say that life in the colony is easy nor is it meant to be. It is almost an insult to a Hutterite to suggest that his life is easy. The material security, behavioural certainty, structural order and emotional intimacy can themselves place strain on the individual, but this is part of his test. To accept the strain of communal life is living proof of one's belief in Christ and one's determination to obtain salvation. Yet there are ways of overcoming strain. Compensation of an innocuous nature can be found (see below); better still, one can avoid many potential strains simply by acting according to Hutterite norms. By not asserting oneself, by not *seeking* responsibility, by not being egoistic, by not being different, one is already avoiding strain. If problems arise, there is no need to rush into action. Things can work themselves out slowly. Solutions can come by themselves; consensus can emerge spontaneously. If something has to be done quickly there are those in positions of responsibility to decide on the appropriate course of action. In this way too one preserves the rule of law. By not making independent decisions or judgements one is not only not asserting oneself, not throwing accepted norms in doubt, but allowing the law, which is given, to take its own course. Any other path would lead to 'the tyranny of the strongest'.[1]

So those in positions of authority merely carry out their responsibilities in order to ensure that the given order is maintained. All others must do the same and accept that those in authority are only attempting to maintain proper order. Therefore their authority must not be undermined.

We have already pointed out that all this does not mean that the Hutterite sees or feels himself as being unindividualistic. On the contrary, within a narrow and restricted frame of reference – whether this refers to personality traits, social practices or religious beliefs – the Hutterite sees himself as being a free and individualistic person. He has chosen this frame of reference freely, and consciously believes that he is as autonomous a personality within it as anyone else is beyond it. This frame of reference is the guideline by which, quite literally, almost every single aspect of and happening in life is judged. Everything in the world can be and is reduced to it. The most mundane incident while working, the jokes they make to each other, their comments on world affairs (and, by the way, Hutterites are, I think, more knowledgeable than at first appears) are all implicitly reduced to religion and a justification for the colony way of life. Very little is said for its own sake (at any rate to the outsider) – the thought of religion and colony life underlies nearly every topic of conversation. Even things a Hutterite may conceivably do beyond the colony will have this basic referent. He would scorn a trip to the Bahamas but get very excited about visiting 'the Brothers in the east' (the Bruderhof in America) or the Holy Places of the Middle East. Partly because of his limited education, partly because of the narrowness and 'givenness' of this frame of reference, the Hutterite is not what we would call intellectual. He is not concerned to show why the way of life and the beliefs on which it is based are correct. He can point to the obvious problems of outside society as proof of their correctness, but he will not, and indeed cannot, attempt to justify them on purely abstract grounds.

We have said that in Hutterite life there are strains and compensations. What form can these take? For one thing there is a fairly widespread desire for greater individuality in housing and clothing and for a higher standard of living. Too much individuality in clothing is against Hutterite belief, but in fact much individuality exists – usually enough for the individual not to feel constrained by absolute uniformity. (This stems from the fact that sewing is done at home, so variations immediately crop up; the material is often chosen from among a small variety of patterns (and in some cases colours); and some items are not much covered by rules or there is laxity, e.g. men's shoes.) There is no Hutterite injunction against changes in the style of clothing, only that such changes must be sanctioned by the Elders of the Leut, who naturally attempt to play a conservative role in this regard. These same Elders pay regular visits to the colonies to see if discipline is lax or not, but a minor degree of leeway is given provided the overall clothing style is not upset. Women too have a set pattern of clothing. Here, perhaps, the desire is not so much for a different style as for individual choice of colours as opposed to the black and white they conventionally wear. This is strictly controlled but one compensation women do take for themselves is to use less durable forms of cloth in making their dresses, so that they will wear out quickly and can be replaced. Even though the style of the new dress is the same, the feeling of having a new one apparently gives satisfaction. Where women do find compensation in the matter of colour is regarding babies. Here there is no injunction regarding colour or style and the opportunity is seized by the women to enjoy this freedom – chiefly by dressing their babies in brightly-coloured clothes.

This is related to another aspect of clothing. Each family is given a quota of cloth relative to its needs. This preserves the principle of equality. However, through persistent complaining or subtle manipulation many women tend to get more than they actually need. Often the surplus is simply hoarded and sometimes it is spread among the family as additional clothing. The important psychological point here is that you have something which is yours over and above what the community would normally give you. It is, in a sense, a 'private' possession.

Generally, among the Hutterites, there is a desire for private possessions. Each Hutterite has his/her own chest in which worldly possessions are locked. To receive this at 15 years of age is a great event in one's life. Strictly speaking, of course, there are no private possessions, but in fact each Hutterite has them and may keep them as long as it is totally surreptitious – transistor radios, perfume, magazines, cigarettes, and so on.

Just as the style and standard of clothing is regulated from above, so is that of living quarters. We should emphasize that among the Hutterites there is no principle of austerity, only of simplicity and saving. There is nothing inherently wrong in enjoying the flesh. One must merely keep it in its proper place. (An anecdote may well illustrate the point: Reverend Jake Klein-sasser, my host at Crystal Springs Colony, showed me a thesis written on the Hutterites. It argued that they are becoming more this-worldly, and 'proof' of this was to be seen in the fact that the Brethren (who are generally abstinent) in this colony drink beer. Jake's reaction was that drinking beer was in itself proof of nothing – what was important was that in the town it was often done in excess or as an escape from problems, whereas among the Hutter-ites it was done in moderation and, he claimed, all the more enjoyable for that.) However, at a grass roots level, there is a quiet but firm pressure to raise living standards. On both ideological and economic grounds the leaders try to resist this, but changes are occurring, albeit in a controlled way. One direct means of raising living standards is simply by getting money privately to buy house-hold items. There are three ways to do this (for males only; in effect there are no such means for females) – to sell goods on the side, to moonlight, to take leave and work outside the colony. The first two are strictly forbidden, but happen nevertheless, though to what extent is not clear.

Among the Hutterites there is generally a need to know the outside world. The Hutterite sometimes has an ambivalent attitude towards the world. He has been taught that it is sinful and corrupt, opposed to the word of Jesus. He believes and accepts this. We saw that he can reduce everything that happens around his colony to a justification of colony life. But there is, too, often a feeling that the big wide world is more colourful, interesting and exciting than one's own, that happiness and success are easy to come by. It seems to promise freedom. One consequence of this is the desire of many men (and to a lesser extent women) to have as much contact with the environment as possible. This can take the form of going to town as often as 'necessary' on business or, conversely, inviting town folk to visit the colony. Reading magazines and listening to the radio, although illicit, are other ways of discovering the outside world. Physical contact with it is not banned, but the Elders make every effort to control it. Incidentally, one form of magazine reading not illicit is professional journals, meaning farming and mechanical periodicals. These are studied closely, not only as a means to improving one's work but, there is little doubt, as a means of learning about or indirectly having contact with the outside world. The Hutterite wants this contact for he feels it is a compensation for the limited life of his colony; it is not the consequence of feeling there is something basically wrong with colony life. In his own eyes it is a harmless means of satisfaction and perhaps it is psychologically necessary.

I have mentioned how the Hutterite sees everything in terms of his religion and way of life but nevertheless he needs, from time to time, simply to have a break from it. Perhaps the most striking way of having outside contact is through officially leaving the colony for a short period. The leaders have come to accept this as a natural, youthful desire and are apparently sufficiently confident that their young men will return to allow it. This is a 'phase', the pre-baptismal period of foolishness and curiosity which, for the Elders, should perhaps best be worked out of a member's system. So far as the leaders are concerned this extended leave is, while not desirable, something to be accepted, and their judgement has proved correct since 90 per cent of the young men return to their colony, in many cases more strongly convinced of their attachment to it (especially because of the closeness of Huttcritc family ties).[2] For the young men concerned they have satisfied their curiosity and in many cases have made some private money. This, strictly speaking, should go back into the colony, but is usually kept by the person concerned or spent in furnishing his apartment when he gets married. Once again, the unwritten rule is that as long as norms are not openly violated (or, if they are, only in marginal fashion) violation is acceptable.

The sphere of work provides further examples of both frustration and compensation. The individual is offered little choice in his/her work place; males and females have a limited range of work opportunities; ambition in the sense of leadership or competition with other work branches is frowned upon. The tensions which spring from this situation are partially overcome in both institutional and non-institutional forms. Although the individual male has little choice in his work place, efforts are made to put people where they want to work. This makes sense economically and socially: people will naturally work with greatest motivation and efficiency if their work gives them satisfaction and an opportunity to express their talent. More than that, it is not uncommon for the Preacher or Boss who is sensitive to individual feelings to put someone in a job, even though he is not particularly efficient, so that he will feel a degree of satisfaction. This may occur at all ages but particularly with regard to older people, who often feel that leaving active work is a sign of old age or inability to keep up with new developments. Where the older male does leave physical work he is often placed on the community's council. This serves a social function (to maintain conservative leadership) and a personal function (to maintain the sense of involvement, responsibility and contribution).

In connection with retirement there is another important consideration. Retirement from active work usually takes place in one's forties. Add to this the fact that the entire male work population might only number about forty to fifty, spread out among five to six branches, we find that the opportunity for an individual to attain a position of responsibility is quite large. In every community almost every male has, by the age of 45, held a position of responsibility. Hence, even though one is not permitted to entertain ambitions overtly in this regard, one knows that one is almost certain to satisfy them anyway.

Also in the work sphere, various ways may be found of attaining satisfaction apart from any inherent job interest. One of these is the acquisition of professional skill. While members go in for little formal study (although this too is changing) they have a voracious interest in improving their mechanical knowledge, and the Hutterites have attained very high agricultural-mechanical standards as a result. Clearly, the willingness of the Elders to invest in mechanization is important here: from the viewpoint of the individual, the more they do so the greater the opportunity he has to improve and express his individual abilities.

A further means of compensation lies in inter-branch competition. This is highly informal and is in fact forbidden since competition is supposed to be unethical. Nevertheless, there is much competition among branch managers for allocation of resources, either in terms of investment or manpower, and there is much pride in running or working in a branch which is economically successful, especially when this success is greater than that of others.

Despite the fact that status divisions are highly formalized, there are informal means of acquiring status. One of these is in work. To be quick and efficient in one's work is a status symbol among the Hutterites. It serves a double purpose – it is a proof of one's superior ability to that of others and it is a proof to the community of how dedicated one is to one's work, and thus, by extension, to the colony as a whole. One index of this is loss of work days through illness. Among Hutterite males loss of work implies (as least in the eyes of the sick individual) loss of status, and therefore they tend consciously to avoid illness. Of course lack of illness may also be an index of job satisfaction. On the other hand, female work, which has a lower status both because it is done by females and because it is non-productive, does not have the same status, and one therefore finds greater readiness on the part of females to stay off work or complain about having to work extra hours. Since the work has little status value there is not much status to lose by not doing it at all or by not showing dedication to it. (This and the preceding paragraph apply equally to the Kibbutz.)

Regarding work, we should note that the larger the colony the more diversified its economy is likely to be. This provides greater opportunities for satisfaction of individual interest and creates the possibility, even for women, to engage in non-traditional occupations occasionally. There is a negative consideration here though: larger colonies leave fewer opportunities for individuals to take on positions of responsibility.

Finally, there are a number of private activities which leave room for individual expression. Hutterites have a strong tradition regarding handicraft, and individuals may engage in these outside of work hours. Activities in this regard include furniture carving, book binding, copying the family tree and sermons (a stylized handwriting is a great Hutterite virtue).

We have now seen that in four aspects of Hutterite life – clothing, housing, outside contact and work – the Hutterite can feel constrained and frustrated, but in each case can find means of releasing the tension generated or of gaining compensation. These means do not violate the colony's basic unity or ideological premises, and sensitive leadership can help sustain the balance between consistency and solidarity on the one hand, and private satisfaction on the other.

Regarding the overall life-style of the colony there are once again positive and negative factors for the individual. On the positive side life in the community provides perfect (literally) social security. As long as a person belongs to the community his needs are taken care of according to the standards set by the community – food, clothing, shelter, medical treatment and education are all absolutely guaranteed irrespective of any consideration. Yet individuals are socialized into accepting their place in the community which, to the extent that they rebel against it, leads to frustration. They are also socialized into certain behavioural patterns or against others: to the extent that these are violated strong guilt feelings emerge.

One consequence of all this is the low rate of crime (against civil laws), delinquency, homosexuality, divorce or suicide. These seem to indicate a society which is stable and a group of individuals not suffering from anomie or insecurity. But another consequence is the mental health problem. In Eaton and Weil's classic study (1955) there was a low rate of schizophrenia and a relatively high rate of manic-depression. They argue that this is the reverse of the position in the wider society. They postulate that schizophrenia is more common among unskilled labourers, farmers and isolated people, while manic-depression is more common among professional and socially prominent people because they have a strong need to live up to expectations. This explains, they argue, the greater degree of manic-depression among the Hutterites. The education system 'orients the people to look for blame and guilt within themselves rather than in others'.

Neurotics, too, tend to blame themselves. There is little attempt to project hostile feelings on to others nor is there much scape-goating. For Eaton and Weil this is a consequence both of the educational values and of the high level of expectation in the community, a level which they feel can sometimes impose an unbearable strain on people. Clearly this cannot be the entire explanation (nor do Eaton and Weil present it as such) since all members go through the same socialization process and all live according to the same set of expectations. Yet only one in forty-three had had any form of mental disorder in their study. The reason may, in addition to the above, lie in genetic factors since, as they point out, three family names accounted for nearly half of the total number of mental disorders. In my conclusion to this chapter I suggest some general considerations which might help to clarify the problem.

But there are forms of depression which do not necessarily fall into the conventional psychiatric categories, 'home-made' depression as it were. The Hutterites themselves talk of *Anfech-tung*. This is a state in which the individual has great feelings of doubt about his own worth, indulges in much self-recrimination, withdraws from social intercourse, and is possessed with strong guilt feelings. The Hutterites' attitude towards this are instructive. For one thing it is considered natural to have *Anfechtung*. This means that there is no need to be ashamed of having it (something the individual may not appreciate at the time but can do so before and after). It is an illness which can happen to anybody and must be treated sympathetically. These considerations naturally make it easier for the family to be sensitive to the onset of *Anfechtung* and to accept the situation without shame or guilt for themselves. One advantage of this is that when the symptoms appear a positive and constructive response is forthcoming instead of attempts, as often happens in our own society, to repress or ignore them through shame, guilt or ignorance. As a result, when an individual suffers from *Anfechtung* all members of the community, particu-larly the family, friends and those in responsible positions, rally round. He is given support and encouragement; he is led into talking about his feelings as much as possible; he is relieved from pressures and only works insofar as he feels he is capable of doing so; he is encouraged to try to live a normal community life.

Eventually most people recover from this period and, what is more important, without stigma to themselves, their families or the community.

These remarks on fundamental sources of satisfaction and dissatisfaction in colony life can be generalized. Basic personal satisfaction and basic personal strain are both intrinsic to communal life. The material security, personal intimacy and ideological certainty are all fundamental sources of personal well-being, but they can equally be sources of strain, and at various times in a member's life he feels it – the desire for more independence and freedom, the need to deviate, guilt feelings, moral doubts. The question is not whether a community can avoid this – it cannot. It is a price that has to be paid for communal living, but the community can provide compensations, consideration, support, concern and flexibility. These can help to reduce the strain and leave the positive side of communal life outweighing the negative. Nor can these mitigating factors be totally institutionalized. There is a point beyond which the institutions of the community cannot help individuals. Only other individuals – family, friends and perhaps leaders especially – can help. The culture of unstructured interactions (cf. section on alienation) in a community is a crucial factor here, at times even more so than the institutions or formal rules. One cannot legislate as to how to relate to other people or handle problems, even if the norms or guidelines are perfectly clear. The informal atmosphere of an intentional community is something members have to be sensitive to, and I suggest that among the Hutterites and the Kibbutz this kind of sensitivity has been crucial to the feeling of well-being members have, and has contributed significantly to their persistence.

Under what circumstances do people actually leave a Hutterite colony? Among the Hutterites defection can take three forms – short-term defection (days and weeks), long-term defection (months, even up to two years) and permanent defection. The temporary defection rate is 7 per cent, the permanent rate 3 per cent,[3] although this seems to be increasing.[4] Defection occurs chiefly among the 18–25 age group, mostly males.[5] Why do people wish to defect, either temporarily or permanently? We have already noted that most Hutterites have a curiosity about the outside world, that they see it as having certain advantages their own lives do not possess. This leads to the desire actually to experience the outside world at first-hand. A further consideration we have seen elsewhere is the possibility of accumulating some capital to be used in furnishing one's room on marriage. (This appears to be more of a side advantage to temporary defection than a prime motivation.)

Yet there are circumstances of a non-personal nature which may encourage defection. The foregoing reasons are applicable to a fairly stable colony, one where, despite the doubts and hesitations, members are basically committed, at any rate in the long term, to colony life and values. Here there is a desire for temporary defection in order to satisfy an urge; the assumption is that the individual will return to the colony (which he usually does). In unstable circumstances though, the situation is different. Here a situation of *basic* doubt, of *weak* commitment, of social *in*stability prevails. This may be peculiar to a family within a relatively stable colony or may apply to a colony as a whole. In certain circumstances, defection can be 'contagious'.[6] This is true but it depends on the circumstances. One or two defections from a strong colony are considered natural or inevitable; no-one expects perfect commitment. If the colony is strong then those who remain do not feel themselves threatened because they know that the defection is numerically marginal, nor does it put their own values in doubt; in fact it may strengthen them. But if the colony is weak in the first place because of coming and going, because of instability of circles of friendship, because of factionalism (see below), because of widespread deviance, because members are uncertain of their own commitment to Hutterite values, then every defection is a warning sign, a further loss of friendship, a further proof that 'we'll never make it', a further reason to doubt one's values and a further sign that 'if you really want to leave you can do it, here's the proof'.

Sometimes defectors may leave for purely personal reasons. There may have been disputes with leaders of the colony over what each side has seen as a major issue, or there may have been family tension (factionalism). Regarding the latter, this is most likely to occur between father and son or between brothers (who invariably live in the same colony) or between groups of brothers. Since males do not usually move from colony to colony, the only choice is to defect should the situation become intolerable. This is partly obviated by the practice of splitting. If a person leaves because of a dispute with the colony as a whole then, in my opinion, the actual external dispute is rarely the fundamental issue. It is often the climax to a period of self-doubt which was taking place anyway. The dispute is frequently the consequence and not the cause of the doubt. Highly committed members also have conflicts with the community. Yet in their case they see that on balance their continuing commitment is more valuable than winning a particular argument. If the individual is not altogether certain in the *first* place about his commitment, then such issues play a far larger role in determining his future commitment. However (preempting our discussion about deviance), if a person or family feels discriminated against directly or indirectly (others getting privileges or being allowed to deviate with impunity) then this may lead from harsh feelings to defection, even in a strong colony.

The presence of the English teacher on the colony may at times help young folk to 'flirt with alien values' (e.g. watch television); they have even sometimes aided them in leaving the colony. To overcome this, some colonies began sending their own members to training colleges, only to find that this intense contact with the outside world led to occasional defection. Naturally, this has only increased Hutterite desire to be as isolated as possible from the outside world.

This also points to a general consideration, namely, that it is those who are least dependent on the colony who are mostly likely to defect in practice.[7] These would be people who are physically young and have few family commitments; it would refer to unbaptized individuals who can be freer of guilt feelings than the baptized; and naturally it is also a matter of personality. Hence the defection rate is highest in the 18–25 age group. Naturally, a weak colony has less moral and emotional claim on the individual: there are fewer guilt feelings and fewer public pressures when a person wishes to leave such a colony.

When I say that individuals may leave because of ambivalences and doubts regarding the Hutterite way of life I do not mean that the individual consciously comes to reject Hutterite belief. Socialization has been so strong that invariably the individual member has no doubt about the correctness of Hutterite theology and even of its application to daily life. Yet, and this is a crucial point, he feels that he personally cannot live according to that daily application. He may well have guilt feelings about his leaving. After all, he has learnt all his life that Hutterite belief and the Hutterite social system are one and the same, that one cannot exist without the other. Nevertheless, he feels that he personally has to divorce them. (This applies equally to the Kibbutz. Few people leave today for 'pure' ideological reasons, only because of the difficulties of putting the ideology into practice – for themselves personally or because the community as a whole has failed to do so.)

In this light, too, we can understand why many temporary defectors return. There is no evidence to indicate that they are incapable of 'making it' on their own. On the contrary, the technical skills they have acquired in the colony, the record of Hutterites being hard workers, the knowledge that colonies are virtually crime-free – these all enhance the possibilities of employers being ready to engage a Hutterite. But having entered the outside world many defectors see that it is not as rosy as they had pictured; they often feel uncomfortable in what is inevitably a culture with different interests, a different pace of life and different values. They will find, too, that although town life provides a higher standard of living than they enjoy on the colonies, this standard is accompanied by tension and insecurity. Finally, and perhaps the single most important factor, they feel a sense of isolation – even more critically than many urban people do – because of the close family and colony ties which they have now had to forego.

For these reasons, many defectors return. They do so without guilt or shame although there are contradictory reports about whether there is stigma attached to it in the eyes of others. Since forgiveness is an essential Hutterite belief, it would seem natural to welcome back the wayward son, as is done in the case of repentance after deviant behaviour. The return of the defector serves a positive purpose too. It is proof to those who stayed behind of the correctness of their chosen path, of the superiority of Hutterite life and values to others. The defector himself comes to see his period off the colony as a childish phase of his life; even expects that his own children will do the same and, like himself, eventually return. To have left as an unbaptized person means that one did not violate the laws of God but acted only through weakness, which can be forgiven. For the defector, then, he has worked his curiosity out of his system, has perhaps profited materially, and while he may still have doubts, has decided that on balance he prefers colony life. Without trying the outside world for himself, these deeper doubts may well linger on. I suspect that when other colonists relate to him negatively (because he left, not because he returned) this is more a reflection of their own weaknesses and ambivalences and even suppressed desire to do the same than a simple value judgement.

What are the factors militating against contemplation of defection? Financially the colony makes no contribution to anyone leaving. (This is a fundamental point of Hutterite belief and practice, so much so that in Manitoba, when an attempt was made to compel the Hutterites to pay defectors compensation, the Elders threatened to leave the province totally if the proposal became law.)[8] On baptism, a person specifically undertakes to surrender everything he has to the colony. For the Hutterite the individual possesses nothing, he only has goods given him by the colony for his private use. Should he cease to be a member (death, defection, expulsion) the goods remain the property of the colony. Should the colony be obliged to pay him on leaving, this would imply the reverse, i.e. that the individual is allowing the colony to enjoy *his* goods as long as he is a member but that as soon as he ceases to be a member the goods revert to him. Furthermore, by paying compensation to an individual who leaves, the colony would be denying its collective nature. Collectivism for the Hutterite does not mean simply sharing (in the sense of pooling what is basically yours) and certainly not conditional sharing. Collectivism for them means that the individual ceases to exist legally and socially as a discrete entity, that the colony is a collection of individuals who, by virtue of their collectivist relationship, have created a unit over and beyond their individual and separate existences. That collective unit is in a sense something apart from its constituent members: if an individual leaves, the unit continues in its entirety without reference to that individual. To recognize that the individual has private claims on the colony would be to recognize his superiority to it and the conditional nature of its existence. Even if an entire colony disbands, i.e. every single member leaves, they have no claims on it: the colony 'belongs' morally (and legally) to the Hutterite Church.

We may assume that a person wishing strongly to defect will find ways and means of overcoming this problem; we may also assume that it helps deter those who are somewhat less determined from defecting. There are three further factors:[9] pattern maintenance (strong socialization into wanting to live the Hutterite way); technical development (provision of work opportunities not available outside); and lack of critical analysis (the socialization system and the ideology do not lead one to compare societies or to try to prove that one's own society is better or to ask questions about it, merely to accept it without reservation). Regarding the latter point my own experience indicated the contrary – that Hutterites *do* indulge in much comparison, *but in order to prove that their own way of life is correct.* I gather though that in some colonies Baden's observations may have been correct. A further factor will be the subsequent relationship of the defector to the colony, especially the loss of family ties. A baptized person defecting is subsequently shunned, which for the Hutterites is particularly difficult to bear.

Given what we have said earlier about the strains and ambivalences of Hutterite life, and the foregoing factors militating against defection, we may accept the view that far more Hutterites contemplate defection than actually do it.[10] Some observers have argued that the defection rate is increasing but there are no statistics available on this point. In fact, information on the subject is generally difficult to come by and this in itself is instructive. Defections give colonies a bad name and this may have important implications for a colony. Leaders of the Leut are more likely to try to intervene in colony affairs; commercial transactions may be jeopardized, especially with other colonies; and Hutterite girls are reluctant to marry boys from colonies with bad reputations (since the wife joins the husband's colony), and difficulties in finding wives, not to mention the effect on colony population growth and economy, may have serious consequences all round.

In Kibbutz society

In what particular ways is the individual likely to find either tension or satisfaction within the Kibbutz? Two things in particular may generate tension – the high expectations people have of each other's behaviour and the closeness of Kibbutz life.

Intentional communities are generally very conscious of their intentionality, of the fact that they exist to manifest a set of ideals. This does not necessarily mean that members reflect on these values night and day; on the contrary, they are generally and implicitly taken for granted in unreflective manner (see Chapter 3). One situation which does lead members to respond consciously to the values of the community is their breakdown. When values are built into communal life and actually work, and when people behave according to accepted norms, there is no apparent need or stimulus to reflect on them. Among these is a high set of expectations regarding personal relationships.

In Kibbutz great store is set by what is called *tarbut ha-yachasim* (lit., 'the culture of human relationships'), i.e. that individuals should relate to each other pleasantly, considerately, with sensitivity and understanding, and especially that members whose task it is to serve others in some capacity or other should do so with maximum effort to satisfy individual members. Now clearly this is not limited to the Kibbutz: most advanced societies would presumably go along with this. The difference, however, lies in the expectations individuals have in this regard and the intimate atmosphere of the Kibbutz.

The point that concerns us here is not the objective standard of interpersonal relations in the Kibbutz, but the reactions of individuals when they find that their expectations are not met. It may well be that by and large those serving other members do so more politely and with greater comradely consideration than one may find off the Kibbutz. It may well be that deviations from this standard are only minimal or temporary lapses. *But this is of no concern to the member who 'suffers' such deviations. What concerns him is the relationship between his expectations and actual practice. An objectively narrow gap may seem to him to be quite enormous.*

Of course, much depends on how sensitive the individual himself is, how often the problem is repeated and whether he sees it as a general trend in the Kibbutz or as a passing weakness. It also depends on his general level of identification with the Kibbutz and to what extent the incident undermines it or 'proves' to him that his negative feelings were justified all along. At any rate it is easy to blow up a small incident into a major injustice and easy to develop a feeling that 'the Kibbutz is failing'.

The problem is compounded by the close relations of Kibbutz life. This closeness is both social and physical. The sheer physical proximity between people makes much social contact inevitable, even if people do not want it. The smallness of the community and its relative isolation require mutual dependence and contact simply to satisfy basic needs. The size of work groups, for example, makes it virtually impossible for members to avoid each other. This has two consequences. Frequent close contact may increase the possibility of friction between members; and should such friction occur, it is difficult to solve the problem by isolating oneself. Theoretically, group life is intended to be intrinsically satisfying; indeed most people do derive much pleasure from the intimate contact they have with so many people – the subtle signs of identity and sympathy, the feelings of belonging and togetherness, and the common fund of purpose, concern and experience. However, it is equally easy to feel that one's life is not one's own, that the smallness of the community breeds narrowness and pettiness, that there is no privacy and that there is too much dependence and pressure to act according to the rules. All Kibbutz members occasionally feel some of the latter; some feel it so much that they see no way out but to leave. This is not a matter of ideology, even though the ideology specifically invokes the joys of group living. It is a matter of individual temperament and of the type of atmosphere the Kibbutz as a whole has developed.

How then are such points of tension overcome? The solution is the same as that required to avoid the problem in the first place – a degree of maturity, thoughtfulness, consideration and sensitivity to the other person's feelings. Where these qualities prevail then, despite the closeness of contact, friction will be minimized. Where it does nevertheless occur, the members concerned will be able to leave it behind them, to recognize that human weaknesses will surface from time to time, to understand that a person is sometimes irritable for reasons which perhaps have nothing to do with the issue at hand, and above all, to put the entire problem in its proper perspective. Whether individuals are able to do this is a complex question. Clearly some do better than others, and some Kibbutzim have developed traditions and an atmosphere – a 'culture of relations' – which guide people in their actions and reactions, while others have not. While it is difficult to argue the point 'scientifically' I would contend that by and large such an atmosphere as a general trend, despite all the blemishes, must prevail, since if it did not, one cannot imagine individuals being prepared to stay on Kibbutz no matter how dedicated they may be to its theoretical values. It is clear that within any one Kibbutz, no matter how 'developed' its atmosphere, some individuals will be able to cope better than others. This is not a slight on the individual who cannot cope thus, since it is also a matter of personal temperament and this is difficult to quantify.

Members are aware that should friction come to the surface life will be made rather difficult for all parties concerned. They often feel therefore that it would be better to overlook many matters of interpersonal relations, to act *as if* there were no problems, to ensure that on the surface good relations are maintained. In this way 'explosions' (as they are called in Hebrew) are avoided. There is a price to pay for this, however: the individual who feels he has suffered may carry his resentments with him and bottle them up inside, so that either he begins to exaggerate them out of all proportion in his mind or eventually a bigger 'explosion' occurs.

This problem should be understood in the context of a wider phenomenon of Kibbutz life. Because of a number of factors – the intentional nature of the community, the high level of expectation, the closeness of social and physical contact and, not least of all, the permanent nature of the community – there is an unstated assumption on the Kibbutz that one should do the right thing even if one does not feel like it, or even if one finds it difficult. The idea here is that adherence to the norms of behaviour and the specific rules of the community should be taken for granted: the community assumes that such adherence does and will occur among all members of the community, irrespective of their personal feelings on the subject. Naturally, commitment is meant to be voluntary and if a member does not act according to the rules there is little that can be done. So whether it is a matter of appearing at work on time or doing extra work hours when needed, of doing one's turn in the dining hall or behaving with decorum when serving in it, of an office-bearer being obliged to help a member in a particular problem or doing it with consideration – the individual is expected to do all these things whether 'officially' demanded of him or not. Should he not fulfil his official obligations or not act in accordance with unofficial codes of behaviour, someone might raise the matter or social pressure might be brought to bear upon him.

On the other hand, wrong behaviour might be ignored, and a corollary of this is the matter of gossip. Gossip is a near-universal phenomenon and is particularly true of small village life, which Kibbutz in so many respects resembles. While many jokes are made about it in Kibbutz life, it serves a serious function. It is a form of communication and an informal means of gaining consensus. More important though, it is a consequence of *tarbut ha-yachasim*: since people cannot always express their true feelings publicly they need to release the tension involved in other ways, and primary among these is gossip. Far from seeing gossip as hypocrisy (talking one way and acting another), I would argue that Kibbutz can only sustain its interpersonal relations through *tarbut ha-yachasim* and this in turn requires a counterbalancing force, in this case gossip.[11] (The opposite occurs among the Hutterites. They have much less, if any, gossip; negative behaviour is 'attacked' institutionally and publicly, hence the need for gossip is much less.)

We should also look at the question of status in the community. While Kibbutz ideology and practice specifically reject material inequality and emphasize moral equality, status distinctions nevertheless exist. There are three main status differentials – occupational role, personal qualities, adherence to Kibbutz values and norms. One's role in the community can lead to positive status, i.e. high evaluation. On the other hand, personal qualities and adherence to values and norms are usually the basis of negative evaluation, i.e. possession of respected qualities and adherence to the rules of the community do not necessarily grant one any special status, but *not* to possess these qualities or to defy the rules can lead to *low* status. However, these criteria may well contradict one another. An office-bearer who performs his job badly or who reveals many negative personal qualities in his execution of the job, may well find that the latter neutralizes the high status of the former. There is an important consideration here. Since so much of an individual's role as an elected office-bearer or, say, branch manager, depends on his ability to handle personal relations, this means that obviously he himself must display socially admired personal qualities. It is one of the more notorious peculiarities of Kibbutz life that an individual officially takes on a central role for the sake of the community (since he has nothing to gain materially) and is thereby expected to set standards of behaviour which are almost ideal – but is then often criticized for not coming up to the standards.

Hence we have here a set of contradictions which we need to understand if we are to explain why individuals are prepared to take on roles in the community. Three factors deterring people from taking on such roles are: there is no material reward; there is the possibility of being subject to too much scrutiny and criticism; you are constantly at the service of your constituency (work branch, Kibbutz as a whole, committees) and must be prepared to devote yourself, even at the expense of personal and family considerations, to your tasks. The factors promoting role occupation are: intrinsic satisfaction at contributing more than usual to a community with which one identifies; an opportunity to lead the community (or work group or committee) in the direction one thinks best; the opportunity to gain in personal status.

One aspect of taking on central roles in the community is the ritual involved. Perhaps it is this ritual which sometimes gives outsiders the impression of reluctance to fill roles. It is rare indeed for someone to volunteer himself to be, say, secretary or treasurer of the Kibbutz, or even to take on relatively minor roles. Invariably the individual has to be approached by the nominations committee (whose job it is to bring nominations to the assembly) and then urged to allow his name to be put forward. At that stage already, and even in the nomination process, the individual invariably goes through the motions of self-deprecation (why he is not suited to the job) and self-pity (why he would rather be doing other things or why he will find it difficult). Sometimes these statements are genuine but frequently they are not. In any event, even if he would really like to do the job the member concerned will enact the ritual of opposition.

This teaches us something about the nature of personal relations in the Kibbutz (and applies to the Hutterites too). It is good that one lives according to Kibbutz principles; it is even better to promote them actively, but in so doing the individual must give no indication that there is any self-interest involved. The slightest hint of self-interest will arouse suspicion, resentment, criticism or lack of co-operation. Ideally, whatever one does in the community one does for the community, or at least, if it is a purely private affair, one must not damage the community. In short, the community's interests come first. It is perfectly legitimate to develop one's interest and satisfy one's ego within the Kibbutz framework, but not through attempting to dominate that framework or any part of it. That is the distinction between leadership and power. To agree to become a leader is one thing: to seek power is another. Even though everyone knows that status accrues to office-bearers, especially if they do the job well and in accordance with accepted standards of relationships, nevertheless the ritual must be observed; the fiction of reluctance must be sustained so as to preserve the distinction between leadership and power.

One aspect of the office-bearer's role related to that of status is his relationship to individual members. We have already noted how important it is not to treat problems mechanically but sensitively and delicately, combined if necessary with firmness. Given that principle, a contradiction develops. To ensure equality of treatment, i.e. the office-bearer relates to people as if they all have exactly the same status, is to reduce the Kibbutz to mechanical equality and inflexible bureaucracy. Besides, it is against the entire ethos of the Kibbutz. But to treat people as individuals inevitably means that they are not necessarily going to be treated equally. Ideally, the office-bearer relates to the individual's problems in the framework of Kibbutz principles generally and the rules of his own Kibbutz – and not in terms of his personal opinion of the individual concerned or the group of friends he belongs to or how long he has been on the Kibbutz or whether the member's wife had a row with his own wife or whatever. However, to divorce the problem from personal considerations is something that has not been achieved in the Kibbutz and probably will not be, unless mechanical equality and rules are introduced. So two individuals with similar problems may not get them solved in exactly the same way or to the same extent. The fact is that some individuals do have generally higher or lower status on the Kibbutz than others and office-bearers naturally react to them differently. Equally, personal relations and opinions, even simply the way individuals and office-bearers 'confront' each other, will go into the final outcome of handling individual needs.

What is also important to note here is that, in practice, handling of individual needs may not play a very big part in the office-bearer's role. Yet the individual member sees the role of the office-bearer very much in terms of his capacity as a problem-solver, and however good the office-bearer may be at handling the wider policies of the Kibbutz, ultimately his status depends, I believe, on his ability to relate to individual members and on their perception of that relationship. Equally significant is the effect of such perceptions on the individual's relationship to the Kibbutz as a whole. If the individual feels that justice is being done, that he is getting a fair deal and that there is no discrimination against him in favour of others, then clearly his identification with the Kibbutz will not be weakened and may even be strengthened. But if he gains the opposite impression, then no amount of ideological commitment is going to support him, especially if he comes to believe that 'that's the way the Kibbutz *really* is'. The individual's attitudes to Kibbutz institutions may be determined not so much by the intrinsic worth of the institutions as by the way in which the office-bearers concerned maintain them.

Having looked at the handling of personal matters 'from the top down' let us see what happens at the level of the individual himself and put it in the context of his status within the community. We recall our earlier comment that status at the individual level is defined more in negative than in positive terms. This means that the individual must not act in ways which will upset the conventions of the community. In personal matters the individual is expected to consider the wider needs of the community, the competing claims of other members, the general rules and standards laid down by the community, the difficulties of the office-bearer in maintaining the particular institution concerned, and the accepted patterns of behaviour (modesty, politeness, camaraderie) of the community. Individuals frequently find that if they do not act in accordance with these unwritten rules, resistance will develop to having their special needs met. However, there is one danger to a Kibbutz here. If an individual does act 'unethically' to achieve goals, and if as a result he succeeds, much resentment will arise among other members ('you only get what you want if you know how to shout') and a feeling of injustice and disillusionment will develop. If this in turn encourages others to seek their own ends by unorthodox means or to become disillusioned with the possibility of Kibbutz realizing its ideals, the dangers for Kibbutz life are apparent.

One aspect of all this shows up some important elements of Kibbutz life. What if an individual feels that an injustice has been done or simply wishes to appeal against a decision which has been made concerning him? Then the Kibbutz democratic procedure comes into play. Ultimately the assembly is the final arbiter of all that is decided in the Kibbutz. So any individual may, if he so wishes, raise any matter, no matter how trivial, in front of the assembly, and its decision will be binding. The advantage of this is that the member need not be dependent on the will of 'the establishment' but can appeal direct to the community as a whole. Clearly, though, he is expected to accept willingly the decisions of the assembly. What is significant is not so much that the member has such democratic rights but that the probabilities are that *he will not take advantage of them*. In most cases the individual would rather accept his position, however reluctantly, swallow his bitterness and frustration and possibly bottle them up, than go through the procedures of confronting the community *en bloc*.

There are two reasons for this. One is that to present one's case before the entire community may well require one to bare oneself and explain publicly various aspects of one's private life, which would be difficult enough even in front of strangers, so how much more so in front of people with whom one is in constant and intimate interaction? It would appear to the individual concerned as public self-debasement. The other reason is similar to that of nominees for office professing their inability and reluctance to do the job. An individual must not appear to be 'pushing himself' too much, to be attempting to impose his will on the community. Even though one's private aims may be perfectly legitimate and even though one is acting in accordance with the rules and with perfect decorum, one should not in the eyes of other Kibbutz members give the impression of putting oneself too much apart from others, too much in control of them. In fact, of course, the very opposite is true. The community controls the individual: *it* decides whether he is to hold office, study or travel overseas, and he cannot decide or act unilaterally, but the community does not want to feel that it is being pressurized into acting in any particular way.

Another factor governing the individual's status in the community and also his general relationship to it is his work. This is hardly surprising in view of the importance of work in Kibbutz ideology, economy and social life.

Work plays a number of roles in the life of the individual on the Kibbutz. It is his means of *self-expression*; it can influence his feeling of *contribution* to the welfare of the Kibbutz; it can be a framework for satisfying *social relations*. Given the fact that work has a high value status and further, that it is the single most time-consuming of all the activities on the Kibbutz, it follows that what happens to the individual in his work can influence everything else concerning his life in the community. By this I mean both his attitude towards others and towards the values and institutions of the Kibbutz, and also the attitudes of fellow members towards him. I think it is fair to argue that an individual's entire perception of Kibbutz life can be refracted through his work situation. Satisfaction in work can generate a positive approach to all the other elements of one's life in the Kibbutz, while feelings of dissatisfaction in work will do the opposite. Conversely, if a person is dissatisfied on Kibbutz for any reason not associated with work, it is in his work that this is first and most obviously expressed. While this is true of all elements of Kibbutz life, I believe it applies to work more than to any other. To feel satisfaction at attending meetings of the general assembly is important indeed, but is not likely to play as great a role as the individual's work in determining his satisfaction at Kibbutz life. One can withdraw if one so wishes from almost every aspect of Kibbutz life, but in no way can one withdraw from work. A work situation, we have seen, is made up of different factors and the emphasis for the individual is no doubt in the following order: personal satisfaction in his work; relations with fellow workers; contribution to the Kibbutz. Clearly these three elements interact: knowledge that one's work is making a good contribution to Kibbutz welfare can influence the morale of the work team and their relations and so on. Also, there is much subtle competition between branches (as with the Hutterites).

The individual's status in the community is partially determined by his work too. This can mean one of two things: how he works and his place of work. Sometimes one is more important than the other. As a broad generalization I would say that where the work is productive the emphasis tends to be on place of work; where it is non-productive the emphasis is more on performance. (The fact that the majority of women work in services thus becomes a matter of major importance in determining their status on the Kibbutz.)[12] Within each sphere (productive and non-productive) there are also branches with higher and lower status and in all cases the good or bad worker's status will be affected by the quality of his work. Hence the two cannot be separated totally. Nor can status in or through work be divorced from other aspects of status allocation in Kibbutz. The good worker who is also a popular individual is likely to have a higher status than one working as well in the same branch, but with an unpopular personality. An office-bearer who has completed his term of office and goes to work in, say, the cotton fields may well receive more status than his predecessor who after his term of office asked for an outside job. The status one derives from work is therefore made up of different variables and the individual's total status is constituted of an even more complex set.

The final factors we shall consider here governing the individual's status in the Kibbutz are his seniority and his circle of friends. We need to note that seniority is the one and only sphere of institutionalized inequality in the Kibbutz, even though on a long-term basis this is only temporary. From time to time the Kibbutz raises living standards, but frequently cannot do so in one fell swoop. Such increases need to be phased, yet how, apart from the few cases of obvious need, is this to be done? The accepted criterion is that of seniority, i.e. those who have been longest on the Kibbutz get preference and so on, down the line. Even this needs to be flexible. If, for example, a certain generation of members is moving into new houses (on the basis of seniority) then someone who belongs to that circle of friends but only joined at a much later stage will not necessarily suffer and may well move with them. This is perhaps a classic example of the need to handle individual situations – even when everything, mathematically, is crystal clear – with flexibility and understanding.

It may happen too that certain groups of individuals have a higher status than others. The reason generally lies not so much in their combined personalities but in their influence at any one time on the Kibbutz. Despite the principle of rotation (whereby offices are only held for one-to-three years) we may find that at any single point in time the rotation is taking place within a particular group of people. This group then comes, collectively, to have a certain status on the Kibbutz and individual members of the group, even if they are less active, may have the group's status rubbed off on them.

We now need to consider some further aspects of the individual's relation to the community and how his perceptions of his own place in it are affected.

We discussed elsewhere that the individual as an individual, and the community as a community, need to combine a degree of ideological passivity and unreflexiveness with a degree of sensitivity, consciousness and doubt. As far as the individual is concerned we may have an ironical situation. The more successfully the Kibbutz functions and the more integrated and contented the individual is, the less he will be stimulated into searching and questioning. The individual and the community as a whole can easily then become smug or self-satisfied. As a result they may not perceive many of the underlying tensions of Kibbutz life. The member may not be responsive to the many changes that are in fact taking place, with the result that when he as an individual, or the community as a whole, faces a crisis or challenge, they may be inadequate to the task. For this reason a degree of tension between the individual and the community can be creative both for himself and for the community as a whole.

What are the sorts of situations in which the individual is likely to find himself questioning Kibbutz values? The general answer is of course when he experiences a discrepancy between his expectations (which may be private or ideological) and reality. This may happen in work, in handling needs, in special requests. It may also happen if the individual feels that the Kibbutz has become anomic, that despite his personal desire to act in accordance with official norms, there is no point in doing so since no-one else is; or since there is little consistency in the way democracy and equality are actually functioning; or because some people appear to be feathering their nests at the expense of others or outside the accepted rules.

An important point should be clarified here. The individual's expectations about communal standards mean that he expects the rules to be observed even when deviance does *not* occur at the expense of others. Consider the following situation. An individual receives a present from his family (off the Kibbutz) of £1,000. He refurnishes his room, buys some expensive electronic equipment and generally enjoys himself. Why should this create resentment on the part of other members, since after all his gain is not made at the expense of other members in any way? Why should such behaviour be considered distasteful? Why should there be resentment even if the individual simply puts the money in the bank and leaves it absolutely untouched?

One answer may be jealousy but that is difficult to prove. I think that two points emerge from this regarding the operation of Kibbutz values and intentional communities generally. They are the questions of homogeneity and dependence. By this I mean that values like equality and democracy, while overtly existing as formal principles, will only be adhered to if there is among the members a feeling of homogeneity and if, in addition, they feel that they are dependent on each other. *A member acting in ways which indicate that he is not dependent on the community poses a threat to the entire community. The community hangs together on the assumption that all are totally dependent on it and that all are equally involved in it.* The member who puts some private money in the bank may be doing nothing to upset the principle of equality, but he is implicitly setting himself apart from other members; he is removing a sphere of his life (a sphere that is legitimately a concern of the Kibbutz) from the control of the community. In a sense he is not a total member of the community. *Only on the basis of total dependence and total involvement (within certain well-defined areas) can the community sustain itself.* This is not to say that all types of communities need these principles, only that if they do not then their structure, and the nature of interpersonal relations, must be different. Put otherwise, deviations from norms create resentment in the Kibbutz not only for widening the gap between the ideal and the real, and not only because they might arouse a sense of moral wrong, but because the deviant is implicitly stating that he is independent of the community, that its norms are not his concern and that he can live quite well without them. No freely structured, cohesive and permanent intentional community can tolerate such independence. (Further aspects of this are discussed in Chapter 10.)

But even if all this is true, does the individual not wish to be more independent of the community? I think that, as with the Hutterites, there is an underlying frustration in Kibbutz life in that many members feel that their dependence on the community is too great. Now, theoretically, the individual is not dependent on 'the community' since he *is* the community.[13] Dependence implies an external force which is capable of controlling one. In Kibbutz thinking the community is not external to the individual: it is the joint effort of a number of individuals, and its form is the reflection and consequence of their beliefs, actions, desires and needs. Since whatever form the community takes is what has been so desired by its own members, members cannot argue that they are dependent on the community. Yet, when all is said and done, this is not quite what happens in the minds of individuals. Whereas *in fact* the individual member has the opportunity to control very many aspects of communal life, including those things which influence him directly, and whereas he is *in fact* consciously aware of this, nevertheless he often tends to feel that he is over-dependent on the community in a way that his friends in the town are not.

Some Kibbutz members have put it this way: the member has

freedom in large matters but has less freedom in small matters. In the town it is the other way round. The Kibbutz member 'knows' that this is true but often *feels* that it is the small matters that are the really important ones. What is important to note about the individual in Kibbutz is not the community's *objective* advantages as compared to other forms of living, but the way in which members *perceive* the relative advantages and disadvantages and how these relate to their expectations. For this reason a small tiff with a fellow member may sometimes counterbalance oceans of consideration and co-operation; and for the same reason while, overall, most Kibbutz members prefer their own lives to a non-communal life, many nevertheless see in the latter a degree of freedom they themselves do not possess. This freedom may take the form of having cash in one's pocket, having a wider choice of films or books or whatever, having perhaps greater freedom of movement. Part of this may be a result of the Kibbutz's distance from the city (although in Israel this is seldom very great), but is more a consequence of the fact that the individual in the town, while living, let us say, at the same standard as the Kibbutz member, can apparently divide his time and his resources with greater flexibility than the Kibbutz members.

Now we need not argue here whether there is more or less freedom on the Kibbutz than elsewhere; that is not the point of this discussion. We are concerned here with how the Kibbutz member sees it himself. So while the Kibbutz member 'knows' that in many respects he has more freedom than his urban counterpart, he also knows that to enjoy it he must be dependent on the community. He has, for example, far more possibility of taking off from work for three years to study than his town friends, but to do it *he has to ask permission from the community*. It thus often seems to the individual member that the freedom he is getting from the one hand is being taken away by the other, and even objective knowledge of his relatively advantageous position may not help him overcome that feeling. He 'knows' that having a bit of cash in his pocket to spend on trivia is not nearly as important as the fact that, compared to the education his urban friends' children are receiving, his own children are possibly receiving a far better one, and if they need special help or advantage, they will get it without any extra cost to him personally (unlike his friends). He also knows that he is far closer to his children's teachers and school culture than his town friends will ever be; he can even decide who shall and shall not teach them, and can influence the Kibbutz's educational policy and practices – but even that knowledge may not stop him hankering after that extra bit of freedom in spending on trivia.

This is one reason why it is necessary that the Kibbutz maintains living standards comparable to that of the urban middle classes – whence most Kibbutz members come. Standard of living cannot be judged simply by computing total income – the way in which that income is distributed and how that distribution is related to individual desires are what affect the individual's *feeling* about his standard of living. So, once again, it is not enough that the Kibbutz member knows his living standard to be equal to the Israeli average[14] – it is how he relates to it that is important. Nevertheless, that standard should bear overt resemblance to that enjoyed by one's urban peers if the Kibbutz member is to feel that he is not greatly losing out by living on Kibbutz. This was perhaps one of the motivations towards the institution of personal, and now combined, budgets.[15] It has also been the reason for members tending towards greater freedom of movement, e.g. provision of more cars for private use.[16] (Paradoxically, town people often suggest to Kibbutz members that the latter are the lucky or privileged or wealthy ones, and Kibbutz members often resent this and will make every effort to prove the opposite.)

However, we should stress that if matters reach a crisis people seldom leave Kibbutz purely for economic reasons. If people leave they do so because of a more basic dissatisfaction with Kibbutz life per se. The increased living standards of Kibbutz have some- what closed the gap between the Kibbutz member and his friends in the town. The possibility of more money will not make him leave if he is happy with Kibbutz life. But if he is already wavering it may make the final decision to leave that much easier. Many who leave have no money to fall back on, while many who stay do potentially have such money. Conversely, I do not believe that people join solely for economic reasons. Primarily, they must find Kibbutz life personally, ideologically and culturally satisfying, or else they would not join. However, if living standards are very low then many who would consider joining might be deterred. There are few today, as in the very early days, for whom austerity was an end in itself: the modern Kibbutz member sees no contra- diction between his ideology and high living standards. What is important though is that his 'total income' is structured in a different way to the average town family. A proportionately high amount may be spent on education, for example. In the end, the member may have little cash in his pocket and this may give him a *feeling* of not having an adequate living standard.

The individual, then, may sense a latent lack of freedom in his life, and especially when he needs some special attention or privilege from the Kibbutz. Part of the reason for this, to come back to an earlier point, is that the 'real' freedom he possesses comes to be taken for granted; it is so much built into the system that he can even forget that it is there. The same applies when the opposite process occurs. Conventional Kibbutz wisdom has it that one sees the strength of Kibbutz not when things are going well for the member, but when they are going badly for him. The result is that just as the member may come to doubt Kibbutz values, or at least his place in them, when he is going through a crisis, there are other times where situations equally critical may make him appreciate those values and even identify with them more strongly. The situations which might lead to *doubt* invariably involve the individual's overall relation to the community; those leading to *satisfaction* usually involve matters of a highly personal nature over which the community itself has little control, such as sickness or death. In times like this one sees to what extent the community can rally round the individual (over and above the material or formal security it may offer) – by individuals and functionaries showing consideration in work matters, extra expenses and so on, and simply by being caring and supportive in all ways. (We have seen that the same applies to the Hutterites.)

We should note that such rallying round does not occur, in my opinion, because Kibbutz members (or Hutterites) are somehow 'better' than other people. The close nature of Kibbutz life, physically and socially, and the fact that the community can absorb the necessary adjustments to accommodate to the individual going through a crisis, including the fact that those people directly giving support do so without any extra material cost to themselves – these are part of the system. But even when 'the system' allows for such supportive behaviour, there is no guarantee that it will be forthcoming. There are two points here. One is similar to the point about doing the right thing irrespective of private feelings. In the Kibbutz, which prides itself on having high standards in this regard, people will rally round an individual even when perhaps they do not feel completely inclined to do so. That leads to the second point, namely, do people receive equal support? Clearly, in the technical aspect of helping a person out of a crisis there will be equality, but in the more subtle forms of support one's status or circle of friends may be crucial and there is no certainty at all that different individuals in similar circumstances will receive the same support.

Another consideration is that an unhealthy state of affairs is created if members identify with Kibbutz primarily because of its ability and readiness to support individuals in times of crisis. I am certainly not decrying the importance of this reason, nor am I viewing them as 'negative' reasons for belonging to Kibbutz. But I do not believe that this is a very strong basis in itself to identification with Kibbutz values and the particular Kibbutz in which one lives. Personal matters, as we have seen time and time again, loom very large in the mind of the individual, and how the Kibbutz relates to them can influence one's overall attachment to the Kibbutz and what it stands for, even when in fact those personal matters only form a small part of the totality of one's life in the Kibbutz. Members are more likely to identify strongly with the Kibbutz (or colony) when they see positive behaviour such as we have been describing in the context of the wider principles of the Kibbutz, of which such behaviour is only a specific expression. The same applies to one's negative feelings about Kibbutz. If the individual sees problems (e.g. of personal freedom) not as specific or one-time problems but as part of a negative, *overall* appraisal of Kibbutz, then clearly it will lead him to reject more strongly, Kibbutz values. Yet, and this is perhaps the crux of the matter, *the individual does not assess Kibbutz in terms of abstract principles but in terms of their application to daily living* – and this concrete application is invariably extrapolated *backwards* by the individual, i.e. on this basis he assesses his overall commitment to the Kibbutz and its values.

Individuality and communality: the existential tension

If one were forced to reduce the problems of the individual in an intentional community down to one single explanation, it would perhaps be that whereas he finds it relatively easy to accept the community's values in principle, it is far harder to live according to them in practice. I am not claiming here that there is a great disjunction between declared values and actual behaviour. On the contrary, one of my arguments is that in ongoing intentional communities a degree of disjunction is recognized as being inevitable and is lived with rather than overcome 'by force', as it were. On the other hand, a communal society can only persist if such disjunction is not too great. How great such a gap will be depends on a number of factors such as whether communal life imposes strains on the individual which make it difficult for him to live according to the professed ideals of the community, or how the community manages to remove such strains, and how conformity emerges and is sustained among members.

We have argued that conformity in intentional communities is not something seen as enforced from above but is part of the means the individual chooses to identify with the values and life-style of the community, both of which are, for him, intrinsically satisfying. Conformity is not absolute; on the contrary, individuality is recognized. Nevertheless, conformity with the values and life-style of the community is ultimately meant to enhance rather than suppress one's individuality. Such conformity need not require members to be automata: conformity need not mean homogeneity nor equality imply standardization. Yet we live in the real world where people, despite their voluntary desire to live in the community and conform to its precepts, and despite the recognition given to their individuality, find from time to time that tensions arise between their individuality and their conformity. Their conformity is voluntary but, when tensions occur, it may seem to the member as imposed conformity. *This is endemic to communal life*: it would be utopian in the pejorative sense of the word to expect it to be otherwise. At any rate the community has collective goals and it may require the individual to sacrifice his personal interests for the greater good.

The challenge facing any communal society – at least of the kind we are examining here – is not to attempt to eliminate such tension totally (only the worst kind of repression could achieve that) but to minimize it, to canalize individuality into spheres which do not upset the basic conformity upon which the community operates, to lessen conformity to the maximum possible extent without breaking value-consensus or organizational stability, and to ensure that on balance the individual finds that his conformity is more satisfying than his conflicts are frustrating.

We could go even further than this and argue that the inherent tension that exists within the individual between his need to conform and his need to 'individuate' should not be seen necessarily as a sign of inherent weakness in him or his community. Rather, provided it is properly contained and canalized, it can be a source of strength all round: the individual's tensions in the community can potentially be as creative and constructive as his conformity, since they lead him to reflect on his purposes in the community and to find positive ways of strengthening his relation to it. *In short, the community requires not absolute conformity nor absolute individuality (not that these are theoretically possible anyway) but a proper balance between them in terms of the community's ideology and its objective needs. It is this balance which is critical to the way in which members perceive, accept and aspire to the community's goals and the community's ability to perform its basic tasks.*

The individual's attitude to his community can be strongly affected by two types of situation. One is his feeling of satisfaction or otherwise at living a communal life generally, especially with regard to the life-style and atmosphere of his particular community. The other is what happens to him in particular circumstances. There is no formula to be had here of how these factors will combine to increase or decrease individual identification with the community. Within each individual member there is a combination of positive and negative feelings. His relation to the community and his willingness or reluctance to abide by community norms will depend on how he balances these various feelings. This is a matter of temperament to a large degree but not of temperament only. Clearly, different members will react differently to similar situations, since these situations have different relative weights in the context of each member's needs and perceptions. Yet this does not mean that the rest of the community need simply accept fatalistically that however individuals react to situations, so be it, there is nothing to be done. There is the possibility of a collective sensibility developing which can help the individual emerge from situations, if not positively, then at least not negatively, and can help the individual attain some overall feeling of welfare within the community. For this reason, not only sensibility but also flexibility is required. But to this flexibility limits must be imposed, since, if they are not, the values on which the community is based may become meaningless, and the chain-effect of this on other members may be ultimately insidious. *The balance between individual and communal needs is highly delicate and sensitive. To find this balance is a fundamental need if the community is to persist.* Whether it does or does not find this balance depends on the experience, insight, personalities and private values of the individual members (particularly the leaders) and how these are reflected in the overall functioning of their community and in the day-to-day interactions of members.

All this is related to the voluntary nature of the community. For an individual to live in a community is an act of choice: at any stage of his life he may choose to leave. Just as no-one forced him to join, no-one is compelling him to stay. The individual member believes that *in principle* his life in the community can be transient. As we have seen, life in these communities has, almost without exception, its moments of crisis. Every time one passes through such a crisis, one asks the same questions: 'Should I be here? Did I make the right decision? Is this my place? Should I act before it is too late?' Now, one can ask these questions precisely *because* one has the opportunity of answering them and actually acting according to the answer. Each time one goes through such a crisis, one has to reassess one's relationship to the community, one's personal needs and aims, the aims of the community as a whole, the nature of the people one is living with. I suggest that the fact that the individual's commitment to the community is entirely voluntary not only allows him to ask these questions but perhaps strengthens his commitment to the community every time he answers affirmatively. This is definitely *not* to say that an affirmative answer implies that the problem is overcome: on the contrary, guilt feelings or resentments may linger on for a long time. However, the individual has decided on balance that his life in the community is worthwhile – and that often leads to some strengthening of his commitment to it, whatever his reservations.

There can be negative consequences though. The individual may still go through the formal motions of being a member, and from the viewpoint of the community's continued functioning no harm may come to it. But the degree to which he is actively involved in communal life – and involvement, as we have seen, is fundamental to the community's culture – may decline and may even spill over into deviance. Much individual dissatisfaction stems from problems at a highly personalized level and for this reason it is necessary to have people in the community sensitive to this kind of situation, to have leaders who can prod others in this direction, and to have a community culture which will make accommodations to individual circumstances. The point about the intentional communities studied here is not that people do not feel personal dissatisfaction; *on the contrary, they feel it often*, and in fact, it is, as we have said, endemic to communal life. Yet, I suggest that one of the reasons for the persistence of intentional communities is that the situation of 'collective sensitivity' has by and large existed and has managed to counterbalance these problems.

There are other relevant considerations here. We have already noted that because the member has joined voluntarily and knows that others have done likewise, because the ideology values the individual and has high moral goals, and because the individual is dependent on the community, the individual's expectation of what life in the community will be like and what he will gain from it, are high. This has the effect of making the individual often blame the community for his failures, shortcomings and problems. In an individualistic society it is often difficult to find someone to blame other than oneself, but in a communal society it is only too easy. This merely adds to the feeling we have mentioned that the individual, however committed he may be, often has a sense of self-sacrifice in living in the community. Even if one can prove to him theoretically that he may be objectively better off in the community than elsewhere, his high expectations and the consequent frustrations may not let him see the point. This is frequently expressed in personal crisis (*Anfechtung* among the Hutterites, *matzav ruach* in the Kibbutz, 'freaking out' in therapeutic communities). The individual 'knows' that he is not at fault; he *wants* to blame the community for his problems but he knows too that he has himself to blame since, if he really wanted to solve his difficulties, he could do so. *Crisis stems from the state of wanting not to blame either oneself or the community, yet then blaming both and knowing that one is caught in a trap, since one could leave if one really wanted to or make the effort to solve the problem within the community.* An individual in a community who, when he blames the community for his problems, and is confident that that is the entire explanation, simply ups and leaves or makes a rational compromise, however unpalatable. He may be resentful but he does not go through a crisis. The individual who blames both the community and himself and yet feels he has absolved both, is the one who goes through the classic crisis of community life.

So we suggest that the voluntaristic basis of the community can have positive and negative consequences. On the one hand, it raises the level of identification and commitment, the feelings of solidarity and the determination to succeed in attaining your goals. On the other hand, frustrations in so doing and in attaining personal satisfaction, can lead to greater sense of crisis, disillusionment, deviance and even defection.

The problem lies perhaps in the fact that to live one's entire life (at any particular time) within a particular and fairly close framework often entails a degree of pressure and strain, physical or psychological. It is inconceivable that every facet of community life will operate exactly in accordance with one's own needs and desires. The smooth operation of the community requires much mutual accommodation. To accept the need for such accommodation is obvious at an 'academic' level of understanding; to accept it for ideological purposes is undoubtedly noble; but to accept it in matters highly important to one at a very subjective level is often extremely difficult. So to live in a community requires a conjunction of, on the one hand, one's ideological commitment and, on the other, one's personal temperament regarding the community's mores, institutions and fellow members – *one without the other can never be a solid basis to identification with the community*.

These observations confirm that the individual's readiness to contribute, in day-to-day terms, to the communal cause is not simply the result of a prior, abstract commitment to that cause. There is no simple monocausality here. Indeed, ideological commitment can equally be the *result* of individual satisfaction within day-to-day community life, whether at a higher organizational level (i.e. whether they join 'the establishment') or in the most mundane and trivial areas of life.[17]

All this is related to the principle of effort which I raised in our discussion on community ideology (Chapter 5). The principle of effort seems antithetical to the notion of play.[18] Play (as opposed to games) is about self-expression, experimentation; play is an end in itself. At first glance play may seem an inappropriate concept to apply to ongoing intentional communities. Applicable enough to 'personal growth' communes, yes, and certainly relevant to any kind of individualistic society. After all, even in therapeutic communities one can hear people saying to the uninvolved resident: 'Stop playing about, you're here to *work* on your problems.' Work and effort are good because they promote community goals and are somehow 'good' for the individual. However, I contend that the distinction between play and effort in our intentional communities may not be as great as implied. In each of our communities individuals do, and *need to*, find room for self-expression, for negotiation, for enjoying the life of the community as an end in itself. Paradoxically, the more permanent the community, the *greater* the need for the play element. A therapeutic community is all about personal growth, but because it is a transient community you are expected to make maximum effort and *not* to see life in the community as an end in itself. By contrast, in our long-lasting communities there is a need to allow individuals freedom of manoeuvre, the opportunity to lead their lives in relaxed fashion, to explore ways and means of finding the most comfortable existence, the most compatible friendships, the most enjoyable work. Freedom, opportunity, exploration, comfort, compatibility, enjoyment (as the community member, not the observer, understands them) – these are what play is about, and in ongoing intentional communities individuals could not survive without them. In such communities, the ideology of effort and the sociology of play find a fruitful meeting ground.

Again, a comparison of our two major communities with therapeutic communities can be instructive. Therapeutic communities should actually be seen as comprising two communities – staff and residents. We have argued that the individual in intentional communities must not totally submerge in, or yield himself to, the community, since he could not sustain this for a lengthy period of time. But in a therapeutic community this can be demanded of residents because their period of stay is *intended* only to be transitory. Not so, however, with staff. They are there for a longer period of time and if they are not to 'burn out' then they need to pace themselves – to confine their work to work hours, to have outside interests, not to get 'over-involved' with residents, and so on. Burnout is a common phenomenon in therapeutic communities, although one only hears of it with reference to staff, not residents. The reason is that staff are the 'culture carriers', the vehicles of permanence and continuity – and if they are to perform this function then they need to see their own needs – personal, professional and material – as being independent of the needs of the community and separate to those of the community's clients.

This means three things which we have already partly noted. The individual must find the way of life intrinsically satisfying; he must also be given a degree of personal room for manoeuvre. Third, and this is perhaps a paradox in the context of intentional communities, he must be allowed for much of the time to forget that he is living in an intentional community. Indeed, even a degree of collective amnesia is necessary to persistence. We have already noted the principle of effort in the ideology of each of our communities. We have already mentioned though that too much emphasis on effort and reminder of goals and principles can be psychologically distressing for the individual and functionally debilitating for the community. (This is closely related to the question of community 'totality' discussed in Chapter 10.) Now, it is fairly easy and definitely necessary for the individual to be satisfied with his life as it is, to feel that as things are everything is fine. People simply do not and cannot go round saying to themselves – 'I did a bit of self-realization today,' or 'I am one step nearer salvation now.' On the contrary, those with unrealistic expectations of themselves and others tend, it seems, to be more frustrated with communal life, leading sometimes to a cynicism on their part and even to the kind of deviance they condemn in others.[19] And, if conventional wisdom is anything to go by, 'the big talkers' are the first to leave. This does not mean that ideological consciousness is totally lacking: the act of joining, the occasional crisis, constant reminders of the real reason for one's presence in the community (through rituals and symbols), crisis in the community as a whole, exhortations to work harder at achieving goals, threats (real or imagined) from the environment, and the presence in every community of ideological watchdogs – all these make it difficult to forget the purpose of the community. So, even though routinization is necessary, if these reminders, crises and reassessments never occurred, there would be a serious danger of apathy, complacency, stagnation and self-interest creeping in.

I suggest that the two major communities we are studying have persisted because they have managed to sustain a balance between these two situations – 'satisfying apathy' and routinization on the one hand, and reminders from time to time of one's purposes in the community on the other. There is tension between the two because, strictly speaking, the act of questioning is the midwife of the community's existence and of one's membership in it. Yet intrinsic satisfaction in community life is essentially passive: to question it persistently, and even to reflect on it, is to vitiate its intrinsic nature. The communities have not totally resolved the tensions; that is impossible. They have managed to give adequate scope to each party to it – and that has been crucial to their persistence.

Another point to be noted brings in our therapeutic communities, since it involves a basic difference in values between them and the Hutterites and Kibbutzim. In a word, this difference is that whereas in the latter the emphasis is on doing the *right* thing, in the former it is on doing the *honest* thing. The two may sometimes coincide but, where not, one or other takes precedence, and which is to do so is closely related to the question of persistence. I suggest that in a therapeutic community the 'honesty' policy is necessary because this is fundamental to the whole therapeutic policy; if people did not react to the behaviour of others or express their own feelings with complete honesty, there would be no possibility of therapy. But what concerns us here is that this policy is made possible in practice by the transient nature of the community. Precisely because the community's population fluctuates and because the community itself does not have collective goals (someone else has collective goals for it, see next paragraph) people can, in a sense, 'afford' to relate to each other in this way. Considerable strain is involved in such cases, but the strain is tolerable because members of the community know that it is only during a short phase of their lives that they need both to bear it and to relate closely to the others with whom they are honestly interacting. If they were trying to build a permanent community I doubt if such persistent honesty could be possible: they would need to be more careful and balanced in their relations so as not to create a bad atmosphere from which there is little escape. This is precisely what happens among the Kibbutzim and Hutterites. Withdrawal is difficult because of the comprehensiveness of the community in time and space. So, constantly to be treading on each other's toes, as a policy of complete honesty would entail, would be to create a tense and possibly unbearable atmosphere. Doing the right thing is a means of sustaining a tolerable culture of interpersonal relations over a lengthy period of time among the same people, even if a degree of dishonesty and suppressed resentment are at times involved.

This is the price one has to pay for persistence. The communities concerned pride themselves on having created a culture of considerateness, helpfulness, and so on. *I am suggesting that this culture may be, as they believe, morally good, but that even if it were not, moral goodness would be functionally necessary. For the therapeutic communities such a culture is not as necessary, simply because persistence of that group is not in itself a community goal.*

This helps to underline a further fundamental difference between the therapeutic communities and our two major communities. In the latter the individual, to a large extent, defines his identity in terms of both the collective good and the supra-individualistic goals of the community. In other words, he sees himself very much in terms of the community persisting over and above his own particular existence. His own existence is to some extent defined by its contribution to the community's persistence. Precisely the opposite occurs in a therapeutic community. Here the aim is for the individual to *learn* to define an identity. To predetermine what that identity should be, or to ask the individual to define himself in terms of collective and transcendental goals, is to deny the basic purposes of the community. But the community would not then persist over and above the presence of the particular people in it. The reason it does persist is that the community belongs to an organization whose centre is committed to collective goals and which emphasizes that aspect of the ideology which relates to expansion in the world, education of the wider public, and so on. In other words, if left to itself entirely, there may not be a desire or basis for community persistence; by someone else external to the community taking upon himself that objective, persistence is ensured.[20] The shortlived nature of many contemporary communes stems from the fact that they have individualistic goals and *only* individualistic goals, whereas in our major communities the individual's private goals and the overall community goal of persistence overlap considerably.

Finally, we need to look at the connection between our ideas on alienation and the three groups of communities we are discussing. Since we defined alienation in terms of the ability or inability (for whatever reason) to sustain an identity, we argued that all societies are potentially alienating. Basically, there are two kinds of alienating situations. In the one, society does not provide guidelines to members for establishing and maintaining an identity. In the other, it does provide goals but does not allow access to them for many members, either because of the structure of the society or because the goals are scarce resources. Nor does it allow for alternative definitions of identity. None of the societies we are looking at falls into any of these categories. Each meets the necessary preconditions for avoiding alienating situations.

(1)   Each society has clear conceptions as to right and wrong, each has fairly clear norms of behaviour, and each has fairly clearly articulated goals which all members are aware of, accept, and are ready to strive for. In short, each community's ideology is a closed universe and members, even if only implicitly, are aware of what it is.

(2)   Each community seems to its members to be democratically structured; they feel that they are in control of themselves; even rules laid down from above are internalized as 'necessary', not as something imposed on them against their will.

(3)   While there is only limited room for establishing an alternative identity with*in* any community, this is partly overcome by having a number of communities and different streams of communities for the individual to choose from.

(4)   In each community the goals are of a kind to which everyone can have access; ultimately too they are individual goals (salvation, self-realization, personal growth).

Where there are also collective goals (to be a beacon of light in a sinful world, to promote the national cause) then everyone can contribute, can feel part of the collective effort, can feel that it is his effort. However, I suggest that it is *only because the collective effort is linked up with individualistic goals* that it can be sustained over a lengthy period of time. None of these communities could motivate members permanently – however much members might internalize and value the collective goals – if there were not an underlying perception by members that their personal, in the sense of private, identities were not also valued, *not only as a means towards an end but as an end in itself*. In short, each level of identity, the private and the public (defined in the section on alienation), draws its strength from the very existence of the other. Neither level is self-sufficient in terms of sustaining a community on a permanent basis. Only a community whose membership is transitory can devote itself only to one or the other of the two levels. To devote itself only to the private level means that it would be unable to achieve collective goals (unless someone else undertook it, as in the case of the therapeutic communities); to demand of members only to devote themselves to the collective effort would be psychologically intolerable over a lengthy period of time. The communities have not overcome the inherent tension between the public and private levels of identity within each member, nor could they ever do so. *Rather, they have recognized the inevitability of tension and so have articulated fairly clearly the scope of each level so as to ensure that there is sufficient conformity, cohesion and collective effort on the one hand, yet sufficient scope for individuality on the other.*

The structure of the community and its *actual* implementation of certain norms are crucial here. I refer to the absolute material security provided to members, the concept of relative equality and the norms of caring, helping, understanding. I am not suggesting that these are the only societies which uphold these norms or even provide material security. But I am arguing that when these considerations link up with the other considerations we are making, then they contribute to the ability of the community to persist.

These three factors contribute to the feeling the individual gains that he is valued in his own right. Yet, as we have argued, to value him in his own right can, if not counterbalanced by collective goals and norms, lead to anomie, which means alienation. By providing for individual values within a complex of clear norms, by developing individual goals together with collective goals, and by maintaining a structure which gives the individual a feeling of evaluation *and* motivation to collective effort – by doing all these things *simultaneously* the Hutterites and the Kibbutzim have managed to persist.

All this points to what I believe is one of the most important factor (internally) in the persistence of intentional communities. Intentional communities which have an element of voluntarism rest on the assumption that each person will do more than go through the formal motions and undertake the minimal obligations of membership. Two other factors are necessary. One is that each member should display a degree of active commitment (as opposed to passive identification). The problem here is not so much a danger of apathy – the community could function quite adequately if only a small number of members were actually active at an organizational or decision-making level. The real problem is that apathy implies that the individual has no concern for the community, is concerned only to satisfy his own needs. But this negates the idea of balancing individual and collective goals: the former can only be attained through or within the framework of the latter but never on its own. The moment members suspect that others are only concerned for themselves the whole fragile structure collapses (or else rights and obligations need to be formalized, as is happening to some extent on the Kibbutz, although not for this reason only).

The other factor is that members assume that they are all totally dependent on the community. Dependence is not simply a matter of control. It may well be that too, but then it is seen as a form of self-imposed control and not as something external to the individual. We remember that even though the community has individual goals and even though the individual is valued in his own right, the individual nevertheless feels that he is giving up something for the sake of others or of the community as a whole. It is almost a feeling of self-sacrifice, however small a sacrifice it may be. This is enhanced by the perception, right or wrong, that those not living in the community have a degree of freedom and independence which they themselves lack. However, the sacrifice and lack of freedom are considered worthwhile because of the individual and collective goals of the community, and this sense of 'it's worthwhile' is strengthened by giving the individual various alternative sources of satisfaction at a purely personal level or even by allowing for a degree of personal deviance. However, the moment members begin to suspect that other members are somehow independent of the community, or have a type or degree of freedom denied to themselves, or are deriving personal satisfaction in ways which are not socially legitimate or not accessible to everyone – in short the moment members suspect that others are in it only for themselves, mutual suspicion results and people begin acting in deviant ways or simply leave the community. *Only when people are equally dependent on the community and know that this is the case will they be prepared to commit themselves unconditionally to it.* The moment they suspect that others are not as dependent and involved as they are, or wish to 'profit' egoistically from the community, they will see no point in making any effort over and above what is minimally required.

This dependence also means that the individual has only one

frame of reference, namely the community in which he lives. As we shall see in our discussion on exclusive relations, this does not mean that the individual must be committed to the community as a whole, and that only. On the contrary, he is expected *not* to do so. But it does mean that all his goals, all the norms he lives by and all the projects he undertakes, exist *within* the community of which he is a member and according to the guidelines, structure and possibilities of the community *as defined by the community*. The point then is not to be dedicated solely *to* the community but solely *within* the community. This is perhaps the fundamental assumption of an intentional community and the moment this assumption is threatened the basis of all other norms and institutions is threatened.

Now we can see further why people are prepared to devote themselves to something without any apparent gain for themselves. We have already explained that the ideology of the community is, for the member, an expression of his identity. His active efforts for the community can also be a source of personal status. We can now see too that the individual has no need to be egoistic. This stems partly from the fact that his means of sustaining an identity do not require egoism (see Chapter 2) and partly from his knowledge that all other members are as dependent as he is on the community. He can also be as committed as he is because the commitment demanded of him is not total anyway: this, we have seen, is one of the crucial factors in community persistence. Of course he does feel doubts about his commitment, but he has means of overcoming them or compensating for them. (One of these is deviance, to which we turn in a moment.)

To conclude, then. One of the keys to analysing the persistence of intentional communities is to understand the mentality of those who belong to them. And the point here is precisely that there is *no* extraordinary, unique or extreme state of mind to understand. Some members are no doubt fired by religious zeal, inspired by revelations of higher truth; some others, for their part, are indeed straw-chewing yokels, good for nothing else; still others may be good at a lot more but are in it only for their own comfort. But these are the exceptions rather than the rule (yet, arguably, still necessary). As examples of typical members they are to be found usually in relatively brief periods of the communities' histories, and then only as the prelude to either routinization or demise.

The average communard is as simple and as complex a personality as the rest of humanity.

In some respects there are indeed differences, but these are more of degree than of kind. Like most of us he proceeds through life – at times plodding along leaden-footed, at other times displaying satisfaction, confidence and determination – simply trying to find pleasure in the mundane things of life – work, marriage, social life, community activity, leisure and the like – usually not seeing himself as much more than most other mortals and strenuously denying assertions to the contrary. He acts within a broad framework of goals and values, conventional wisdom and social pressures, adapting his most personal desires and needs to them and 'demanding' of them to adapt to him. On those occasions where his supra-individual or intra-individual needs and perceptions are threatened he may reflect on, articulate and rationalize them – with the outcome invariably being a fuzzy process of mutual accommodation between the conflicting and problematic areas. As I mentioned in the discussion on alienation, this is the way most of us act anyway. The difference between the communard and 'the rest' is that he lives in a community whose goals and values are more explicit, more determined, more demanding of the individual than others – but the difference, as I have said, is more of degree than of kind.

So, on the one hand, there is the similarity – the haziness, the lack of reflection, the attitude of 'let's just get on with the job', the desire for private satisfaction in the most banal of matters, the irritations suffered in the most trivial of matters, the half-inchoate attachment to a set of meanings and the readiness to balance those meanings with all the other dimensions of one's life in a way which is not always strictly logical or consistent or idealistic or maximally efficient, but is a way which simply works and so makes it possible for life as it is to persist, perhaps a bit better, perhaps a bit worse. On the other hand, there is the difference – that extra bit of goal-articulation, of sensitivity to values, of readiness to subordinate oneself to a greater good, of a conscious desire to envisage and actively construct a more meaningful present and a more valuable future, without all of which the drive, solidarity, cohesion, morale, pride and sense of purpose of the community would be lacking.

It is when both these dimensions of individual life in the community are present that communal persistence is made possible.

Chapter 9
Deviance and conformity

For the good of self and others: control among the Hutterites

Basically, there are two ways of limiting deviant behaviour among the Hutterites. One is to ensure in advance that members will not want to deviate; the other is to ensure that if they nevertheless do deviate, they can quickly be brought back into line. The two are related in that prior knowledge of the consequences of deviation is in itself meant to deter people from it.

The main means of ensuring a non-desire to deviate are discussed elsewhere – socialization to Hutterite values and behavioural patterns and the inculcation of guilt feelings and responsibility to the community. The two most important means of detecting deviant behaviour are surveillance and reporting. Surveillance is possible because of the authority structure of the community (since most people need permission from above for a wide variety of actions, leaders of the colony know what is going on and what people should or should not be doing), because of its size (the smallness of the community makes observation of the behaviour of others quite easy) and because of its intimacy (one does not have a 'private life' in the community, doors are not locked, withdrawal is difficult). So all members of the community are aware of what everyone else is doing.

That in itself would not ensure detection of deviance. In addition, members must be sensitive to deviant behaviour not only in themselves but also in others, and must wish such behaviour to cease. Hence the institution of 'reporting'. We have seen that, in Hutterite thinking, all Christians are responsible for and to one another. This means too that you are accountable to others.

Responsibility does not only mean assisting other Christians, but also helping them to live a Christian life. Hence, if someone deviates from the True Way, other Christians are obliged to help him back. This is done by reporting his misdeeds to the preacher – who then takes the appropriate action. This principle is strongly entrenched in Hutterite consciousness. It obliges even members of a family to report on each other, and while we cannot know how much unreported deviance exists, we do know that much reporting does occur, even within families.

There are various actions the preacher can take, and various degrees of punishment he can mete out. He may feel the matter to be too marginal or too unclear to warrant making an issue of it. However, if he learnt about it through reporting he is obliged to take action, or else he is undermining the whole system of reporting and encouraging deviant behaviour. Initially the preacher will simply lecture the individual on his deviance. In most cases this is sufficient to evoke a word of repentance from the sinner and a promise not to indulge in such behaviour again. Should he refuse, however, further steps are taken. The individual is summoned before the entire male congregation and, as a further step, the entire adult congregation to repent his sins. Refusal here leads to *Meidung* (shunning). This means that no individual in the colony, not even family members, may have anything to do with him. It is a form of internal excommunication. The individual is not punished physically: he continues to eat, pray and work – but in his own corner, away from others. Invariably this is a fairly short period which ends with the individual indicating his remorse, appearing before the congregation once more and asking for forgiveness. It is important to note that once forgiven the matter is regarded as closed: the individual carries no burden for his sins, nor may anyone refer to it again or attempt to make him suffer for it in any way.

There are two reasons for dropping the matter in this way. (The incident is, however, recorded in the community book, but this is only for future reference should an incident occur again.) One is that forgiveness is part of the Hutterite ideology. Forgiveness is a form of love and charity, an expression of the desire for Christians to support each other. To make the individual continue paying for his sins would be to make him something less than a true Christian, for it is to say to him that even if he recognizes the error of his ways, he is still a sinner. However, and this is the second point, no person is perfect; man is inherently sinful. The true Christian is not an idealized, perfect man but one who knows what sin is and is prepared to fight it. Should he succumb to temptation – as all people inevitably do – this is not in itself a sign of his being unChristian. Only the refusal to recognize that he has sinned is such a sign; conversely, he who admits to his error and undertakes not to repeat it thus affirms his Christianity. The person who refuses to forgive is the one who is ultimately acting in an unChristian way. He who does not forgive is setting himself up as a judge of others. This is pride and egoism; it implies superiority and one's own perfection. To forgive others is to recognize one's own inherent weakness. Put otherwise, in Hutterite thinking deviant behaviour is not a consequence (necessarily) of a rejection of Christian values. The individual may hold the values wholeheartedly and still act wrongly. The aim of punishment must be to show him how he has been weak and how his weakness has led him to wrong behaviour. Punishment is not meant as retribution but as moral education. Conformity to Hutterite values should ideally be voluntary. Hence the individual should internalize colony values and act accordingly, so that he will act according to them of his own free will. He should not act correctly through fear or through mechanical thinking. He must act correctly because he *actively believes* (both words are operative) his actions to be correct. The aim of punishment is to help him to understand and accept this, and once he has done so there is nothing further to be said and done. (The only exception is in regard to office-bearers. If they sin they are deprived of office: this is meant to ensure that they set a good example and also to maintain the confidence of members in their leaders.)

Should even shunning be unsuccessful in bringing the sinner into line, then the individual may be banned, i.e. totally excluded from the brotherhood (not only his own colony) and ultimately he may be excommunicated (*Ausschluss*) from the Church. Should he then wish to return, he needs to go through the entire procedure of a new member before being reaccepted. (In fact, excommunication is only applied to acts of rebellion against the faith itself, because that is deliberate, whereas most other sins are the product of weakness.)

One reason why matters seldom reach such an extreme stage (and this too is an important factor in discouraging defection) is that Hutterites are generally highly attached to their families, friends, colonies. People are dependent on the colony for all material and social needs. They are taught not to assert themselves; they are intimately close to their families; they have been taught that only the Hutterite way is the True Way. In short, the Hutterite virtually sees his entire identity in terms of being a colony member. For an individual to take upon himself the threat of the ban or excommunication, would require him to be in a position where he feels he can dispense with the security, emotional intimacy and support his colony, and especially his family, provide; it requires the conscious laying aside of deeply entrenched guilt feelings; it virtually requires a reconstruction of one's personality. Most Hutterites, in repenting their sins, genuinely seek forgiveness but, even if they are not convinced that they should seek it, few will take the drastic step of provoking major confrontation with the community. We should also note that anyone leaving the colony permanently, for whatever reason, gets no support from it whatsoever, and this no doubt reinforces doubts about entering the wider world.

This is related to the more general point that the Hutterite has been socialized into thinking that the group is superior to himself and that he is dependent upon it in all ways. Hutterites are thus highly dependent on others for their approval and acceptance. It is as important to be seen doing the right thing as actually to do it (in the eyes of the doer). Knowledge of the opprobrium incurred by wrong action is in itself strong enough to deter individuals from deviant behaviour. The fear of rejection is as strong as the desire to do good deeds.

There is a great difference between the transgressions of a child (which technically you are until baptism) and those of an adult. Misbehaviour before baptism is regarded as something silly and misguided. Misbehaviour after baptism is an infraction of divine rules. The child who misbehaves must be taught the error of his ways; he must learn the superiority of the group over his own world; he must learn to accept the consequences of his actions. Punishment for the child is a preparation for his future life in the colony. He may be punished by the preacher or by his father, sometimes in front of the adult congregation. He is not deprived of food, work, education or self-respect (no mocking, no stigma).

However, a child's transgression is not the same as that of an adult. He must be taught a lesson; an adult must be prepared to repent. In either case the persistent offender is not considered as especially immoral, rebellious or sinful. Rather he is seen as a sick person, one in need of assistance. The argument here is that a colony member who repeats his sins continually must be weak; a stronger personality who opposed colony rules would be highly unlikely to want to stay on the colony, to reject its discipline and to incur repeated punishment. Such an individual would be more likely simply to leave the colony. Hence the persistent sinner who continues living in the colony must be acting through a defect in his personality more than through a conscious and deliberate rebellion. Conversely, for the Hutterites, and this is crucial to their self-perception, a person who lives in a colony and abides by its rules must have a strong personality.

We have seen that in Hutterite thinking all human beings are weak. Discipline is a means of helping them; it is not intended as a means of oppression. For this reason the persistent offender is treated with sympathy more than with anger. Among all Hutterites though, one is expected to accept colony discipline and punishment in the spirit in which it is meant. The child is taught this both formally and informally, virtually from birth. When one is baptized one is clearly instructed regarding one's commitments: the actual ceremony involves both a confession of previous sins and repentance from them, plus an undertaking 'to accept brotherly punishment and admonition and also to apply the same to others when it is needful'.[1]

Under what circumstances is deviant behaviour likely to increase and how do the Elders respond? Among the Hutterites themselves conventional wisdom has it that the inability or reluctance of the leaders to control their colonies is the chief cause of deviance. Here we must remember two things about the Hutterite's mentality. He has been taught all along that he is basically sinful, that the discipline imposed from above is for his own good. However, we have noted that Hutterites sometimes have ambivalent feelings regarding their way of life. They see it as the only morally valuable way of life; it is, too, meant to be personally satisfying. Yet they sometimes see it as somewhat narrow, rigid and demanding of the individual. The individual therefore at times seeks, albeit with guilt feelings, ways of compensation and deviance (not necessarily consciously and perhaps only in marginal ways).

He has guilt feelings because he knows his actions to be wrong – in both the moral and legal senses. However, I do not wish to give the impression that there is a perpetual, constant and pressing strain in the Hutterite's life, so that he is constantly on the lookout for ways to act deviantly. This may be the case here and there regarding people with meagre identification, but, if it were generally true, a colony could not hope to survive. For the Hutterites, life in the colony is generally not a matter of wishing to act deviantly (yet being prevented from doing so) but rather of wishing to conform (both for instrumental and intrinsic purposes) while occasionally and marginally stepping beyond the accepted norms. At this level, they do not get over-upset about minor acts of deviance in others, nor do they have tremendous guilt feelings within themselves. They do not see these acts as being threatening to the basic principles of Hutterite life. Nor indeed do they want to threaten those principles. To the Hutterite, then, deviance in himself and in others is not a crucial question of daily life. On the contrary, marginal deviance is considered normal and natural, while 'perfect behaviour', especially if the person concerned trumpets his 'perfection', is viewed with suspicion. (We explain the reason for this in our comments at the end of this chapter.) The point is that the Hutterites are under no illusion that people can and will act deviantly. Nevertheless, they still wish to uphold the rules, even if only as a legal fiction, since these constitute the concrete expression of the community's beliefs. At the same time, they wish to ensure that deviance is well-contained, marginal and not injurious to the faith.

To this end, discipline must be imposed – it is both morally and socially imperative in Hutterite eyes. For this reason the Elders of the Leut keep a close scrutiny on the internal life of the colonies. This also helps to explain why they are so careful in their choice of leaders, the long probation period they undergo, and the regular visits paid by Elders to each colony. (The Ordination Vows specifically enjoin the preacher 'to exercise punishment and admonition with the right courage and discipline'.)[2]

Preachers may not always be able to impose discipline, even if they want to. The size of the colony may not allow for adequate surveillance of members. Closeness to towns may allow people to slip out unnoticed or make it easy for outsiders to come in. Economic pressures may give him less flexibility than he would desire in appointing people to positions or rotating them between jobs so as to prevent situations which lead to anti-social behaviour. It follows that the process of splitting colonies in order to keep them at a manageable size and the principle of being isolated from the environment are relevant to the needs of social control.

Where leadership is weak certain consequences follow. Office-bearers begin to break rules; this creates bad feeling and encourages others to do the same. If people see their peers getting away with it they see no reason not to try as well. The whole process becomes a vicious circle. The more indiscipline, the more bad feeling; the more bad feeling, the more indiscipline.

If we recall a point from the previous chapter, there is an important aspect of communal life to remember here. Every member, no matter how strongly committed, consciously feels at times that he is making a sacrifice of sorts in living in the community. He is often proud of himself for having the strength to make these sacrifices – they may be economic, professional, social – but feels that the price is worthwhile. All this, however, is predicated on the assumption that others are doing the same. The moment one sees others enjoying the advantages of communal life but wriggling out of the disadvantages, reaction sets in. First of all the 'righteous' member is dismayed, that is, in moral terms. However, if nothing is done about it he cannot help being angry, leading to disillusionment, a feeling of cynicism ('why am I the only righteous one?') and ultimately to deviant behaviour on his part, possibly even to defection – either through a decline in commitment to colony values, or through a desire to seek a more strongly committed framework elsewhere. This line of progression is in fact over-simplified, but it helps to show how easy it is for successful deviant behaviour to become contagious in a communal society.

Similar results can occur where the leaders are too weak to handle problems with the right tact regarding the parties themselves or the right sensitivity regarding the community as a whole. If the leader is himself outmanoeuvred by one party or another or gives privileged treatment to any individual, feelings of discrimination arise, leading once again to a chain of resentments, and ultimately to deviant behaviour.

The Elders of the Leut are the ultimate arbiters of what is and is not legal. They have a record of conservatism combined with flexibility in this regard. A law will remain a law as long as it is enforceable. If they should see that infringement of a law is so widespread as to make the law unenforceable or, if enforced, will lead to widespread dissatisfaction, then they are prepared to be flexible. If the contentious issue is not a matter of faith, this is naturally easier; if it is a matter of faith, then it can be relegated from that status. If the issue is not likely to affect the basic stability of Hutterite life, then once again they are prepared to be flexible.[3] Both the leaders of the Leut and of the individual colonies are aware of the need to distinguish between essential and non-essential matters (although the leaders of each Leut have different standards as to the degree of 'liberalism' or 'conservatism' required). In general, though, they realize that communal life imposes strains; they 'know' that men tend to sin. They are sensitive to the need not to turn every item of behaviour into a matter of principle, that a little leeway on relatively minor and unessential issues may give the individual a feeling of satisfaction which, in its turn, will help him to adhere more faithfully and more willingly to those matters that really *are* essential. Rules are an attempt to contain change, to prevent contamination, to avoid excesses and to maintain simplicity. The attitude behind the making of laws or changing them is not to prevent change at all costs, nor to impose unnecessary strains on the individual, since these will only lead to more not less deviance. They are aimed at ensuring continuity of tradition and adherence to the faith, and if minor changes of a 'technical' nature need to be made, which will add to individual satisfaction but not upset continuity or faith or viability, then so be it.

The hidden hand: control in Kibbutz society

In the Kibbutz there are no formal sanctions for rule-breaking. If matters get very serious, members can be expelled, but so rarely does this happen that it can be virtually ignored. What forms can deviant behaviour in the Kibbutz take?

In work it may be refusal to accept work-norms (punctuality, readiness to work overtime, readiness to co-operate with other members of the work team, refusal to accept job assignments, unreasonable requests for leave, 'sickness', irresponsible actions causing financial loss). In consumption patterns, deviance can mean use of external sources of income to raise one's living standard beyond the accepted levels, or indulging one's tastes in financially legitimate fashion but unacceptable style, e.g. outlandish clothes. In the decision-making processes, deviance can mean refusal to accept decisions made in the accepted way, or even not referring certain matters to the appropriate body. This can apply to both office-bearers and other members. The former may not carry out decisions made by the assembly or some committee; or they may simply act in a way which offends members personally; or they may execute their job inefficiently; or they may act against accepted principles, (e.g. by showing favouritism or by taking advantage of the job for personal gain). Members may refuse to abide by decisions of the community or may simply do something of their own accord without asking permission first. Deviance here may also refer to the way in which requests are made, e.g. by threatening to leave the Kibbutz, getting hysterical, demanding undue sympathy, implying that you are superior to others ('I've worked my fingers to the bone for twenty years now, so I deserve such and such' – it may be true but one should not say it). Finally, there are the informal codes of conduct in personal behaviour – how one relates to one's children and one's neighbours, forms of speech, sexual morality and so on. The details of many of these rules vary from Kibbutz to Kibbutz. Hence I am not concerned here with specific rules and specific deviations (what is a deviation in one Kibbutz may not be quite so in another) but rather with the sources of deviation and reactions to it.

One of the most important means of pre-empting and preventing deviance in an intentional community is selection of new members. Unlike the Hutterites who, with their high birth rate and general suspicion of the outside world, do not need or seek converts, the Kibbutz does. While its own children add to the Kibbutz's population, there is always the danger that one day they might not do so. Hence the Kibbutz actively seeks and welcomes new members, although this itself creates dangers, since newcomers have frequently not been socialized to Kibbutz patterns of behaviour. We have already noted that it is one thing to know in advance what the rules are; it is quite another actually to live by them comfortably. So it is difficult to know how newcomers will relate to Kibbutz rules; and even if they do so positively, then they may well bring in their own attitudes or interpretations. This is not to say that the Kibbutz is somehow afraid of new members from the outside. On the contrary, most Kibbutzim welcome them, since they frequently add much to the cultural atmosphere, the range of friendships and the economic possibilities of the Kibbutz. Further, the very fact of their joining satisfies the Kibbutz's need to be involved in the wider world and to its feeling of expansion and dynamism. Most Kibbutzim, though, go cautiously in this regard. Prospective members are sifted out by a special committee; if accepted they go through a probation period of up to two years; they can then only be accepted by a two-thirds majority of the general meeting (the discussion is closed to members only and vote is by secret ballot, emphasizing the gravity of the decision). If an individual has gone through the entire probation process (during which period he does nothing special but simply lives and works on the Kibbutz like anyone else) then it seldom happens that his application is refused. Candidates who are not likely to be accepted invariably drop out along the line.

(Parenthetically let me add something to this point not directly related to deviance. The Kibbutz will not allow a person to stay indefinitely without committing himself one way or the other; you cannot be half in and half out of the Kibbutz. The same applies to the Hutterites. They do not demand formal membership necessarily, but do demand that after some time a person does act and dress in all ways like a Hutterite. The Kibbutz demands formal membership because one cannot be a Kibbutz member by external appearance only. The same applies in both communities to people who leave temporarily. After some time they must make up their minds where they stand. It is characteristic of intentional communities that they demand unequivocal membership or none at all. They would rather lose a member than compromise on this issue. If they do compromise, this is usually a sign of inner weakness on their part.)

So homogeneity of membership or, to be more precise, compatibility, is the first means the Kibbutz chooses to ensure that individuals will conform to its rules. The point here is not one of control but of maximizing the probability of conformity. (We should remember here too our earlier argument that one of the advantages in having many Kibbutzim and different Kibbutz movements is that it enables each individual Kibbutz to maintain its homogeneity.)

Many Kibbutz norms are not easily identifiable, even by members themselves. In the absence of specific sanctions, one is not always sure what ways of behaving are expected of one. This, I believe, has positive consequences for Kibbutz life by and large, but also has its dangers in terms of deviant behaviour. The positive consequences are that lack of norm-specifity allows for greater flexibility in individual behaviour. In a community where individuality, up to a point, is highly valued, and where satisfaction of private needs is seen as a basic right, a narrow interpretation of norms would create tension, frustration and a feeling of external constraint. It is far more satisfying for the individual that he is able to use his own judgement as to how he should interact with others or respond to and assess situations. But, and this is the problem, the spectrum cannot be too wide. The range of private interpretations must conform to the values and needs of the community and the total range must allow all interpretations within it to be mutually compatible. To step outside the range is to be deviant, but how does the individual know what the range is? The lack of specifity can now become a hindrance rather than a help. The possibilities of subtly overstepping the accepted limits or of moving beyond them unconsciously are great where no clear guidelines to actions are available. What the community has won on the one hand ('freedom of reaction', hence greater satisfaction, for its members), it can easily lose on the other (greater possibilities of deviant behaviour).

When deviant behaviour does occur, the lack of formal sanctions may aggravate the situation. In a community with clearly defined norms and formal sanctions, and where such sanctions are clearly applied each time norms are breached, everyone learns what is right and what is wrong, and more important, what will happen if and when wrong behaviour occurs. But what if nothing happens, or what if there is simply nothing to happen? The result will inevitably be despair or cynicism on the part of other members; disillusionment and apathy will set in; jealousy and competition will surface; and in view of the possibility, now clear to everyone, of acting in defiance of accepted norms with impunity, some members are bound to see this as an invitation to do likewise. *In an intentional community the problem of deviant behaviour is not so much the deviant act itself as the consequences of the act for the sense of commitment in other members.*

The factors most likely to restrict the incidence of deviant behaviour in the Kibbutz are the commitment members have to the norms of the community and their sensitivity to the opinion of others. In practice the two link up: one's status in the community is partly defined by how others assess one's commitment to community norms. Furthermore, you know that this is the case – and it is important to you. As with the Hutterites, it is very important on Kibbutz not only to do the right thing but to be seen to be doing it. For this reason individuals will frequently do things they might not otherwise do – whether this refers to work, expressing an opinion at the assembly, helping a neighbour clean his house, the way one dresses or the way one talks to one's children. I do not for one moment suggest that the thought of public opinion is always uppermost in one's mind whenever one does anything; at any rate, one mostly acts in ways which seem to be natural and acceptable to oneself, and this coincides with public opinion or has perhaps been shaped by it. But when one does want to act deviantly, sensitivity to public opinion is important, since it inhibits one from so doing. One proceeds to act deviantly either because public opinion is not very important to one generally, or because the issue is so important that one does not care about the threat to one's status, or because one is simply not aware of what public opinion is.

What can be done about this? We have already discussed how the Kibbutz tries to obviate the first possibility – by simply trying not to accept individuals to whom public opinion is likely to be secondary in their considerations. There is a further means. The intimate nature of Kibbutz life means that one is highly dependent on others, both in terms of services the Kibbutz provides and in terms of simple, informal, personal contact. Withdrawal and independence are difficult to effect, so a person with low status can very easily be made to feel his status in all sorts of subtle ways. He will not specifically be refused service, but the important thing in Kibbutz (as we have already seen) is not only the fact of receiving a service but the way in which one receives it. An individual can feel very quickly that attitudes towards him are negative. So if, for example, a person is obviously buying more clothes than he can possibly afford on a Kibbutz budget then, when he comes to get his share of clothes from the clothing store, he may well feel the attitude of the person in charge, without her even saying anything directly. Similarly, in informal contact with individuals one can be made to feel a lowering of status in the eyes of others simply through gestures, manners of speech, evasion and so on.

Regarding the second source of deviation – the importance of the issue – the way in which the Kibbutz handles problems is crucial. We cannot over-stress the importance of flexibility in handling personal matters, although equally important are the limits to this flexibility. We have also stressed the importance of handling problems justly, i.e. that equal problems be given equal consideration, more or less. Frequently, deviance occurs precisely because the Kibbutz has been inflexible, or because an injustice has been done. In these circumstances the individual feels that he has no choice but to leave or deviate. He knows only too well that his actions may incur public opprobrium but this is not enough to deter him. On balance he prefers personal satisfaction to public status. *It is important to note that, as with the Hutterites, you receive no material, moral or social compensation for accepting the alleged injustice – it does not increase your status, although a deviant reaction to the injustice will reduce it.* This puts the Kibbutz in a delicate situation. Members must relate to each other flexibly and considerately. That is both a matter of principle and simple sociological common sense. If members are aware that such attitudes prevail then the temptation to deviate is lessened. But if the Kibbutz stretches the limits of such flexibility and consideration, then expectations are going to soar beyond what the Kibbutz can reasonably provide, thus leading to disappointment and feelings of injustice – and this will result in people leaving or deviating. We have then an apparent paradox. To prevent deviation, one must be flexible in handling personal matters, but in being flexible one may well be encouraging deviant behaviour in others. By being either too flexible or too inflexible, an atmosphere can develop of 'I'll simply have to manage on my own'. It seems to me that most Kibbutzim manage to steer a middle course, but clearly whatever they do some members will feel dissatisfied and they will either leave or begin to act unilaterally.

The third source of deviation – not being aware of public opinion – depends on the means of communication in the Kibbutz. Such channels are of two kinds – the formal and the informal. Here the leadership of the Kibbutz is important. Through meetings, the assembly, 'house-groups' or the Kibbutz newspaper, they should try both to communicate their own views and to hear the views of members. Clearly much depends on the readiness of members to respond, but I emphasize the role of leadership because unless meetings take place regularly, unless discussions at the assembly are wide-ranging and open, and unless the Kibbutz magazine comes out regularly, members will have no framework in which to communicate their opinions. It is not enough that the formal right exists for *any* member to take the initiative. If the assembly is not held regularly, very few members are likely to call a meeting on their own accord. If there is no regular newsletter, the chances of an 'ordinary' member coming forward to volunteer are slim. By and large, the initiative comes from the leadership and, if such initiative is lacking, formal means of communication will be poor.

Then there are informal means of communication. Here the relative smallness and intimacy of the Kibbutz are important. Communication, including the much-maligned institution of gossip, is easy. The role of sub-groups is relevant here. In complex societies one may have a family, a work place, and a circle of friends. What happens in any one sphere may not be of concern to the others; at any rate these may be three distinct groups. In a communal society there is tremendous overlap: the sub-groups are like intersecting circles and information filters rapidly from one to the other. Add to this the fact that members use the same services, are in contact with the same functionaries and share the same cultural activities, and we find that members have a large fund of common activity and experience. In this way the individual can be aware of public opinion and can learn both the norms expected of him and the limits to the range of private interpretation allowed him.

Having made all these observations about deviance and its relation to public opinion, and about how public opinion can be communicated, we need to make two 'counter-observations'. The first is that even though status is lost through deviance, and even though communication is meant to help the individual know how he should act and what people think of him for not doing so – despite all this Kibbutz members are reluctant to confront each other directly. We have already said that sometimes Kibbutz members prefer to keep up pretences rather than show what they are really thinking, especially when it comes to highly personal matters. This is not so much a matter of appearance for appearance's sake as one of believing that relating to people in sophisticated and delicate fashion is both worthy in itself and socially necessary if an atmosphere conducive to satisfactory personal relations is to be maintained. Just as the individual does not wish to have a showdown with the community, so does the community prefer not to have a showdown with him, especially if this involves certain members having to be hard on him, even if they feel they are perfectly justified in doing so. Put crudely, there is fear of creating a 'bad atmosphere' on the Kibbutz. This means that deviance sometimes occurs and no-one is prepared to do anything about it directly. One can only hope then that the individual will be sensitive to public opinion. However, if the deviance is so great that the consequences of not doing anything are more dangerous than are those of ignoring it, the Kibbutz may well confront the member directly.

It is tempting to think that perhaps focusing on an individual is an opportunity for the group to assert its solidarity, but I do not believe that this is a primary motivation; rather, when the Kibbutz feels it is forced to have a showdown with the member, a certain feeling of sadness at having had to do it prevails, of preferring not to have had the situation at all. Kibbutzim will differ in this regard. Some will prefer to have direct confrontation only as a last resort, while others are more ready for it. There can be no general rule since this is a consequence of the type of personalities one has on the Kibbutz and their perceptions of what living on a Kibbutz means, especially in terms of individual-community relations. So each Kibbutz has to find its own ratio of direct to subtle control. Which ratio to adopt is not a matter of formula, only of it being concomitant with the type of members the Kibbutz has and their attitudes towards it and each other. The healthy Kibbutz is the one which finds the correct balance in terms of its own needs, and since needs differ from Kibbutz to Kibbutz, so will the ratio vary. Nevertheless, we should note that confronting an individual or family is a means of sustaining group solidarity (even if it was not a motivation) and of reaffirming publicly and consciously the values and rules of the Kibbutz.

Finally, I wish to make an observation (applicable to the Hutterites too) which apparently contradicts all I have said so far. We have said that status depends partly on conformity to norms, that individuals are aware of the norms and that they do not wish to lose their status. Hence, they are discouraged from deviation. The corollary should be that he who adheres most faithfully to the norms and also does so most obviously should be the one with the highest status in the community. In fact this is not the case at all. The fanatic, if I may use the term, is likely to be seen somewhat as a deviant too, and his status may not necessarily be high. His 'deviance' is admittedly less damning than the person who offends norms 'negatively'. 'Over-conformity' in Kibbutz can lead to loss of status in the same way that 'under-conformity' does. If the Kibbutz gets angry at deviant behaviour (of the negative kind) it can just as easily be cynical, mocking and suspicious of publicly trumpeted self-righteousness. Our explanation of this is found in the following comments.

Discussion: social control in intentional communities

Theories of deviance vary as to whether deviant acts are deviant in themselves or only because they are so labelled. At any rate, the concept of deviance implies that there are accepted norms in society which, for whatever reason, are being violated or are thought to be violated. Deviance is inherent to every society (although why this should be so is a subject for basic debate). A certain 'quota' of deviance is tolerable to every society.[4] Deviance, it is further argued (e.g. by Durkheim), can also serve positive functions for society, e.g. in establishing norms or clarifying group boundaries. I would like to suggest a few aspects of this relevant to our own considerations.

We need to distinguish between the *ideal* standards of behaviour and the *prescribed* standards of behaviour. The two are not necessarily congruent. It makes sense to argue that people in society are expected to act in accordance with the ideal standards, and are considered deviant when they fail to do so. I am arguing, however, that, in intentional communities at least, they are expected *not* to act in accordance with ideal standards; in other words, a degree of non-conformity to the ideal standards is not simply accepted it is (unofficially) *prescribed*. Deviant behaviour is not that which departs from the *ideal* standards, but that which departs too much from the *accepted* standards. Generally, this refers to behaviour which moves even further away from the ideal standards than accepted behaviour does. But equally it can refer to behaviour which moves *too close* to the ideal standards. So, to give two examples from everyday life: being kind to one's friends is normative, but if every time you visited friends you took them a lavish gift they would not be very likely to consider you a paragon of friendship; they would be more likely to view you with suspicion, embarrassment or resentment. Similarly, to make lots of money is highly valued in our society but to do this very early in life or very quickly is not necessarily viewed with favour. There are four reasons for this 'prescribed deviance':

(1) The ideal standards are often contradictory or mutually exclusive (in our latter example there is a conflict between two values – making money and working hard for it). To prescribe strict adherence to any one norm may lead to conflict with the others.
(2) The prescription of absolute adherence would demand standards of behaviour which most people would find psychologically difficult to sustain.
(3) If absolute adherence were demanded there would have to be explicit sanctions for non-adherence. This applies to prescribed deviance too, but there is far greater flexibility in that case. With fundamentalism there can be no such flexibility; absolute consistency both in behaviour and in the application of sanctions against deviance would be necessary.
(4) Similarly, absolute adherence would not allow for adaptation to changing or problematic situations. Norms, as we have already explained, cannot cover every conceivable situation and ambivalences can easily arise, to which absolute norms can provide little guidance.

So both under- and over-conformity are deviant: the one is criminal, the other self-righteous. Both have to be punished or brought closer to the accepted standards of behaviour. This is done through judging the deviants (in contrast to ourselves) not by the accepted standards but by the ideal standards. The over-conformist is subject to a degree of ridicule and is judged by the standards he himself sets. His occasional lapses are condemned for falling short of ideal standards, even though they may still be closer to those standards than to the accepted standards. This helps to bring him down somewhat and helps his critics to feel that his standards are unnatural, unhealthy and unattainable. It is not the ideal standards themselves which are being attacked. On the contrary, these are upheld, since these are the reified guidelines and taken-for-granted meanings around which we construct social structure, behaviour and morals. But, by and large, they are meant to be a frame of reference not a literal prescription for action.

The under-conformist, too, is judged by ideal standards so that the *actual* extent of his deviance is overstated. The critics have ambivalent feelings about their own deviance, inevitable and necessary though it may be. By judging others according to the ideal standards, they (the critics) uphold their moral adherence to those standards and confirm in their own minds that they (the critics) are not as deviant as in fact they are (in other words, it is the critics who are being self-righteous this time).

Deviant behaviour – whether as under- or over-conformity – is threatening to society, since it will easily lead to chaos or to inflexibility. Yet if the deviants are to be judged by actual standards of behaviour, then the under-conformist will seem more like us than we would like to think, while the over-conformist would appear better than we are. We would then be faced with two groups of people, regarding whom we would have to say respectively, 'they are not so bad after all' or 'if they can be so good then we must be failing in not being equally good'. Yet under-conformity and over-conformity are sociologically and psychologically threatening, so we adopt the above means of assessing and controlling them. (I put forward this argument not only to explain the hostility of commune members to their own self-righteous comrades but to some extent also the attitude of the host society to the emergence and existence of the communes themselves.)

Clearly, conformity and deviance are both facts of life. What we need to consider is why the individual in an intentional community should conform in the first place, why he does at times deviate, and how his society responds to this.

First we need to distinguish between three types of rules. The first is *organizational* rules. These ensure a minimum of order, continuity, co-ordination and predictability, e.g. what time to start work or eat meals. These rules are in most cases ideologically neutral, although the fact that a person should start work on time is an ideological norm. Then there are *formal rules* derived directly from the ideology, e.g. from the principle of equality we have the system of clothing allocation. The rules here are often quantifiable (how much clothing, how many work hours, and so on). Finally, there are *informal rules (conventions)* such as how to talk or relate to others, when and what sort of emotions to display publicly or to hide, sexual morality and so on.

Now, one obvious explanation for conformity is that unless the individual abides by the rules there will be chaos in society and, in the end, he is as likely to suffer as anyone else. Just in case he is not aware of this, sanctions exist to coerce him into conformity. This argument is indeed important but it constitutes only a part of the explanation for conformity in intentional communities. I suggest that the individual member conforms to the rules *because he wants to* and that the problem of intentional communities is to *sustain his desire for conformity rather than to prevent deviance*. In other words, *conformity must be seen more as a positive and self-fulfilling state than as a negative and self-interested act*. This is an extension of our arguments about commitment and identification.

To a large extent the individual lives in the community in order to conform with its rules. Conformity is the overt and concrete expression of his commitment to the community. It is one of the key concrete means he has of stating both publicly and to himself that he has an identity and what that identity consists of. One does not live in an intentional community in the abstract. One actually does certain things and it is these things which, put together, mean 'living in the community'. It is by doing these separate things that one derives personal satisfaction, expresses one's sense of commitment and meets one's needs. One of the things one chooses to do is to live according to the rules. Put otherwise, one does not live in the community and *in addition* behave in accordance with the rules. Even less, does one live in it and accept the objective need for a certain set of rules. On the contrary, living in the community in many respects *means* 'living according to the rules'.

For the individual member, then, following the rules is an intrinsically satisfying activity. The rules express his ideological beliefs; he believes they are socially necessary and morally right; and he finds his personal needs – subjective and objective – met by them. It follows that the more these reasons operate the more the individual will wish his commitment to the community to continue. Each reason plays a different role for different individuals, and each has a different weight. Conversely, the less these reasons apply, or the more they are threatened, the less is his commitment likely to be sustained. This will lead either to defection or to deviance.

So, individuals generally appear at work on time. Now clearly, among both the Hutterites and the Kibbutzim, there are some who would not be punctual if there were no punishments for it.

But for the majority this is simply not the case. To the extent that the member sees his work as personally satisfying, as socially useful, as a means of attaining status, as a concrete manifestation of his commitment to community goals and as an intrinsically moral activity – to that extent punctuality is not a fear of punishment but simply a natural concomitant to one's overall relation to one's work, which in turn is a concrete expression of one's overall relation to the community. For all these reasons, the member does not generally see rules as being externally imposed. To the extent that he does see the necessity for rules, he will argue that they do not exist for the member who wishes to act correctly anyway, only for the potential deviant. (In Hutterite conventional wisdom, the fence exists not for the sheep who is grazing contentedly but for the one who might stray. The analogy is agriculturally false but sociologically enlightening!)

Like some other aspects of communal life there is here too a certain duality in members' thinking. On the one hand, the rules (or, to be more precise, their foundations) are considered external. They have an autonomous moral authority; the member simply knows they are inevitable, necessary and right. Yet, on the other hand, he sees his community as a voluntary group and a democratic one at that. The rules, at least in their concrete details, are of his own making; he believes that he has control over them, that they are not imposed from above. *Rule-bound behaviour is therefore a simultaneous expression of the closed universe which marks out his identity, of the autonomy of that universe, and of his control over it.* (This follows our earlier argument about the duality of members' relation to their ideology.)

Rules must meet a number of conditions. They must be morally good *and* instrumentally effective *and* personally satisfying (or at least not break the member's psychological threshold). Failure to meet any one of these conditions is a threat to the status and effectiveness of the rules, and thereby (depending on the centrality of the rule) to the solidarity of the community. There is a contrast here between our major communities and the therapeutic communities. Whereas in the former the rules are frequently subsumed under the moral imperatives of the ideology (even if only post hoc), in the latter they serve an instrumental purpose only. Because the therapeutic communities have no transcendental goals, they need appeal only to the therapeutic effectiveness of the rules as a justification for them. If we recall our earlier discussion about ideological debate within and between intentional communities, we can now see why such debate is less ferocious in the arena of therapeutic communities. Rules and practices here are to be judged 'scientifically', and anyone who can prove that his practices are effective for the problem at hand need not seek further justification for them. (Although others might find those practices distasteful, that is a personal more than an ethical problem.) This leaves greater room for experimentation, and there is less scope for a priori arguments. (Debate in the sphere of psychiatry becomes intense as in sectarian movements precisely when schools develop whose principles are proposed as being a priori correct and are based, as in intentional communities, on a *pre-conceived* model of the universe.)

The individual in therapeutic communities, unlike in our major communities, sees the rules as externally imposed, but he accepts this as necessary to solve his problems and not because he (necessarily) believes the rules to be morally good. This is possible because of the temporary nature of the community and its limited functions (e.g. there is no economic activity). The wider the scope of an intentional community and the more its rules are couched in terms of intrinsic moral worth (for the therapeutic communities only the ultimate goal of the community, emotional health, has this status), the finer a balance has to be found between the three conditions of rules mentioned above. In the therapeutic communities there is far less danger to the community's persistence if the rules are applied too mechanically or too flexibly. It may be bad therapy to do so but the community can still persist. Among the Hutterites and the Kibbutzim the balance between ideology, social organization, social solidarity and personal satisfaction is highly delicate, and only if the balance is carefully maintained is persistence possible.

None of the foregoing is intended to deny that there is deviance in intentional communities. On the contrary, as we have seen, deviance is implicitly understood to be natural. Paradoxically, then, deviance is a sign of identification *with* the community. In our theoretical discussion on alienation we saw that individuals need to 'conspire' against their society. The greater the external imposition, the greater the need to find expression of individuality, to assert one's 'private' identity against the public domain. The fact that the individual engages in (minor) deviance is therefore a sign that in other respects he is committed to the community.

Deviance in intentional communities is sometimes a matter of gratifying some immediate private need, but much more significantly it is a means of declaring to oneself that whatever one has in common with others, whatever the sacrifices for the greater good, one *is* an individual. (For this reason, private possessions, however modest, are important to the individual.) As I argue repeatedly, minor deviance is not a threat to the community, not only because it acts as a 'safety valve' for individual self-assertion, but because the areas in which deviance occurs, and the extent to which it occurs, do not upset one of the fundamental conditions of communality, namely, that it is the community that has ultimate authority over individual life. We now explore this, and other themes, in our next chapter.

Chapter 10
Exclusive relations

The problem of exclusive relations

While at first glance the role of the family in communal societies may seem to be a very specific and limited topic, this is in fact not the case at all. The question of exclusive relations raises some of the most fundamental issues we need to understand, and for this reason I have left it until last.

Most theories about communal societies have had to deal with the problem of exclusive, intimate or familial relations. Most communal societies, too, especially those who see their goals as being something higher than the existence of individual members or private goals, have had to take a stand on this issue. The generally accepted view of observers, and indeed of many directly involved, is that a fundamental conflict exists between commitment to the community and the existence of exclusive relations. No doubt the fame of certain communities which adopted this argument, for example the Shakers (with their celibacy) or the Oneida (with their sexual communism) has strengthened this view. This line of thinking stems from viewing the basis of communal life as enforced commitment or intense socialization. The orthodox argument goes along the following lines:

A communal society which aims to be a total community has an all-embracing set of goals, and life in the community encompasses all aspects of the individual's existence. The reason one's involvement with the community must be total is that there can be no compromise regarding goal-attainment. One cannot have one foot in and one foot out and still satisfy the purposes for which one is a member of the community. One must dedicate the totality of one's life to the attainment of these purposes. The words 'dedicate' and 'totality' are operative. To attain one's goals is not easy – hard work is required. One cannot be diverted from the task by other or egoistic considerations. At any rate, since the community entails a total revolution in one's life, all one's daily activities must be directed towards completing that revolution successfully. One's entire life in the community is relevant to attaining one's goals. Also, the community as a whole has to work together. It faces certain difficulties – threats from outside, economic problems, and so on. All members must therefore put their shoulders to the wheel and must not be diverted by private needs or interests. The only needs and interests one has are those of the community as a whole. In short, one has one loyalty and one only – to the community. This means that individuals cannot enter into intense or exclusive diadic relations since these, by their nature, direct one's energies – emotional, physical and mental – in upon the relationships themselves, hence away from the community.

Exclusive relations (the argument continues) have a further quality, that of protection. Total communities need to control their members. For this various practices exist – supervision, reporting, confessions, punishments, and the like. But a community can never control its members totally if they are being 'buffered' by intimate associates. Will a husband report on his wife? Will a person accept public criticism if he can find refuge in others? Clearly, then, control is limited if exclusive relations are allowed to prevail. If it is sexual satisfaction people want, then institutionalized means must be found of providing it without affective content, or else they must renounce it altogether. At any rate, to the extent that diadic relations *are* permitted, however reluctantly, the community is divested of its ability to control members and demand loyalty from them.

Even where the purpose of the community is not surrender to a higher cause, as in a transient commune, the nuclear family is antithetical to community cohesion. Such a commune is a revolt against the kind of personal relations found elsewhere, of which nuclear family ties are one expression. Only by creating 'familism without the [nuclear] family'[1] is this possible. Whatever the reason for the transitoriness of modern communes, one appears to be that they have not 'absorbed' the traditional nuclear family or created a viable alternative to it.

A further argument for abolishing the nuclear family is that invariably such families represent the prevailing values, ethos and social relations of the surrounding society – parental domination over children, inequality between man and wife, and so on. Thus the structure of the nuclear family also contradicts the value-goals of intentional communities. (Alternatively, if there are to be families then they should *emphasize* the traditional nuclear family structure, i.e. greater dominance of man over women, parents over children – since this can free men for commitment to the community and allow parents to socialize their children in the community values.)[2]

So far the conventional argument. What we wish to do here is to show that while there are points in it which hint at the real nature of communal societies it is basically a lopsided view of the problem and stands in contrast to what has happened in our communal societies. Of the three most successful communal ventures in modern western history – the Hutterites, the Kibbutzim and monasticism – the first two have not only 'accepted' or 'tolerated' family life but have actually incorporated it fundamentally into their culture. This 'paradox' – of family recognition and community persistence coinciding – is too strong to be ignored. We are therefore led to ask whether exclusive relations have perhaps been a *contributory* rather than a detrimental factor in the persistence of our two major groups of communities. In fact, we need to distinguish between different kinds of exclusive relationships and it is partly the failure to recognize such distinctions which vitiates the orthodox argument.

The family

We must begin by distinguishing between family relations and other expressions of intimacy or exclusiveness. The problems involved in each case are basically different and throw different light on our subject matter.

The Hutterites and Kibbutzim have never rejected the legitimacy of the family in principle. The role and structure of the family have changed considerably over the years but neither community has ever attempted to abandon it entirely. The Hutterites have moved away considerably from the early Moravian days when parents could not even take their children for a short walk without permission from the preacher, where a woman picked a husband from among three unknown men, and where couples lived together (apart from their children) under the same roof. Among the Kibbutzim the founders decided that they had to postpone marriage because of the economic situation; when within two years people decided to marry anyway, they agreed to defer having children; within a year the first child was born. The marriage ceremony was rejected because it was religious and enshrined sexual inequality; couples were frowned upon if they displayed affection publicly or became too protective of each other; and rooms were for sleeping in (once again with others if need be) but not for any other purpose. So in both cases the extent of one's involvement with one's family was severely curtailed but the right to family life was never really denied. Today, in both groups of communities, the family is a stable unit, apartments are modestly furnished, children and parents have a close relationship, and the family has a degree of self-responsibility (e.g. among the Hutterites wives sew for their family; in the Kibbutz there are budgets for personal consumption).

What has all this meant for commitment, solidarity, control and collectivism? When we talk of the totality of a community, it is an oversight to see it (totality) only in terms of the individual's community involvement. Totality also means that the total individual is involved in the community, that is, all his needs have to be met within the community, and it is the community's responsibility to see that this is done. Totality also means that the community attempts to be a single integrated whole, i.e., ideally, all aspects of community life are integrated around the basic meanings and goals of the community. This is something of a two-edged sword. Total involvement in an integrated community means that when one aspect of the individual's life is not adequately satisfied, his sense of dissatisfaction inevitably spills over into other spheres of his life in the community, even those having apparently nothing to do with the specific area of dissatisfaction.

Now it is clear that the kind of affective satisfaction one gains within familial relations is basically of a different kind to that gained from overall community involvement. However much the individual invests his emotions and 'whole personality' in the attainment of communal goals, these can never be a substitute for primary affective relations (if he wants them). Conversely though, and equally significant, even if he has primary affective satisfaction, he is unlikely to see these as a substitute for collective involvement. Within a communal society there is no need to assume that one kind of emotional investment has to be made at the expense of another, since basically they are non-substitutable. On the contrary, we may assume that the individual seeks not to invest himself entirely in one kind of relationship only, but in different kinds of affective satisfaction. When satisfaction of one kind is thwarted the other kinds do not present themselves to him as a substitute, but as a further hindrance to a sense of balanced satisfaction in the community. *I suggest that for a community to persist the members need to find balanced satisfaction – emotional investment in a single sphere of community life can only represent a temporary period of the individual's life in the community.* The individual – to the extent that a particular problem weighs upon him – tends to see his entire life in the community from the perspective of that problem, even, as we have said, in areas which have nothing to do with the problem. This applies to work, circle of friends, living standards, leisure time, the education system and – one's ability to find primary affective satisfaction. Conversely, the more one is satisfied in particular spheres, the easier it is to find satisfaction in others, and more important, the readier one is to commit oneself to the collective cause, since it is the embodiment of that cause, the community, from which and within which satisfaction has been gained. From this perspective, then, familial relations, far from being a hindrance to community involvement, can be a positive encouragement to it. (At any rate, there is no evidence whatsoever that unmarried members are more dedicated, committed or involved than married ones.)

Much depends here on the relation of the family as a unit to the community. The foregoing is only true if certain structural conditions are met. Traditionally, we associate four functions with the family – affective, biological, economic and educational. In our two major communities, the last two functions are virtually totally removed from the family. This stems from a further aspect of communal life, namely the importance of dependence. This means that the individual should be totally dependent on the community as a whole for the satisfaction of his needs; indeed, that it is the community which decides what those needs are and how they shall be met. What is crucial here – and this is where confusion frequently arises – is not so much *what* the community decides, but the fact that *it is the community that is deciding*. The

community is able to grant the individual spheres of independence
– *as long as ultimately he is still dependent on the community*. So
the community may give the individual clothes or money for his
own private use. The fact that they are now his does not mean
that he is independent, since it is the community which has given
it to him and has determined what and how much to give.

Now, the fact that the individual belongs to a family does not
in any way affect his dependence on the community. The family
in these communities is an affective-reproductive unit only: it has
no educational or economic functions and in these respects the
individual is still totally dependent on the community. (As we
have argued, he is not dependent on the community for primary
affective satisfaction, since the community could not provide it
anyway.) Provided the principle of dependence is maintained, the
goals of collectivism and equality need not be vitiated by the
existence of the family. Collective consumption still prevails and
there is no scope for inheritance or automatic privileges through
financial or familial status. (However, there are informal inherit-
ances and statuses, and we will mention these below.) We should
note, too, that while family members are dependent on each other
affectively, they are dependent on the community *as individuals*
and not as family members. Their personal allocations, rights and
obligations stem from them each being a separate member of the
community, not from their family status or family's status.

There are other respects, too, in which family members are
independent of each other. Because of the smallness of the
community, its intimacy and its egalitarian atmosphere, we find
that at a 'purely' social level family members are often not 'thrown
upon' each other. I generalize here on the basis of impressionistic
observation and suggest that there is much social intercourse at a
personal level which is free of family ties. Since other members
of the community are so accessible, socially and locationally, individuals need not 'go out' socially as a family. There is a constant
and 'shortlived' interaction with others who, even if they are
only workmates or functionaries, are at the same time fellow
community members and, even if not intimately, friends.

What then of social control? Does the existence of the family
vitiate the community's ability to ensure conformist behaviour?
Can the individual, because of family ties, avoid being subject to
public pressure, formal or informal? I suggest that (1) the family
does indeed buffer members from public control; yet (2) this

buffering cannot be so great as to make the individual entirely independent of control; at any rate (3) a degree of protection is necessary for the individual; and (4) there are even times when the family strengthens rather than weakens control.

This follows partly from our earlier point about the need the individual member has for the balanced satisfaction of needs. Bearing that in mind, we readily see that it is impossible for the individual to submit himself to the absolute control of the community. By absolute we mean *total* control at any point in time, and *permanent* control, i.e. for his whole life. This is the heart of the matter. There are two dimensions of totality, the synchronic and the diachronic, and the community cannot sustain totality in both. It can demand *total* commitment for a *short* period or *less than total* commitment for a *long* period (the person's entire life in effect); it can indeed demand *total* control over an individual but only if *part* of his life is involved in the community and not if his total life is involved.

In short, except for very short periods, there is no such thing as totality, since the individual could not sustain it psychologically. Either he must be totally involved for a limited period of time, in which case the rest of his life is uninvolved (as in the therapeutic communities); or he can be totally involved for a long period, but in certain spheres of his life only – in which case he has certain spheres of uninvolvement; or if he is to be involved for his whole life span, and if all aspects of his life are to be lived within the community (as with the Hutterites and Kibbutzim), then he *needs* certain spheres and degrees of independence, protection, withdrawal, and even deviance. If the individual's only criterion of how to act or not to act was consideration of public opinion, communal morality or institutional demands then, I suggest, the strain would be, for most people at any rate, intolerable. This would require sustained rationality, surrender of independence and social-moral sensitivity to a degree which would weigh too heavily on most members. The problem then is not one of demanding *total* commitment and control, but of finding *just enough* to make sure that solidarity, conformity and striving for collective goal attainment is sustained.

In connection with the family I am therefore suggesting that, as the classical argument claims, the family protects members from public control, but that if the family did not take on this role, the individual would have to find 'refuge' somewhere else anyway –

and if he could not, then this might have negative consequences for his overall commitment to the community and its behavioural norms. The question then is not whether the family should or does protect the individual – I am arguing that it does and should – but to what degree.

In the case of the Hutterites, we need to note that socialization has been so strong and norms so internalized that even one's family members will frequently act as complete outsiders regarding socially or morally unacceptable behaviour. So it is not uncommon for wives to report on their husbands to the preacher when the latter have been miscreant. If punishment is applied, e.g. shunning, family members act like any other member of the community. (As we have said, we cannot know how much spouses do not report on each other but the fact that reporting occurs to the extent it does indicates the high degree of internalization of norms.) The interesting phenomenon here is that, at times, far from preventing control over the individual the family strengthens it. The fact that the family is a unit in its own eyes and in the eyes of the community often leads individuals to feel directly responsible for the behaviour of others in their family. So parents often feel a moral responsibility regarding their children's behaviour. The misdemeanours of children can reflect back on the parents, and this can affect the status of the entire family in the community. For this reason family members are often the first to attempt to control deviant behaviour in one of their number. I do not wish to go to the other extreme about family control here; I merely wish to assert that even in 'total' communities two conflicting functions have to be met – protection and control – and among the Hutterites both functions operate within the family unit. (This applies to the kibbutz too.)

With the Kibbutzim, unlike the Hutterites, there are few formal codes of behaviour. Control is exerted primarily through informal public opinion. The family does indeed protect members from criticism. One reason for this is that criticism may lead to other family members suffering for the sins of one. An anecdote will illustrate the point. A member of one Kibbutz wrote an article for the Kibbutz news-sheet. The article irritated many members. The author was not of high standing in the Kibbutz but his wife was. One member said to me: 'I would like to write a reply and tear him to pieces, but I don't want to hurt – [his wife].'

At the same time a member's life on a Hutterite colony or

Kibbutz is, as we have already noted, not restricted to his family. He belongs to a work group and a circle of friends, too, and has contact with many other members. These groups are often less sensitive to the member's private feelings, and through them public opinion is communicated to him. Since he lives closely with these people, since the structure of life within a community makes withdrawal difficult, and since he is dependent on them for the satisfaction of his needs, he cannot ignore their opinion or pressures, however much his family may protect him. The member is not a free agent. Dependence once again enters our discussion. If the member has a request to make which is out of the ordinary, or acts in socially unacceptable ways, it is with the community as a whole that he has to have the 'showdown'. It is their attitudes towards him and the consequences thereof which (because of the intimacy of the community) he cannot avoid, and this often deters him from taking things to extremes. Whatever the member does he still needs the community – he has to work with others, eat in the dining hall, use community services – and in a variety of subtle or not-so-subtle ways other members can communicate directly their disapproval of him, and this he cannot avoid. Most people, too, cannot accept the strain involved: in the Kibbutz they need to be particularly thick-skinned to do so and among the Hutterites they must be prepared to accept increasing degrees of punishment even as far as excommunication. In fact, it often happens in practice that family and friends will deter a person from unusual or deviant behaviour even before he does it, both for his own and for their own sakes.

In contrast to everything we have said until now, we need to note certain negative effects the development of the family has had in these communities. In both communities we find the problem of divided loyalties. This applies particularly when the interests of one member of the family are affected. It is also more noticeable on larger and more established communities where we may have not only families, but whole family groupings. The type of problem that may occur among the Hutterites is the appointment of someone to a particular position. Here there may be competition between or even within families. Many observers of Hutterite life have pointed to factionalism – for example, groups of brothers pitted against each other. Also males tend to direct their loyalties to their family of birth, females to their family of procreation.[3] A related problem among the Hutterites is that of inherited positions. Sons often take over their father's work role. This may be partly a matter of inherited ability and partly due to the fact that from the age of 16 children begin adult work, and sons naturally gravitate to their father's work. By the time sons are in a position to take on responsibility they are often the natural heirs to their fathers. But over and above this, and more problematic, is the fact that certain positions are sometimes 'reserved' for certain family groupings. This creates resentment and hostility among less 'privileged' families, which is clearly detrimental to the sense of community solidarity. The Hutterites, we have seen, have certain means of overcoming this, e.g. splitting up colonies, or ensuring that almost all males take on at some time in their lives a position of responsibility, but this does not solve the problem entirely.

In the Kibbutz there has been an increasing trend for the family to see itself as more than an affective-biological unit. The most 'advanced' situation to date is that of the family apartment, the children sleeping with their parents, personal consumption budgets allocated to the family as a whole and in one lump sum, provision for private (if limited) cooking facilities. To some extent, either as cause or effect or both, the family has become more inward-looking, that is, it may see family activity as being more important than community activity, e.g. celebrating an anniversary with friends at home at the same time as a public lecture is taking place. Then of course there is an increased responsibility placed on family members – looking after the flat, choosing and tending to children's clothes, baby sitting, etc., all of which divert time and energy away from the community to the family. Finally, and this too may be cause and effect, there is a parallel rise in materialism – a desire for higher living standards beyond the merely comfortable (although austerity for its own sake has never been a Kibbutz value). The last point is significant in terms of Kibbutz principles because it can affect Kibbutz economic practices (e.g. hired labour) and Kibbutz collectivism (e.g. turning to families off the Kibbutz for 'a little help'). One thing we should note, though, is that very often the desire to be housebound is related to the standard of services the Kibbutz provides. The better its meals or laundry services or cultural programmes, the less members may feel the need or desire to rely on their own private efforts.

However, in the Kibbutz's case it is not clear to what extent the extended family has a negative function. There is no indication that the family serves as a springboard for power, influence or privilege. The evidence is inconsistent on this point. What is true though is that the existence of an extended family, as with the Hutterites, is likely to cause members to want to stay in the community, thus providing it with stability and continuity.[4] This applies to the Hutterites too, indicating that the member's desire to live in the community stems less from fear of losing family connections than from an intrinsic desire to maintain them.

Finally, we need to note a positive function of the family, its biological role. Clearly, no community needs to be dependent on internal reproduction for continuity. But there are three advantages to it:

(1) Recruitment from outside requires canalizing manpower and resources into missionary activity; reproduction represents a saving here.
(2) Although pregnancy, motherhood and the need to maintain an education system somewhat offset the saving, at least reproduction is something that can be relied upon and even controlled, whereas one can never be certain how many recruits one will get from outside.
(3) Perhaps most important of all, recruitment usually involves adults, hence people who need *re*socialization, but whose residual behaviour patterns from earlier days are always suspect and can never be obliterated; with reproduction the community has new members from birth and can educate them totally to its values, goals and behavioural norms.[5,6]

Non-familial exclusiveness

So far we have invoked the concepts of control, dependence and totality and demonstrated the role of the family in regard to them. There are two further dimensions to communal life – sharing and involvement, and here we need to examine close, intense and exclusive relations not connected with the family.

Sharing is the most fundamental social characteristic of communal societies. There are many kinds of sharing – material goods, sense of fate, goals, responsibility, and sharing of one's personality, emotions, problems. Now, we have seen that our communal societies aim to satisfy simultaneously collective and transcendental goals on the one hand, and individual, here-and-now goals on the other. The transcendental goals are attained through collective effort and solidarity, and only through sharing of the kinds we have mentioned can this be sustained. In addition, a life of sharing is meant to be inherently moral and intrinsically satisfying. *This dual role (instrumental-intrinsic) of sharing is a fundamental condition of community persistence. The value of sharing will not be upheld in the abstract if members do not find it intrinsically satisfying. Conversely, sharing creates many strains for the individual, and only an ideological commitment to it is likely to help one accept these strains.* It is also clear that sharing is the antithesis of withdrawal and independence. Sharing implies involvement and is a source of control, so it is not simply a formal institution or technical procedure. Sharing is the fundamental existential fact of communal life – *each kind of sharing is only one overt expression of that fact.*

Given this assumption, it follows that anything that violates the principle of sharing can potentially sabotage the raison d'être of the community. On the other hand, given our earlier comments about totality, or more precisely, the inevitable need for a *lack* of totality, we must argue that sharing too cannot be total. What we need to examine is how sharing is conceived in terms of community solidarity, yet does not impose impossible strains on the individual. The place of close interpersonal relations is significant here.

We argued earlier that family relationships are both permissible and necessary because they are non-substitutable. However, such is not the case with other intense relations. Here the problem is their possible exclusiveness. Unlike family relations, these are potentially shareable among all members of the community and anything which is potentially shareable (material or non-material) must not be used or held in any way by any members exclusively. Exclusive interpersonal closeness may (and does) lead to feelings of suspicion (what are they talking about? Are they doing things behind our back?), jealousy (why are they doing things without us?), partisanship (our group is better than theirs), power (perhaps we can pressurize the community into seeing things our way?).

The sense of solidarity which sharing engenders turns into an us-and-them feeling. This applies whether we are talking of an exclusive group or a single 'excluding' individual. Furthermore, and once again because of the integrated nature of the community, the disruption of sharing in one sphere begins to express itself in others. For example, if an individual denies that he shares responsibility for the community's collective goals, inevitably others will feel that they do not share personal responsibility for his welfare and so on. So it is legitimate for people to have *close* relations but the moment these become *exclusive* the shared sense of solidarity becomes disruptive. *The person who excludes others is not only not sharing himself with them – he is not allowing them to share themselves with him. In essence, it is no different to having private money or seeking power in the community – they all deny the principle of sharing.*

There are further aspects to this. When we spoke earlier of dependence, we were mostly concerned with its material expression; however this, like sharing, is only one dimension of dependence. The communal principle is that in all respects one is dependent on the community, just as in almost all respects one needs to share. People who have exclusive relations are in effect saying to others that they (the excluders) are somehow independent of the rest. Implicitly they are proclaiming that they do not need the rest of the community, that the content of their relationship is of no concern to the community and perhaps even that they are superior to the others.

We have already said that no community can demand total dependence, involvement or sharing. But neither can it go to the other extreme. What precisely is to be shared are *all those things which are potentially shareable* (without violating the member's sense of individuality or his psychological threshold) and all those things which are *relevant to the community's goals* . The point is that not all aspects of a person's life are considered relevant to the community. *Each community chooses spheres which are relevant and grants the individual autonomy in the rest, or in those spheres which cannot be shared anyway (such as family life).* In so doing, it does not demand of him to share himself totally with others since, we have said, this is impossible. So, among the Hutterites or the Kibbutzim your relations with your parents are of no concern to others; but in economic matters total sharing is demanded. Compare this to a therapeutic community where your family relations, your sex life, your daily states of emotion may all be open to public discussion – but there is no demand for economic sharing. For this reason, then, the Hutterites and Kibbutzim recognize the autonomy and exclusiveness of the individual in certain spheres of life and up to certain points in others, but they stop at the point where the overall concept of sharing might be violated and the goal of solidarity upset. So while close relationships are permissible, resentment arises when these develop into exclusiveness. (We should note that these arguments apply whether exclusiveness is based on attraction or hostility. The latter is problematic not only because it creates an unpleasant atmosphere but because the relationship is removed from the control of the rest of the community.)

Exclusiveness is a kind of withdrawal. Now, while withdrawal must be legitimate up to a point, each community needs to set limits. The problem is not so much withdrawal in a physical sense, though this too is frowned upon. Physical withdrawal entails problems of control and, as we saw above, to the extent that he finds it difficult to withdraw, the individual can be controlled. But far more important for communal societies is 'existential withdrawal'. If the goals of the community can only be attained on the basis of sharing then a person (or group) who withdraws is implying that in effect he is not part of the community on the same basis as everyone else. Under their noses, as it were, he is denying the we-feeling, the sense of common fate and goals. He is implying that somehow they have personal failings or are unacceptable to him, or that the goals of the community are not of his concern, or that the intrinsic value of communal life stops at his doorstep. Any person who lives in the community and goes through the minimal motions of membership, but in all other respects erects a barrier between himself and the others, is striking directly at the very basis of communal life. These points can be more fully demonstrated by looking at two rules of a therapeutic community – that there must be no sex on the premises and that there should be no passing or holding of confidences.

We have seen that a basic assumption of a therapeutic community is that most if not all aspects of one's life can be relevant to therapy. The aim of the community is to allow one to engage in a variety of activities and to experience a variety of situations so as to test oneself, to learn and grow, and to examine literally every thing relevant to one's life. Given this assumption and this aim, it follows that everything one does in the community is potentially 'up for grabs'. Since everything is relevant to therapy, everything that happens in the community, and even beyond it, must be open to discussion, analysis, exposure, criticism, encouragement. Members need to accept this, since only in so doing is therapy possible; and members can be expected to commit themselves to this kind of totality *because totality is not demanded of them in other spheres*.

The point of there being a no-sex rule in a therapeutic community is not so much concerned with sex itself as with the problem of exclusive relationships. Any kinds of exclusive relationships in a therapeutic community are taboo. Just as the community cannot accept private intimate relationships, it cannot accept private relationships based on extreme hostility. For two people to dislike each other so intensely that as a result they cannot interact in any positive way is as much a threat to the nature of the community as is exclusive intimacy. Nor can the community tolerate withdrawal on the part of a single resident, that is, if he refuses to interact with other residents. Whether exclusiveness is based on intense attraction (the couple is detached from the rest) or intense repulsion (the two are excluded from each other) or private withdrawal (the individual excludes himself from the community as a whole) the effect is the same in each case. Once exclusiveness appears, a barrier has been erected to the totality of the culture as a therapeutic agent.[7]

This means two things. One is that certain aspects of the individual's life are then considered not to be the concern of the other members of the community. This not only denies the basic principle of social therapy, it is also an effective way of the 'excluder' saying to the others that somehow he is above them or is able to control them. The other is that the basic 'technique' of social therapy, namely free and constructive communication between individuals, is being undermined. Exclusiveness of any kind not only removes certain aspects of life in the community from therapy, it is likely to hamper the ability of individuals to communicate even in those spheres which have not been so removed.

This stems from another basic principle of the therapeutic community, namely, that in order to communicate constructively individuals must be able to both give and receive negative and positive responses regarding each other's behaviour, thus responding to each other in ways which are therapeutically useful – to criticize when necessary, to protect when necessary, to demand when necessary. Once exclusive relationships emerge this will no longer be possible since the reason for the relation being exclusive in the first place will inhibit others from responding in what may be the most constructive way. People might begin to protect each other from necessary criticism, or make unnecessarily harmful criticism, or simply not allow themselves to be criticized or encouraged at all, and this is inconsistent with the aims of a therapeutic community. (And this, by the way, is the reason therapeutic communities place so much emphasis on group meetings and insist that attendance at some group meetings is compulsory: this prevents the individual from total withdrawal.)

Another aspect of exclusiveness is the question of confidences. There is a rule in a therapeutic community which says quite simply that nothing shall be listened to under the prior guarantee that it will be held in confidence. Someone may tell a staff member something and they may decide between them that it be kept from other residents, but a staff member will never listen to a resident, or other staff for that matter, *on condition* it is kept confidential. There are two broad reasons for this. The first is simply therapeutic. For staff to perform their job properly, they need to know all there is to know about residents and even other staff, therefore they must not keep information from each other. (If there is something you want to keep to yourself, that is entirely your privilege; if however, you choose to reveal it to someone, you must realize it may well become public knowledge.) Furthermore, it is extremely difficult for a resident to know something about another resident and have to keep it to himself. Experience shows that the stress placed on residents in such circumstances can be destructive.

The existence of these two rules helps to explain a basic aspect of intentional communities. This is that the rules (formal or informal) must have all the following characteristics; (1) they must promote the ends for which the community exists; (2) they must promote the principle of communality; yet (3) they must not put intolerable strains on the individual. In each of our communities this is precisely what happens. Regarding (1) we find in the two major communities an insistence on economic sharing, a shared sense of history and purpose and shared responsibility. In the therapeutic communities we find sharing of one's personality, emotions, private life. Talking is the 'currency' of therapeutic communities. Sharing one's feelings about one's parents is as irrelevant to a Kibbutz or Bruderhof as sharing one's Social Security payments is to a therapeutic community. But what is important is not only that the rules suit an ideological end – they are rules about sharing. *By creating a culture of sharing they are creating a life of community, since sharing is in itself the basic quality of community and helps sustain dependence, control and involvement,*

But surely, it can then be argued, the more sharing there is in the community, or is demanded of members, the more intense the community atmosphere will be and the more successful the group will be as an intentional community? The answer to this is categorically negative. We saw in our theoretical discussion on alienation that where individuals find themselves faced with an overbearing public identity, they are going to seek a private level of identity. So, to demand total sharing is not going to create total community. Quite the reverse. People are then going to seek various illicit and subterfuge ways of opting out and conspiring against the system.[8] But which spheres they will choose and to what extent they will act deviantly is beyond community control. The communities we are studying here have chosen a different strategy. They accept the need for spheres of individual autonomy, so they define those spheres explicitly and say to the individual (meaning, say to themselves) – let us each go our own way in those spheres but let us each give ourselves up to the community in other spheres. Which other spheres? We have already given the answer in this regard – they must share in those spheres relevant to the goals of the community. Now we can expand on this.

We need to note one essential difference between the therapeutic communities on the one hand, and our major communities on the other. For the former, communality is instrumental only, while for the latter, it has an inherent value. The therapeutic community in its own right does not have collective goals. (It does have collective goals, e.g. economic support or recognition from outside, but this is met by the headquarters and not by the community itself.) Since the community is in one case an end in itself it needs to demand of members that they share collective goals – this leads to a common sense of fate, responsibility to each other, subordination of private interests for the public good. But to demand these in a therapeutic community would go against the individualistic goals of the community. It would divert the

individual away from his private goals – the definition and attainment of which are the very purpose of the community. Yet
communality nevertheless needs to be attained, since this is an
essential instrument for attaining one's ends, however private. So
sharing has to be implemented in such a way that the act of
sharing promotes communality *and* individual therapy, yet without
the two contradicting each other. Sharing of one's 'whole personality' serves this dual purpose and the point is that it can demand
this kind of total sharing precisely because it does not demand
sharing in any other spheres of the member's life. In the case of
our major communities the principle is the same, but the emphasis
is reversed. The demand for communality is basic and the specific
forms of communality (economic, 'historical') uphold this, but
precisely for this very reason, spheres of individual autonomy
have to be granted.[9]

So in each case the rules serve the purposes of the community
and promote communality, but leave the individual with spheres
of autonomy. By defining spheres of individual autonomy clearly
the community is, paradoxically, *increasing* control over members,
since it knows precisely what can be demanded, and can be totally
demanded, in other spheres. At the same time, an individual need
not feel alienated, both because the definition of public identity
is explicit and unambiguous, and because the private level of
identity is recognized as being legitimate. (He may, however, be
alienated for other reasons.)

The denial of communal totality

From these and earlier observations, we see that the persistence
of a (voluntary) communal society is based on its ability both to
sustain its fundamental defining characteristics and to attain its
goals. Yet it must do this without violating the ability of the
individual member to commit himself to those characteristics and
goals. We mentioned earlier that what is important is not only
that the individual has spheres of autonomy but that the
community defines the parameters of those spheres. For this
reason the viable 'total' community does not aim to be *total* – it
aims to be *comprehensive*. The community has to meet each need
and its opposite. (We have already mentioned this in our
comments on ideology.) So we speak of totality-partiality, sharing-

exclusiveness, dependence-independence, involvement-with-drawal, exposure-protection, control-tolerance of deviance. To meet only the first side of the duality (as the 'total-community' theory implies) will lead to an intolerable burden being placed on the individual (which I suggest has been a most significant factor in the inability of so many communities to persist). To meet only the latter side will vitiate the development of solidarity and collective effort (equally significant to non-persistence). A balanced situation is a sine qua non of community viability.

The presence of the family in successful, comprehensive communities, like Hutterite colonies or Kibbutzim, has helped them to sustain the necessary balance in most respects (and has certain straightforward functional advantages), although certain family trends in each group of communities sometimes upset this balance. Non-familial exclusiveness in these communities would upset the balance more seriously, hence is not legitimate.

Part C

Chapter 11
Summary and conclusions: the nature and persistence of intentional communities

Throughout this book we have presented numerous comments, observations, suggestions, hypotheses and postulations. We need now to bring all this together and to summarize the main arguments. (For the reader who is tempted to begin with this section it should be clear that most of the points below assume that the main text has already been read.)

While the conclusions are based on our discussion of three specific groups of communities, they stand as possible springboards for a wider analysis of intentional communities. They are not presented as a formula for success or as a list of necessary conditions for persistence. Many of the following comments could be equally applied to other intentional communities, including those which were only shortlived, but cumulatively they have contributed to the persistence of the communities we have studied; they help us to understand the basis to their communality, the problems involved in sustaining it, and how they have overcome them.

Our comments below concentrate on the Hutterites and Kibbutzim. Most of them apply to the therapeutic communities we studied too, but on a lesser scale, appropriate to their shorter time-span, smaller size and more limited aims, although some aspects are fundamentally different.

I must emphasize that we are not suggesting that all the conditions mentioned below have been met perfectly by all the communities. On the contrary, the communities have at times fallen far short of ideal attainment and this is the reason for many of the crises they have faced. Our conclusions are based as much on the observations of failure and crisis as of success. But by and large the communities have followed the patterns, embraced the conditions and displayed the characteristics we present here, albeit in different ways and in different degrees. They have done so in sufficient 'quantity' to allow them to persist. Therefore we can present them as common characteristics and perhaps some as universally necessary conditions regarding this type of community. Only further and much wider research can confirm or refute their relevance to a generalized understanding of intentional communities.

1 The basic ideas and motivations of our communities were firmly rooted in their society of origin and not in total contrast to it. The difference between them and the surrounding society lay in their synthesis of different trends of the time and in giving to new trends which were already becoming accepted in the base society a radical interpretation.

2 The communities also emerged at a time of great social change, a time of social and moral uncertainty. Traditional ways of understanding were being questioned, while a desire and need for experimentation in new ideas and social forms were strengthening. Rapidly changing circumstances and the climate of uncertainty left a vacuum regarding the nature of, and the means of attaining, the new needs.

3 Because the communities were not completely incongruent elements within the wider society they successfully appealed to some groups of people within it: they helped satisfy personal needs which had given rise to or were the product of changing times, and they 'made sense' in the context of new moral ideas.

4 To some extent they also met certain needs of the wider society as a whole, i.e. the latter had an interest in their existence. This interest was mainly economic-political.

5 Yet there were other forces – political and religious mainly – which strongly opposed the existence of the communities. This opposition came from both straightforward ideological opponents and from elements in the same movement as the community itself who could not accept the community's interpretation of their common beliefs and goals, or who saw the community as a flight from reality.

6 This meant that the communities managed to get off the ground because they satisfied various types of needs in the base society; yet they were also in a state of tension with that society, which helped them to preserve their sense of uniqueness and mission.

7 These communities were not the only response to the changing times. Of the other responses some were more radical, others less so. The new trends had given birth to some very broad goals which were open to a wide variety of interpretations at the levels of both belief and practical application.

8 At the same time, each individual community was not isolated. It became part of a network with a degree of centralized control and support.

9 These circumstances (7, 8) together helped the individual communities. Individuals or groups seeking a particular interpretation of some new beliefs or goals could find one compatible with their personal ideas and needs. There was less danger of foreign and potentially disruptive elements creeping in. Even within any one network, where the interpretations and applications were fairly consistent, a potential member could choose a community compatible with his particular needs. Each trend, and each community within each trend, could therefore be more selective and homogeneous, yet the movement could still be fairly widespread and encompassing.

10 The existence of the network meant that communities could benefit from mutual support in times of need. The central authorities of the movement could also represent the communities in the outside world, protect their interests and extend their influence.

11 None of the communities began with any blueprint for social planning nor even with a very clear ideology. The founding of the communities emerged from a desire to satisfy certain societal needs, certain intensely held but vague ideological beliefs, and also some personal needs. What precisely those beliefs consisted of or how the needs were to be met was not at all clear. The overt ideological justification for the existence of the communities came at a later stage of development, and it took some time for a stable structure to emerge.

12 The life-style of the founders was a reflection of their personal needs and relations. Among the circumstances which had given birth to the new trends was a break-down of traditional community ties and traditional roles. Yet for some these ties had been based on morally defective foundations. The founders now sought to recreate a community culture with clearly defined roles,[1] but based on a new belief system.

13 The early lack of clarity was strategically advantageous. The institutions, as they became clearer and more formalized, were a product not so much of ideological planning as of trial and error, experimentation, responses to environmental demands, responses to internal and economic needs and responses to personal needs. There was no contradiction between these emerging forms and the ideology, simply because the latter was so vague and generalized. (Just as order and meaning stand in a dialectical relationship for the individual and emerge over time for him, so too does a community only 'find' its full identity after a period of time.)

14 Nevertheless, the founders were highly conscious of their values and goals, however vague, and highly sensitive to the need to relate institutions to abstract beliefs.

15 The communities have had ambivalent attitudes to change. On the one hand, because of the reifying effects of institutionalization (i.e. granting to the concrete forms of social organizations a reality or necessity which stems from 'out there' and so takes on an untouchable quality) there has been reluctance to change, and this has often caused conflict with younger generations. But neither have the communities been totally resistant to change; pragmatism has had a very strong say.

16 Hence the ideology and the actual institutions which developed were a product of the interplay between them, each shaping and 'vindicating' the other. The relation to the environment was similarly established and adapted. This meant that the community could meet its various practical needs and satisfy its 'pure' ideological goals in ways which both made its physical existence viable and were, to its members, true to its beliefs.

17 The subsequent development of the communities to this day

has followed a similar pattern. Even though the ideology and institutions are fairly formalized, the former still remains open to differing interpretations and applications. The 'higher' elements of the ideology have remained vague enough to justify all sorts of accommodations to economic, social, personal, organizational and environmental demands. In addition, many areas of daily life are simply 'ignored' from an ideological point of view. Hence the communities have allowed themselves structural and ideological change, yet still see themselves as being essentially the same community as before, and still faithful to the same ideals.

18 Even where ideological lapses have appeared, these have been pragmatically accepted as such – problems to be resolved in the future. The lapses are even used to stress the need for more determined effort regarding goal attainment.

19 The communities have to a large extent routinized their institutions and beliefs (i.e. given the concrete forms of social organization a regular and predictable pattern, and codified the ideology). This has had a number of consequences:[2] (a) it is a means of conveying the underlying reasons for the community's existence to the second generation. (b) It reduces psychological strain on members. If questions were to be asked every time a problem arose as to which was the correct response from an ideological viewpoint, many problems would not be adequately faced and there would be too much debate and conflict. For the same reason many activities are engaged in or situations responded to without any ideological references. (c) Routinization is a necessary precondition for innovation. (d) The communities were founded as a result of people dereifying the beliefs of their societies of origin. In order to legitimate the new beliefs, reification was needed and institutionalization was one means of doing so (i.e. forms of social organization are adopted which not only serve a practical organizational purpose but come to be seen as the concrete manifestation, the vehicle, of ideological belief).

20 The communities have generally not seen a conflict between economic success (which is based on technological advancement) and their ideological purity. On the contrary, they have almost always emphasized economic progress and efficiency. Where they have refrained from this or have had economic difficulties, there

have usually been negative consequences – loss of influence, declining membership, lowered morale.

21 Except in the early days, or in times of crisis, a modicum of economic equality between the community and the environment has also been seen as necessary. The communities have never tried to outdo the environment regarding living standards, but they have also avoided being 'over-primitive' in relation to it. (In therapeutic communities, too, a living standard comparable to that of peers outside the community is necessary.)

22 Technological efficiency and economic success have been a crucial factor in the persistence of the communities: (a) It has helped them maintain a reasonable (in their own eyes) standard of living. (b) It has allowed the communities to do other things which it considers necessary. For the Hutterites this means land acquisition (for splitting); for the Kibbutzim this means releasing people from productive work, either to engage in social-political activity on the Kibbutz or to do non-productive but personally satisfying work. (c) It has been intrinsically satisfying to those directly involved. Efficiency and modernization have partly served as a compensation for not deriving material gain from one's work. They are to a large extent ends in themselves. (d) It has been a source of morale to the community as a whole – a further sign that the way of life works, that belief can be translated into practice, that if one is determined enough one can do what is right and necessary. (e) The communities have felt that they cannot achieve their goals without economic stability – their energy would be consumed in fighting for survival and they would be at the mercy of forces stronger than them.

23 Nevertheless, economic success can be a complicating factor in the life of the community. It need not detract from the principles of authority, dependence and sharing, but it can vitiate the 'we-feeling' of the community. More significant though is the possibility that economic success can create a labour surplus, which, if not managed carefully, can create groups of people who are marginal to the community because they perceive both that they do not need the community nor does the community need them. They can be extricated from the processes of collective

production and consumption and this can attenuate their commitment to the community.

24 At times conflicts have arisen between economic efficiency and basic principles. With the Hutterites this involves commercial practices, with the Kibbutzim, hired labour. Both communities have acknowledged these problems but they have not simply abandoned the economic practices as a result. They have preferred to live with the problem, partially but never totally adjusting to or eliminating it (the Hutterites by increasing inter-colony trade, the Kibbutz by increased mechanization, fines for hiring labour, hired worker involvement in the industrial enterprise). The need for economic viability has, by and large, not conflicted with ideological principles, but where conflict has arisen, viability has taken precedence and the conflict has been seen as an unfortunate deviation which will be solved in time.

25 So, by sustaining a determined idealism, yet combining it with a shrewd pragmatism, the communities have managed to be highly motivated to attain their goals, and have managed to meet the needs of day-to-day living internally and externally. The communities have been decidedly non-millenarial and non-utopian. Their goals and values are considered as given: the rest simply means getting down to the job of making them work.

26 This has been partly facilitated by the fact that leadership has never been charismatic (except possibly in the very early stages) at an individual or group level. This has allowed for greater flexibility and change, and greater response to grassroots thinking. In the Kibbutz there has been much rotation of leaders. Among the Hutterites, whose leaders are appointed for life, there is much emphasis on responding to problems either firmly or pragmatically, as the situation dictates. In each case founders are seen as heroes and models, but not as supra-human beings. The founders derive their authority from their dedication, not from their very being.

27 Despite all the changes that have taken place and the variations that exist in the community's structure and even in its ideology, there is a strong sense of continuity with the past, identification with other communities and orientation to the future. These have

served to strengthen the community's sense of moral worth, purpose and uniqueness.

28 These feelings have also been strengthened by internecine conflicts. One negative consequence of having 'variations on a theme' has been that at times each has considered itself to be the correct interpretation of the basic beliefs. Much energy has been used up in conflict with other movements, at times over 'petty' issues. But this has positive consequences too. Each community (or group of communities) has preserved its own identity, sense of purpose, feeling of moral superiority. Each has needed to articulate its ideology more clearly and to emphasize to itself why *it* has the right approach. Sometimes the internal struggles have been the consequence of lack of motivation, purpose and identity in the communities, and have thereby served to motivate members to greater effort. Phenomenologically, challenging or redefining interpretations of basic beliefs serves the purpose of 'conspiracy' (see the theoretical discussions on alienation and ideology, Chapters 2 and 3).

29 The communities (or groups of them) often feel the need to endistance themselves from each other and from the world. For this reason they might pick on small issues for dispute; communities of the same group might engage in subtle rivalries and they often exaggerate certain aspects of the environment (negative) and of their own structure (positive) to show how different they really are.

30 Influence on the environment and expansion in it have been intrinsic to the ideology of each group of communities. This has served a number of purposes: (a) recruitment; (b) acceptability; (c) enhancement of feelings of rightness of cause ('if we are expanding we must be right'); (d) it provides further motivation to members to strive for collective goal-attainment; (e) it provides feelings of tension with the environment, hence of uniqueness and possible danger, resulting in a greater sense of collective identity; (f) it gives a sense of dynamism, progress and success; (g) it provides some members with an intrinsically satisfying occupation.

31 Yet, where attempts to influence the environment or to expand within it have posed dangers to the community, it has tended not to seek confrontation or over-involvement, but rather to accom-

modate its beliefs, practices and relations to the host society just enough to defuse dangerous conflicts – yet not so much as to allow itself to be absorbed by the environment. The sense of uniqueness has been maintained even though ideological distortions have emerged (e.g. with the Hutterites – no missionary work, alternative service, English School; with the Kibbutzim – hired labour, a degree of materialism). The loose structure of the ideology and the sense of pragmatism already mentioned have allowed the communities to live with these problems.

32 In order to sustain collective efforts towards the attainment of supra-individual goals, the individual needs to be treated, and needs to see himself, as a means to an end. For the community to persist over a lengthy period the individual must, up to a point, subordinate himself to the satisfaction of collective, functional needs (unless individual needs and collective needs are met by two different bodies within the same framework, as with the therapeutic communities). The need to give oneself up to the collective effort is partly accepted through imbuing the community as a whole with purposes over and above the lives and needs of those presently in the community. Hence the need for both a past and future orientation. This is also a major source of solidarity in the community.

33 On the other hand, the community could not survive for very long if only collective needs were to be met. The individual has to see himself also as an end in his own right, since the strain of 'personal surrender' could not be indefinitely sustained.

34 In each of our communities the individual is valued in his own right and is given various forms of personal satisfaction on a daily basis. But numerous tensions arise in the life of the individual, although the tension between the positive and negative aspects has generally been resolved in favour of the former. For certain individuals the negative outweighs the positive, but this has not led to such large-scale defections as to endanger the existence of the communities. (Even though a few specific communities have collapsed, perhaps more would have done so if not for the efforts of the centre of the network, e.g. additional manpower, finances, guidance.)

35 The community as a whole has been flexible in its approaches

to ideology and to collective practical necessities and it has done the same regarding the individual in relation to the community. A balance has been obtained in which the tenets of faith have been broadly maintained, the needs of the community as a whole have been met, and the satisfaction of the individual has been attained. The latter serves to strengthen his identification with the community and his readiness to direct some of his energies to the collective effort.

36 There can be various sources of strain and dissatisfaction for the individual:

(a) He cannot simply live and let live – he feels that he is under too much moral obligation to others and to the community as a whole.

(b) He may feel a lack of privacy.

(c) The member may feel that he is too dependent on others and on the community as a whole, even, or perhaps especially, in relatively trivial or even very private matters.

(d) Life in the community may seem to him to be narrow, petty, claustrophobic.

(e) The community may not meet his expectations – in ideology (there is a huge gap between the ideal and the real), in interpersonal relations (people do not act as they should), in the community's readiness to satisfy his own personal needs (a feeling of injustice).

(f) He may not find the general collective life-style (e.g. communal eating, collective education, collective distribution) intrinsically satisfying.

(g) He may not find specific sources of satisfaction which he considers necessary, e.g. work or leisure.

(h) He may feel under pressure to conform – the smallness of the community may leave him unable to be as individualistic as he likes, i.e. he has to take the opinion of others too much into account.

(i) Individuals in these communities possibly suffer less loneliness, less injustice, less neglect, less indifference from others than in a non-communal framework, but when they do suffer them, then they feel them *very* intensely.

(j) The member may feel he has sacrificed his interests or needs or private life for the sake of the community.

(k) He cannot divorce one aspect of his life in the community from others. All aspects of his life in it interlock. A problem arising in one sphere tends to express itself in others, hence magnifying it out of all proportion and becoming a larger burden and strain than it might otherwise be.

(l) He may sense a lack of freedom in small matters, which others in non-communal society possess. The specific sphere in which there is lack of freedom may then be extrapolated to a feeling that this characterizes his entire life in the community.

(m) It is easy for the individual to blame the community for his problems, but he may know in his heart of hearts that the solution lies in his own hands. This can produce a feeling of personal crisis.

(n) Expectations can be very high, sometimes unrealistically so, hence easily dashed.

37 The communities we have studied have all had to deal with at least some of these problems. *They are endemic to communal life, and the communities have never pretended or assumed that they can overcome personal problems absolutely.* Yet they have had certain basic characteristics which help overcome them and they have been sufficiently conscious of them to make necessary accommodations to the individual.

38 The factors which can provide individual satisfaction are:

(a) The ideology is ultimately reducible to an evaluation of the individual in his own right (even though a collective framework is considered necessary to attain individual goals).

(b) The ideology in each case expresses the norms of care, understanding and sympathy, both in institutional and spontaneous inter-relational terms.

(c) This has been expressed in practice and has not simply been a hollow ideal.

(d) The community has not demanded total involvement from the individual. It does not expect the individual to give himself up entirely to the community, nor does it consider every aspect of the individual's life to be of concern to everyone else. Which spheres are to be total and which private depend on the goals, time-span and beliefs of the community.

(e) The individual has sources of personal satisfaction, e.g. in varieties of work or positions of responsibility.

(f) A degree of latitude is allowed regarding deviant behaviour. The individual needs to be partially deviant since this asserts his individuality (see the theoretical discussion on alienation (Chapter 2) and the discussion on social control (Chapter 9)). The community chooses not to have a 'show-down' on issues which are marginal and not likely to cause any breakdown in community solidarity or basic belief. 'Show-downs' are usually left to more fundamental matters.

(g) The democratic structure (as each defines it) gives individuals a feeling that they are in control of their own lives and that the community as a whole controls its own destiny. Significantly, though, when decisions are made with which the individual disagrees, or which have negative consequences, it is easy for the member to opt out of responsibility ('the community decided, not me').

(h) The principle of *general* equality leads to a feeling of justice, i.e. that you are as valuable as anyone else; while the principle of *relative* equality means that your personal circumstances are taken into account.

(i) The community provides absolute material security for the individual.

(j) Individuals may find the communal life-style intrinscially satisfying and adjustments are sometimes made in the institutions to ensure that this feeling of well-being exists.

(k) While the communities emphasize the positive advantage for the individual of being a member, they also emphasize the difficulties involved and the need for individual effort. This has tended to lower expectations.

(l) The fact that there are a number of communities in each network has meant that the individual can join a community which satisfies his particular needs and in which he can find interpersonal compatibility.

(m) In each community the individual has certain means of attaining status.

(n) The member can find certain means of endistancing himself from others (yet can never do so entirely).

(o) The member has been able to enter family relationships which have provided him with affective satisfaction and have served to buffer him from community control and criticism.

(p) Each community can seem to its members to be not only the repository of abstract beliefs, or a particular social system, or a unique force in society, but – over and above all this – simply home.

(q) The member may take great pride in his particular community and its way of doing things – a sense of superiority over other communities of the same network or in his network over other networks – not so much in ideological as in practical matters (the 'subtle rivalry' mentioned earlier).

(r) The communities have recognized that the individual cannot sustain conscious purpose continuously, since the strain will be too great, so a degree of 'legitimate apathy' is permitted. This allows the individual to live the community life in routinized fashion with the emphasis on intrinsic satisfaction therein, rather than on the ideological connotations.

(s) The individual may find great pleasure in intimacy, close interaction, the we-feeling.

(t) He may derive great pride in having made a 'sacrifice' for the greater good; it can give him feelings of moral superiority over outsiders, and a sense of purpose and satisfaction in life.

(u) While the ideology and actual workings of the society theoretically form one grand and interlinked scheme, we see that this is not altogether the case in practice. This is an advantage. It means that within one broad and fairly coherent scheme, different individuals can find different points of identification, can emphasize different goals, and can relate to different parts of the ideology with different motivations – yet none of this need necessarily upset the balance of the whole and the solidarity of the community.

(v) The individual sees his community as 'home' in the most private and subjective sense and at the same time as the concrete expression of his impersonal and transcendent beliefs.

39 Yet these are all 'strategies' or 'techniques' *after* the individual's readiness to commit himself to the community. They help to explain how the individual manages to sustain a sense of well-being in the community, *given the fact that he wants to commit himself to it in the first place.* In themselves they do not explain that commitment.

40 The individual joins the community because it gratifies his

identity needs. He believes that the beliefs, goals, norms and life-style of the community, as a totality, are for him non-alienating.

41 'As a totality' means that the individual would not join or remain in the community if only his abstract beliefs were being met. Conversely, the endemic strains of communal life would be intolerable, despite all the 'compensations', if he had no ideological identification. Adherence to beliefs and goals, on the one hand, and acceptance of the life-style, on the other, are equally necessary – each cannot exist without the other, at least not in a voluntary communal society. If 'ideology' were the only consideration, the strain on the individual would be too great. If the personal level of identity were all that mattered, egoism would take precedence over all else, leading both to the breaking of 'mutual faith' and the inability to undertake collective tasks.

42 The communities have met the necessary preconditions for not being alienating societies. They provide guidelines to identity; there is equal access to the means of attaining identity satisfaction (since the goals are not scarce resources, and because of the structure of the community); having a network of communities and 'variations on a theme' means that individuals can find alternative means of identity satisfaction; at the private level of identity attempts are made to overcome strain; the universe of the community is neither 'over-open' nor 'over-closed' (taken from the *member's* standpoint); the societal and private levels of one's identity are recognized as being equally legitimate and are satisfied in mutually compatible fashion.

43 The individual's identity consists of the totality of his biological and affective needs, his personality traits and personal interests, his experiences, values, beliefs and goals, and his relationships with others. He identifies with the community because he feels that within it each of these elements will be satisfied, and in ways compatible with each other.

44 Strains can and do arise in the actual practice of this, and crises develop regarding his identification. The majority of members on balance accept that compromises are necessary, and so choose to sustain their identities within that framework. If any specific need is seriously jeopardized and is very important to a member, he

has to make a radical choice between continued identification with the community and an alternative framework.

45 The particular forms of communal life are not therefore to be seen as externally devised (in the eyes of the individual) or as a means of control over the individual. They are the means by which the individual expresses his commitment to the community and affirms his solidarity with others. For him they are part of his identity, not something imposed on him from beyond it. Therefore the formal rules of the community exist for him as a concrete expression of his moral beliefs and as a means of attaining his personal-moral goals. They are not a necessary evil (for him personally, although they may be for potential deviants) but an extension of what he wants and needs anyway.

46 Even so, the individual has a basic need to deviate in marginal ways: this satisfies his feelings of individuality ('conspiracy') but does not upset the cohesion of the community, and so leaves both that cohesion and the framework of his identity intact.

47 The voluntary nature of the community means that anyone not satisfied with its goals, structure and personnel is free to leave, so need not feel he is coerced into or by them.

48 It is when the norms and institutions cease to satisfy the individual's identity needs that he feels alienated and is convinced that the institutions are imposed on him. (And we have seen that since communal life is so integrated, one serious problem can upset his entire relation to the community.) Even if the individual sees that on balance he is happier in the community than out of it, he can still feel coercion – hence resentment and lack of solidarity – in specific circumstances. Under such circumstances there is naturally a greater propensity to act deviantly.

49 Whatever the causes of deviance the communities all recognize its existence and also its necessity. So while formal and informal means exist of containing deviance, such containment is not absolute nor is it meant to be. Each community attempts to sustain sufficient control to allow for efficiency and solidarity. Yet it permits a degree of deviance which allows for individual satisfaction and relieves personal strain; at any rate, 'legitimate deviance'

avoids the institutional, ideological and interpersonal problems which would arise from having over-explicit and rigid codes of behaviour and sanctions for breaking them.

50 So the spheres of personal identity, community ideology and social structure we have been considering should not be seen as neatly slotting into each other. They do not and cannot, and the communities have implicitly recognized this. There is a broad congruence between these spheres but each shapes and is shaped by the others, while each also changes – sometimes with the others, sometimes independently of them and sometimes even in conflict with them. Compromise, adaptation and change have characterized our communities as wholes and also their individual members – yet within a consistent frame of reference. This has led on the one hand to an ability to function efficiently, change and adapt to new needs and circumstances, yet on the other hand to maintain a sense of past and future continuity and overall satisfaction in having achieved, sustained and promoted the purposes for which the community exists.

51 An important source of solidarity is the member's identification with the supra-individual needs and goals of the community. This creates a common focus of identification which is beyond private need, and so not subject to egoistic considerations or private interpretation. These collective goals are reified.

52 Fundamental to the sense of solidarity is the development of mutual faith, i.e. a perception that all members are equally and fully committed to the goals of the community. Because the individual goals are of a non-exclusive kind (salvation, self-realization, personal growth) there need not be competition to attain them. Mutual faith is broken when members suspect that others have egoistic goals – either they seek ends to which others have no access or they are not concerned to make maximum effort for others, neither individually nor for the community as a whole.

53 Sharing is a sine qua non of communal life. It is meant to be both an end in itself and a means of attaining higher goals.

54 The principle and practice of sharing upholds and stems from mutual faith. Since there is sharing, no individual need feel that

he is giving but not receiving, or giving and receiving but in disproportionate amount. Sharing means that there need be no competition within the community. But sharing is not exactly equal. Relative equality means that individuals give and receive different amounts. Only where there is mutual faith or trust do individuals accept this kind of equality rather than contractual or mechanical equality.

55 Individuals must live by the accepted (as opposed to ideal) standards of behaviour, and not make themselves out to be models of community ethics. They need to be humble and modest and not appear to be seeking power or influence. Individuals must do the right thing even if they do not wish to. (The therapeutic communities are a partial exception to this, because they are concerned with personal growth and not with the creation of a long-lasting culture.) Not to do so would seem to place the individual in a position of being independently able to interpret the norms. Nor must individuals engage in activities or set up relations which appear to be exclusive or which give the impression of seeking power. Exclusiveness implies private possession, superiority, detachment or independence. These negate the basic qualities of communality.

56 This is another way of saying that whatever democracy means and however much the individual is valued, he cannot have independent authority, even in many private matters (which may seem to him to be a threat to his individuality, in which case the community's authority is seen as coercion and not as a reflection and extension of his identity). *The important thing for community cohesion is not so much what is decided but what the source of authority is for it.*

57 Hence solidarity is based on having collective goals and on lack of competition, exclusiveness, superiority or private authority. The particular institutions of democracy, equality, material security, flexibility and sympathetic handling of personal problems can all function not simply because of any technical efficiency but also, perhaps primarily, because they are rooted in the fundamental sense of solidarity which pervades the community. If this solidarity and its concomitant, mutual faith, did not exist, then their specific institutional expressions could not function properly.

58 Conversely, the technical ways in which the institutions are managed can strengthen or weaken the sense of solidarity and mutual faith. Here a special obligation is placed on leaders to manage their tasks flexibly and with understanding, yet clearly within the norms and traditions of the community.

59 It also means that the community must simply have a sufficient proportion of members who are organizationally and occupationally efficient. (This has implications for community democracy, i.e. democracy can only exist where there is an even spread of knowledge and skills.) It must have leaders who are far-sighted, have clear conceptions about community values and goals and can exhort members to strive for them – yet are also flexible, sensitive and politically astute. The quality of manpower at all levels and in all kinds of activities is as crucial as anything else to the community's persistence.

60 Leadership in intentional communities is particularly important. It is crucial that leaders provide intellectual, moral and organizational authority internally and can negotiate effectively with the outside world. They also need to be, quite simply, sharp and shrewd. They need good business sense; in effect, they are no different to the managers of large corporations, except that in addition they provide social-moral leadership. What is crucial is not only that they assume authority but how that authority is accepted. And what is relevant here to all our communities is that their authority ultimately does not depend on charisma, tradition or bureaucratic power, however formalized.[3] Authority rests simply on the leaders successfully carrying all the above functions, while being sensitive at the same time to members' needs, grass-root feelings and ideological demands.

61 All this also means that any particular rule must serve three purposes: it must be morally good in itself; it must promote the basic qualities of communal life (sharing, dependence, involvement, control); it must be an intrinsically satisfying activity or state. A threat to any one of these purposes is a threat to the rule as a whole and to the community's persistence (because the community becomes ideologically bankrupt or loses its communality, or because members become disaffected).

62 In each community there is a kind of anti-intellectualism, a suspicion of the consequences of splitting intellectual and practical activity and a suspicion as to whether 'pure' intellect can really solve the problems at hand. This has been both a motivating factor in setting up the community in the first place and a consequence of the community's successful persistence. For them, thinking and doing are each sterile if not accompanied by the other. In all three groups of communities the concept of action and its integration with the intellect is primary.

63 This is related to the principle of effort. Each individual in each community and each community as a whole feels the need to strive consciously to attain its goals. The need for effort is often impressed on the individual through crises or threats (real or imagined) from within or without. The communities have never seen themselves as having absolutely attained their goals; nor, for that matter, do they see themselves as having failed in their task. The perception of success has strengthened morale; the perception of failure has generated more determination to succeed – and this is strengthened by the ethic of striving, hard work, doing and not talking. (Hence the ambivalent and even lowered status of those who engage in or seek only intellectual work.)

64 This is based on an implicit assumption that if human beings are to improve, and if society is to be more moral, it is not enough only to restructure the institutions of society. On the other hand, unless institutions are restructured, the individual could not possibly have the means of improving and leading a more moral way of life.

65 Despite the principle of effort the individual is allowed to a large extent to act mechanically and live apathetically. Not to allow this would impose intolerable strains on him.

66 This is only one aspect of how the communities have acted to sustain solidarity, purpose and ideological consistency without breaking the individual but rather by enhancing his feeling of well-being in it. Despite the need to ensure solidarity, to express their defining communal characteristics, to promote operational efficiency and to adhere to their ideological tenets the communities have not demanded of the individual that he play his part to the extent that his private existence is considered irrelevant or his

psychological threshold is broken. Apart from the specific sources of individual satisfaction (above) the communities have therefore balanced not only the need for both effort and apathy but, overall, have adopted a policy of both 'totality' and 'partiality' (see the conclusion to Chapter 10).

67 Each community has emphasized socialization of children. It has spent large proportions of its budget to sustain an independent education system. The principles of this system have been consciously geared to raising a generation to whom the beliefs of the community are unquestionable, to whom the way of life is intrinsically satisfying, and who are capable of taking their place occupationally in the community. They have succeeded sufficiently in these aims to ensure continuity in both demographic and cultural terms. In each case the education system has been an integral part of the social system as a whole. Life in the community is meant to be an education in itself.

68 However, there can be difficulties: a strong emphasis on education can lead to the educational process being 'detached' from the community. This can lead to a generation being created which feels that it is not part of 'the system'. This has implications (as with economic success and a labour surplus) for their commitment to the community.

69 A point not hitherto mentioned. The agricultural setting of the communities seems (I put it no higher than that) to have something to do with their persistence. A possible reason is the isolation of farm life but, without wishing to move from sociology into mysticism, there seems to be more to it than that. Farmers seemed less concerned with competition than those living in the towns or engaged in industry. Perhaps, as has been suggested, farmers are more concerned with fighting nature than each other; or perhaps, as the community members themselves believe, a natural setting induces more ethical behaviour. Clearly, simply to move to an agricultural setting is in itself no prescription for success; on the contrary, hardships can be many. Perhaps we should simply conclude that while the numerous factors facilitating persistence can be applied to any intentional community, their potential is substantially increased when operating in a 'natural' setting.

Notes

1 The study of intentional communities

1 Examples are to be found in Abrams and McCulloch (1976);
Bettelheim (1969); Cornfield (1983); and Rothschild-Whitt (Aug.
1979).

2 Abrams and McCulloch (1976) put it this way: 'It is as though we
wanted at one and the same time to convince ourselves that our
most licentious fantasies could neatly happen and to stigmatize those
who suggest, however modestly, that social life might be possible on
terms other than those of our own tightly constrained system.'

Two personal anecdotes will illustrate this point. For many years
Kibbutzim were seen as repositories of 'free love', a place where
children do not know who their parents are. The image exists to this
day. In the Jewish marriage ceremony, the groom says to his bride
at one point: 'Harei at mekudeshet li' ('You are sanctified unto
me'). Only a few years ago an Israeli from the town asked me if
it was true that at the wedding ceremony on Kibbutz the groom has
to add the words '. . . ulechol ha-meshek' ('. . . and to the entire
Kibbutz'). Regarding the Hutterites, I had read in books that
rumours persisted amongst Hutterite neighbours that in order to
'vary the stock' (since the Hutterites are endogamous) they brought
in young men from outside to impregnate the women. Not only
did I not believe the story (and still do not) I did not even believe
that such rumours existed – at least, until I went to Canada only to
find that on telling people that I was going to visit a Hutterite
community, the reaction I got in *every* case was one of nudge, nudge,
wink, wink – 'we know what you're *really* going for!'

3 Goodwin (1978).

4 Sometimes the word 'Hutterian' is used. Generally, 'Hutterite'
applies to individuals and 'Hutterian' to collective entities, e.g.
Hutterian belief. However, I have come across so many
inconsistencies in this regard that I have opted for the term
'Hutterite' throughout.

5 Erasmus (1977).

2   A theory of alienation

1 This phrase is based on Gouldner (1965).
2 While there is no space to enter into a discussion of other alienation theories I would like to state briefly why I have not appropriated any existing theory as it stands. Ideal-typically all alienation theories fall into one of three categories: (i) ontological (i.e. inherent to human existence, e.g. existentialist, Freudian theories); (ii) 'structural', i.e. in a given social structure all people are alienated (Marxist, mass-society theories); (iii) 'particularist', i.e. people can be alienated in certain spheres of their lives but these have no *necessary* relation to other spheres, e.g. occupation, politics, family education, etc. (In practice, of course, some theories fall into more than one category, e.g. Marxist-Freudian or Marxist-existentialist theories.)
I have developed an argument which is indebted to all three approaches. I argue that alienation is inherent to being human; that some societies are by their nature more alienating than others; yet that within any one society alienation can be 'differentially distributed'. Alienation is indeed ontological, but I argue away from fatalism or despair and show that it also has sociological and individual dimensions. Yet, while showing that it is possible to move away from alienation, I also show that some societies are by their nature more alienating than others.
3 While I do not equate alienation and deviance (below) this has been influenced by Merton's theory of deviance (1966).
4 Buber (1949) refers to 'the need of man to feel his own house as a room in some greater, all-embracing structure in which he is at home, to feel that the other inhabitants of it with whom he lives and works are all affirming and confirming his individual existence' (p. 140). Simple community of views and aspirations are insufficient, as are co-operative organization, production and consumption, since these 'touch the individual only at a certain point and do not mould his entire life'.
5 Other analogies between family structure and intentional communities are to be found in Abrams and McCulloch (1976), Cornfield (1983) and Ogilvy (1972).

3   A theory of ideology

1 See Kuhn (1970), p. 78. This idea is the application to communal societies of one of Kuhn's arguments about how scientific paradigms change. In fact, if we change the term 'paradigm' to 'ideology', we could apply many of Kuhn's ideas to ideological change in intentional communities.

4   Origins and development

1 Horsch (1931), Clasen (1972). Estimates vary regarding their numbers.

2 Yearbook of American and Canadian Churches, Abingdon Publishers, Nashville, National Council of Churches of Christ in the USA, 1983.

3 Source: Cook (1954). There appears to be no decline in the birth rate since then.

4 Source: Statistical Abstract of Israel (1983).

5 I am treating all the relevant developments of the previous thirty to forty years cumulatively since I am concerned with their overall effect rather than their chronological order.

6 The term 'therapeutic community' was coined by Tom Maine in 1946.

7 See Koestler's (1970) idea of bisociation, and also his idea of the 'ripeness' of a culture to receive innovations.

8 Ben-Rafael (1980) develops an interesting argument here, namely that the Kibbutz movement's lowered influence after 1948 led it to feel free of national burden, thus allowing members to be more self-absorbed and to indulge themselves after years of restraint.

5   Ideology

1 In particular, this is to be found in the organization's *Staff Manual*, albeit in limited form. See also Jansen (1980).

2 Bienkowski (1981).

3 See Sorokin (1962) on the relationship between solidarity and the non-material nature of society's goals.

4 Mannheim argued that all knowledge is rooted in our place in the social structure, hence there is no such thing as 'objective' criticism or analysis. The only ones who can attain this are those people in society – intellectuals – who are 'classless' (or who are drawn, as a group, from every class), i.e. have no vested interest or clearly-demarcated function (apart from their intellectual function) in the social structure, or attach themselves to a social group but are marginal to it and serve its intellectual interests.

6   Ideology, structure and change

1 Gross (1965).

2 The most detailed analyses of changes in Kibbutz society are in Talmon-Garber (1972) and Cohen (in Bartolke, 1980).

3 This book cannot enter into a discussion regarding the economic life of Hutterite and Kibbutz communities. Experts on the subject have emphasized their economic efficiency. Bennet (1967), in particular, stresses this regarding the Hutterites. Ryan (1976) points out that their productivity is much higher than that of individual farms; however, their costs are also greater, so profitability per unit of production is actually less. It seems, though, that communal consumption is in itself an enormous source of saving, hence the ability to maintain living standards. Barkai (1977) argues that the Kibbutz economy flourishes because, among other things, it has

seen growth as a priority. For this reason, industrialization was a *necessity*, one which could not have been achieved without hired labour in the first instance (i.e. the trend we see today of capital-intensive, high-technology production could not have been instituted in the early industrializing phase). According to statistics in Krausz (1983) the Kibbutz's contribution to Israeli agricultural production is (as expected) very high; remarkable, though, is the proportion the Kibbutz occupies in certain sectors of the country's *industrial* exports.

4 The Hutterites have been accused of depleting the countryside (by buying up private farms) and of causing a decline in local village life (by buying in bulk elsewhere). This was partially the reason for attempts, which eventually proved unsuccessful, to limit their concentration (see below, note 10). The Kibbutzim have been accused of being parasites, not paying taxes and exploitation of Sephardi labour. This was actually an issue in Israel's 1977 general elections. See Oz (1983).

5 According to Frideres (1972) some $0.5m was then required to set up a new colony.

6 Except in the 1950s, when it was introduced as a response to the unemployment resulting from the mass immigration of Jews from North Africa and the Middle East. The government pressurized the Kibbutzim to develop industries and absorb labour, on the grounds that the Kibbutz's commitment to national goals over-rode its commitment to internal ideological purity. This is a classic example of how different components of an ideology can be contradictory. In recent years the extent of hired labour has declined. Kibbutzim are fined by their head offices for hiring labour, and new industries cannot be established if this would necessitate hired labour. Special subsidies are given to facilitate mechanization so as to reduce the need for hired labour. Interestingly, the biggest spurt to decline in hired labour has been the awareness that, in pure *economic* terms, Kibbutz industries are generally more successful when based on capital-intensive, high-technology plant. Hired labour is almost obsolete in agriculture (except sometimes for seasonal work) and in services.

7 These are two types of Moshavim: in one there are individual small-holdings side by side, with common marketing and co-ordination of services; the other is like a Kibbutz but members receive salaries, and there is less communalism.

8 See Greenblatt (1959).

9 In each of these cases conflict arose between members of the colony and leadership of the Leut, either because of the adoption of a new religion (Interlake) or because of (by Hutterite standards) immoral practices (Forest River). In the Interlake case members were expelled, so they demanded a share of the colony's assets. In 1966 the Canadian Supreme Court decided that individual members have no private share in the assets of the colony (Hostetler, 1974, pp. 277–82).

10 The problem here is not so much the physical availability of land as where that land would be situated. Hutterites have always tried to keep their colonies close together, but in response to public pressure (Manitoba, Saskatchewan) and legislation (Alberta, Communal Property Act 1947, repealed 1972), Hutterites have had to spread their colonies out and limit their acreage. If their growth rate continues (population doubling every sixteen to eighteen years), they will have to become increasingly widespread (because of splitting), which has implications for the control the Elders of the Leut can exercise over individual colonies.

11 Kubassek brought with him a small group from Hungary. He was a dynamic personality and the Hutterites made him a bishop (1936). But he began to implement his own interpretations of Hutterite belief. The Hutterites eventually excommunicated him and lost about forty members in the process.

12 Arnold founded the Society of Brothers in Germany in the 1920s. They had Anabaptist beliefs and Arnold himself became a Hutterite bishop. After expulsion from Germany in the 1930s the Brothers went to England and Paraguay. The Hutterites gave them financial support but became disenchanted with the Brothers in Paraguay because of their un-Hutterite practices (e.g. smoking, dancing). The Brothers for their part felt the Hutterites to be anachronistic in their practices, although not in their beliefs. The two groups broke off relations, with the Hutterites losing some members in the process. Since 1974 there has been full reconciliation despite continuing differences in their respective practices (e.g. the Bruderhof economy is based entirely on light industry).

13 Until the early 1970s Hutterites did not pay tax as they had the status of a church. They then agreed to pay personal income tax (i.e. computed as if the member had a private income, although naturally the colony would pay a lump sum on behalf of all members). The Lehrerleut opposed this and went to court. The court ruled that indeed they should not pay personal income tax – but that they must pay *company* tax instead, and that this applied to *all* the Hutterites. The other two Leute are deeply resentful of the Lehrerleut for this. (Information based on private conversation with Hutterite members.)

7 Socialization

1 Baptism is not a condition for an adult to live on a colony, but unless baptized one cannot marry, vote or hold office (for males). One may live on a colony as long as one abides by the rules.

2 Kibbutz education is subsidized in the same way as all education in Israel (although high school education is not free). In fact though it costs the Kibbutz more, for two reasons: (i) the Kibbutzim tend to have smaller teacher-pupil ratios and have many para-educational staff (the subsidies only pay for ratios and staff as determined by the government); (ii) local authorities are required to pay the

difference between government subsidy and total cost (less, in the case of high school, parental contribution), but this is done in effect by deficit funding, which ultimately falls back on the government, whereas the Kibbutz (which acts like a local authority in this case) cannot do this. The only advantage the Kibbutz enjoys is that parental contribution, assessed according to income, is uniform to the entire Kibbutz movement, which puts some of the wealthier Kibbutzim at an advantage. (Source: internal communication of Kibbutz Tzorah, 1.7.77.)

3 The phrase usually used in Kibbutz language is 'new man'; this is a translation of the Hebrew *adam chadash*, and since *adam* can mean equally man or person, I have chosen to translate it as 'new person'.

4 Kibbutz teachers are usually called not *Moreh* (teacher) but *Mechanech* (educator).

5 Bartolke *et al.* (1980).

6 Indeed, some writers, such as Abrams and McCulloch (1976) and Roberts (1971), see this as *the* criterion of communal success, not only regarding children but regarding all members.

7 See Turner and Killian (1957) for the observation that social movements are fragile if based only on ideology or on participation, and stronger if based on both.

8   The individual

1 Gross (1965).

2 Flint (1975).

3 *Ibid*.

4 Boldt (1980).

5 Boldt (1968).

6 Baden (1967).

7 Boldt (1968), following Gouldner, says this is a product of 'functional autonomy'.

8 My impression is that this threat is serious. While the Hutterites are glad to be in Canada because they are free from persecution (but not prejudice) they will have little hesitation in moving if a fundamental matter of faith is threatened.

9 Baden (1967).

10 Boldt (1968).

11 See Davis and Olesen (1971) on how people in communal societies can endistance themselves from each other, including the use of gossip.

12 What is perhaps significant is the fact that many service branches, e.g. the sewing room, are productive in that they *save* the Kibbutz huge sums of money each year, but because they do not actually *make* money their status is still limited.

13 See Evens (1970).

14 During the 1960s the average income (a notional calculation) of a Kibbutz family was 80 per cent of the Israeli average (Barkai, 1977). One can confidently assume that this has not changed and may even

have improved. However, the *distribution* of family income is almost certainly very different in each case. For example, the Kibbutz member, despite rising living standards, probably spends less on consumer items than his urban peer and more on health and education.

15 In the early days of Kibbutz people received what they needed, if the Kibbutz could afford it. Eventually, though, as Kibbutzim grew in size, personal allocations (budgets) were introduced. Under this system there are separate budgets for each item of expenditure (clothing, entertainment, etc.), so that each budget is self-contained and cannot be used for any other purpose. It was then proposed that this should be changed to a combined budget which would bring them all together into one total, 'inclusive' budget. This clearly allows for greater flexibility in personal budgeting. The moves towards this arrangement were accompanied by much soul-searching in Kibbutz circles, an example yet again of how matters which are apparently only organizational can in fact reflect deep ideological tenets – in this case, the greater the degree of budget integration, the greater (so it is feared) the autonomy of the individual and the greater the opportunities for abuse and deviance. A further argument against budgets is that Kibbutz is about providing goods and services communally (according to need) and not about providing a 'salary'. The protagonists argue that abuse can take place under any system, and that the greater freedom which the budget system affords the individual is what Kibbutz is all about.

16 No Kibbutz, though, provides members with private cars, although most people expect this will happen some day.

17 Bromley and Shupe (1979).

18 Abrams and McCulloch (1976) discuss the relationship between play and communal life, which they see as correlative in the context of small, 'self-realization' communities, but by implication (a view I reject) as antithetical in the context of 'utopian communities'. See also Roberts (1971).

19 Blasi (1977).

20 This is not to say that 'one-off' therapeutic communities cannot survive. On the contrary, there are many which do. The reasons for persistence are many and complex, and this issue – of outsiders taking upon themselves the continuity role – is only one.

9 Deviance and conformity

1 Hostetler (1974) appendix 7, p. 338.

2 *Ibid.*, appendix 9, p. 344.

3 Historical examples of change and flexibility (taken from Eaton, 1952) are the introduction of personal allowances (to combat the practice of selling goods on the side or of 'moonlighting' to get extra money); the fact that the rules are not meant to prevent worldly pleasures (e.g. in food, drink, household decoration) but only to limit excess, with the extent of the limits changing; changes in

clothing style so that greater adornment and variation are possible; and the various technological changes in areas of consumption, e.g. refrigeration in houses or use of vehicles for non-economic purposes. (In the early days in America there was resistance to technological innovations in production but this has been virtually turned on its head with, to some extent, an attitude of change for change's sake.) However, and this is crucial, change is always meant to be controlled, and even if the limits of freedom expand, those limits are still clearly defined (even if not always adhered to). The rules are frequently a re-assertion of old edicts and practices as much as a recognition of the need for change.

4 Mauss (1975).

10 Exclusive relations

1 Abrams and McCulloch (1976).
2 Wagner (1982).
3 Hostetler (1974).
4 Ichilov and Bar (1980).
5 The Hutterites refrain from recruitment and the Kibbutzim seek it for reasons not always related to these. The Hutterites' high reproduction rate makes recruitment unnecessary and even burdensome; yet it was abandoned originally to avoid conflict with the host society. The Kibbutz needs recruitment partly for demographic reasons, partly because influence on the environment is basic to its ideology and internal dynamism, and partly to give certain members different occupational opportunities.
6 See Toch (1971) on this last point.
7 We should mention, though, that sexual relations pose further problems which other forms of exclusiveness do not. One is that, given the physical layout of the house, i.e. a number of people living together in a confined space, sexual affection is either going to be displayed publicly or demands are going to be made for privacy ('don't go into the TV room for the next hour'), which causes either embarrassment or inconvenience. This is related to the fact that even though a hostile relationship is problematic for the community, at least others can discuss it and get the parties themselves involved without too much agitation all round. But, for whatever reason, people are very hesitant about discussing sexual relationships (their own or others) publicly, making attempts to use the relationship constructively, or even to discourage it, so much more difficult.
8 See Goffman (1968); also our discussion on 'conspiracy' in Chapter 2.
9 All this helps explain the observation that in all persisting communal societies there is *some* sphere from which the individual cannot withdraw entirely. In the Kibbutz it is work; among the Hutterites there is virtually no privacy; in the therapeutic communities attendance at group meetings is compulsory. In each community the

member cannot avoid confronting or being confronted by other members absolutely, however much he may want to.

11 Summary and conclusions

1 See Klapp (1969) on the question of new roles.
2 This is based mainly on Berger and Luckmann (1971).
3 Roberts (1971) says that effective leadership in communal societies does not derive its authority from 'tradition or bureaucratic structures'.

Select bibliography

1 General

Abrams, P. and McCulloch, A., *Communes, Sociology and Society*, Cambridge University Press, Cambridge, 1976.

Becker, H. S., 'Notes on the Concept of Commitment', in *American Journal of Sociology*, Vol. 66, No. 1 (July 1960), pp. 32–40.

Berger, P. and Luckmann, T., *The Social Construction of Reality: A Treatise in the Sociology of Knowledge*, Penguin Books, Harmondsworth, 1971.

Berger. P. and Pullberg, S., 'Reification and the Sociological Critique of Consciousness', in *History and Theory*, Vol. 4, No. 2 (1965), pp. 196–211.

Bienkowski, W., *Theory and Reality: The Development of Social Systems*, Allison and Busby, London, 1981.

Bromley, D. G. and Shupe, A. D., 'Just a Few Years Seem Like a Lifetime: A Role Theory Approach to Participation in Religious Movements', in *Research in Social Movements, Conflict and Change*, Vol. 2 (1979), pp. 159–85.

Buber, M., *Paths in Utopia*, Routledge & Kegan Paul, London, 1949.

Clark, B. R., *Organizational Adaptation and Precarious Values* in Etzioni (1965).

Cornfield, N., 'The Success of Urban Communes', in *Journal of Marriage and the Family*, Vol. 45, No. 1 (Feb. 1983), pp. 115–26.

Coser, L. A., *Greedy Institutions: Patterns of Undivided Commitment*, The Free Press, New York, 1974.

Davis, A. and Olesen, V., 'Communal Work and Living: Notes on the Dynamics of Social Distance and Social Space', in *Sociology and Social Research*, Vol. 55, No. 2 (Jan. 1971), pp. 191–202.

Erasmus, C. J., *In Search of the Common Good: Utopian Experiments Past and Future*, The Free Press, New York, 1977.

Etzioni, A. (ed.), *Complex Organizations: A Sociological Reader*, Holt, Rinehart & Winston, New York, 1965.

Fellman, M., *The Unbounded Frame: Freedom and Communality in*

Nineteenth Century American Utopianism, Greenwood Press, Westport, 1973.

Gide, C., *Communist and Co-operative Colonies*, George C. Harrap, London, 1930.

Goffman, E., *Asylums*, Penguin Books, Harmondsworth, 1968.

Goldschmidt, W., *Comparative Functionalism: An Essay in Anthropological Theory*, Univ. of California Press, Berkeley, 1966.

Goodwin, B., *Social Science and Utopia*, The Harvester Press, Brighton, 1978.

Goodwin, B. and Taylor, K., *The Politics of Utopia: A Study in Theory and Practice*, Hutchinson, London, 1982.

Gouldner, A. W., *Metaphysical Pathos and the Theory of Bureaucracy* in Etzioni (1965).

Hall, J. R., *The Ways Out: Utopian Communal Groups in an Age of Babylon*, Routledge & Kegan Paul, London, 1978.

Infield, H. F., *Co-operative Communities at Work*, Routledge & Kegan Paul, London, 1947.

Infield, H. F., *Utopia and Experiment: Essays in the Sociology of Co-operation*, Frederick A. Praeger, New York, 1955.

Infield, H. F. and Maier, J. B. (eds), *Co-operative Group Living*, Henry Koosis & Co., New York, 1950.

Johnson, H., *Sociology: A Systematic Introduction*, Routledge & Kegan Paul, London, 1961.

Kanter, R. M., *Commitment and Community: Communes and Utopias in Sociological Perspective*, Harvard University Press, Cambridge, Mass., 1972.

Kanter, R. M. (ed.), *Communes: Creating and Managing the Collective Life*, Harper & Row, New York, 1973.

Klapp, O. E., *Collective Search for Identity*, Holt, Rinehart & Winston, New York, 1969.

Koestler, A., *The Act of Creation*, Pan Books, London, 1970.

Kramer, W. B., 'Criteria for the Intentional Community: A Study of the Factors Affecting Purposeful, Co-operative Community', Ph.D. Thesis, New York University School of Education, 1955.

Kuhn, T. S., *The Structure of Scientific Revolutions*, Foundations of the Unity of Science, Vol. II, No. 2, Univ. of Chicago Press, Chicago, 1970.

Levy, M. J. (Jr), *The Structure of Society*, Princeton University Press, Princeton, N.J., 1952.

Manuel, F. E. (ed.), *Utopias and Utopian Thought*, Houghton Mifflin Co., Boston, 1966.

Mauss, A. L., *Social Problems as Social Movements*, J. B. Lippincott, Philadelphia, 1975.

Merton, R. K., *Social Theory and Social Structure*, The Free Press, New York, 1966 (revised edn).

Mumford, L., *The Story of Utopias – Ideal Commonwealths and Social Myths*, Harrap & Co., London, 1923.

Ogilvy, J. and H., *Communes and the Reconstruction of Reality*, in S. Teselle (ed.), *The Family, Communes, and Utopian Societies*,

Harper Torchbooks, New York, 1972.

Parsons, T., *The Social System*, The Free Press, Glencoe, Ill., 1951.

Remmling, G. W. (ed.), *Towards the Sociology of Knowledge: Origin and Development of a Sociological Thought Style*, Routledge & Kegan Paul, London, 1973.

Rexroth, K., *Communalism – From its Origins to the Twentieth Century*, Peter Owen, London, 1975.

Rigby, A., *Alternative Realities: A Study of Communes and their Members*, Routledge & Kegan Paul, London, 1974.

Roberts, R. E., *The New Communes: Coming Together in America*, Prentice-Hall, Englewood Cliffs, N.J., 1971.

Rothschild-Whitt, J., *Conditions for Democracy: Making Participatory Organizations Work*, in J. Case and R. C. R. Taylor (eds), *Co-ops, Communes and Collectives: Experiments in Social Change in the 1960s and 1970s*, Pantheon Books, New York, 1979.

Rothschild-Whitt, J., 'The Collectivist Organization: An Alternative to Rational-Bureaucratic Models', in *American Sociological Review*, Vol. 44, No. 4 (Aug. 1979), pp. 509–27.

Schutz, A., *Concept and Theory Formation in the Social Sciences*, in D. Emmet and A. MacIntyre (eds), *Sociological Theory and Philosophical Analysis*, Macmillan, London, 1970a.

Schutz, A., *On Phenomenology and Social Relations* (Selected Writings, edited by A. R. Wagner), The University of Chicago Press, Chicago, 1970b.

Shenker, B., 'Continuity and Change: A Strategy of Community Survival', in *Shdemot*, No. 17 (1982), pp. 90–8.

Skinner, B. F., 'The Design of Experimental Communities', in *International Encyclopaedia of the Social Sciences*, 1968, Vol. 16, pp. 271–5.

Sorokin, P. A., *Society, Culture and Personality*, Cooper Square, New York, 1962.

Tiryakian, E. A., *Existential Phenomenology and the Sociological Tradition*, in Remmling (1973).

Toch, H., *The Social Psychology of Social Movements*, Methuen & Co., London, 1971.

Turner, R. H. and Killian, L. M., *Collective Behavior*, Prentice-Hall Inc., Englewood Cliffs, N.J., 1957.

Wagner, J., *Sex Roles in Contemporary American Communes*, Indiana University Press, Bloomington, 1982.

Wallace, S. E. (ed.), *Total Institutions* (incl. his own 'On the Totality of Institutions'), Transaction Books, n.p., 1971.

Wallis, R. (ed.), *Sectarianism: Analyses of Religious and Non-Religious Sects* (incl. his own 'Introduction' and 'The Cult and its Transformation'), Peter Owen, London, 1975.

Wallis, R. and Bruce, S., 'Network and Clockwork', in *Sociology*, Vol. 16, No. 1 (Feb. 1982), pp. 102–7.

Whitworth, J. M., *God's Blueprints: A Sociological Study of Three Utopian Sects*, Routledge & Kegan Paul, London, 1975.

Whitworth, J. M., *Communitarian Groups and the World*, in Wallis (1975).
Zablocki, B., *The Joyful Community*, Penguin Books, Baltimore, 1971.

2 The Hutterites

Alberta Dept of Agriculture, *The Hutterites and Social Policy*, Edmonton, 1972.
Baden, J. A., 'The Management of Social Stability: A Political Ethnography of the Hutterites of North America', Ph.D. Thesis, Indiana University, 1967.
Bainton, R. H., *The Reformation of the Sixteenth Century*, Hodder & Stoughton, London, 1953.
Barkin, D. and Bennet, J. W., 'Kibbutz and Colony: Collective Economies and the Outside World', in *Comparative Studies in History and Society*, Vol. 14, No. 4 (Sept. 1972), pp. 456–83.
Bennet, J. W., *Hutterian Brethren: The Agricultural Economy and Social Organization of a Communal People*, Stanford University Press, Stanford, 1967.
Bennet, J. W. 'Communal Brethren of the Great Plains', in S. E. Wallace, *Total Institutions* (above, general bibliography).
Boldt, E. D., 'Conformity and Deviance: The Hutterites of Alberta', M.A. Dissertation, University of Alberta, 1966.
Boldt, E. D., 'Acquiescence and Conventionality in a Communal Society', Ph.D. Thesis, University of Alberta, 1968.
Boldt, E. D., 'Rejoinder' to Frideres, *Phylon*, Vol. 41, No. 4 (Dec. 1980), pp. 390–5.
Clasen, C.-P., *Anabaptism: A Social History*, Cornell University Press, Ithaca, 1972.
Conkin, P.K., *Two Paths to Utopia: The Hutterites and the Llano Colony*, University of Nebraska Press, Lincoln, 1964.
Cook, R. C., 'The North American Hutterites: A Study in Human Multiplication', in *Population Bulletin*, Vol. 10, No. 8 (Dec. 1954), pp. 97–107.
Eaton, J. W., 'Controlled Acculturation: A Survival Technique of the Hutterites', in *American Sociological Review*, Vol. 17, No. 3 (June 1952), pp. 331–40.
Eaton, J. W. and Weil, R. J., 'The Mental Health of the Hutterites', in A. M. Rose (ed.), *Mental Health and Mental Disorder: A Sociological Approach*, W. W. Norton & Co., New York, 1955.
Flint, D., *The Hutterites: A Study in Prejudice*, Oxford University Press, Toronto, 1975.
Frideres, J. S., 'The Death of Hutterite Culture', *Phylon*, Vol. 33, No. 3 (Dec. 1972), pp. 260–5.
Gross, P. S., *The Hutterite Way*, Freeman Publishing Co., Saskatoon, 1965.

Hofer, P., *The Hutterian Brethren and Their Beliefs*, The Hutterian Brethren of Manitoba, R.R.I., Starbuck, 1955.

Horsch, J., *The Hutterian Brethren 1528–1931: A Study of Martyrdom and Loyalty*, Mennonite Historical Society, Goshen, 1931.

Hostetler, J. A., *Hutterite Society*, Johns Hopkins University Press, Baltimore, 1974.

Hostetler, J. A. and Huntington, G. E., *The Hutterites in North America*, Holt, Rinehart & Winston, New York, 1967.

Littell, F. H., *The Anabaptist View of the Church: A Study in the Origins of Sectarian Protestantism*, Starr King Press, Boston, 1958.

Peter, K., 'The Hutterites: Values, Status and Organizational Systems', in *Variables: The Journal of the Sociology Club* (University of Alberta), No. 2 (Feb. 1963), pp. 55–9 and No. 3 (Feb. 1963), pp. 7–8.

Peter, K., 'Rejoinder' to Frideres, *Phylon*, Vol. 40, No. 2 (June 1979), pp. 189–94.

Peters, V., *All Things Common: The Hutterian Way of Life*, The University of Minnesota Press, Minneapolis, 1965.

Ridemann, P., *Account of Our Religion, Doctrine and Faith (Confession of Faith)*, Hodder & Stoughton, London, 1950.

Ryan, J., *The Agricultural Economy of Manitoba Hutterite Colonies*, McLelland & Stewart, Toronto, 1976.

Schludermann, S. and E., 'Paternal Attitudes in Hutterite Communal Society', in *Journal of Psychology*, Vol. 79 (Sept. 1971), pp. 41–8.

Schludermann, S. and E., 'Maternal Child Rearing Attitudes in Hutterite Communal Society', in *Journal of Psychology*, Vol. 79 (Nov. 1971), pp. 169–77.

Serl, V., 'Stability and Change in Hutterite Society', Ph.D. Thesis, University of Oregon, 1964.

Sorokin, P. A., *The Ways and Power of Love: Types, Factors and Techniques of Moral Transformation*, Beacon Press, Boston, 1954.

Williams, G. H., *The Radical Reformation*, Weidenfeld & Nicolson, London, 1962.

3   The Kibbutz

Baratz, J., *Degania: The Story of Palestine's First Collective Settlement*, Palestine Pioneer Library, Zionist Organisation, n.p., n.d. (revised 1931 edn).

Barkai, H., *Growth Patterns of the Kibbutz Economy*, North-Holland, Amsterdam, 1977.

Bartolke, K. *et al.*, *Integrated Cooperatives in the Industrial Society – The Example of the Kibbutz*, van Gorcum, Assen, 1980.

Ben-Rafael, E., 'Dynamics of Social Stratification in Kibbutzim', in *International Journal of Comparative Sociology*, Vol. 21, Nos 1–2 (March–June 1980), pp. 83–100.

Bettelheim, B., *The Children of the Dream*, Thames & Hudson, London, 1969.

Blasi, J., 'Is a Common Ideology Critical to a Kibbutz?', in *Eloistics*, Vol. 44, No. 263 (Oct. 1977), pp. 231–5.

Buber, M., *An Experiment that did not Fail*, in Buber (1949, above, general bibliography).

Cohen, E., 'Progress and Communality: Value Dilemmas in the Collective Movement', in *International Review of Community Development*, Nos 15–16 (1966), pp. 3–18.

Cohen, E., 'The Structural Transformation of the Kibbutz', in Bartolke *et al.*, 1980.

Cohen, E. and Leshem, E., 'Public Participation in Collective Settlements in Israel', in *International Review of Community Development*, Nos 19–20 (1968), pp. 251–70.

Cohen, E. and Rosner, M., 'Relations Between Generations in the Israeli Kibbutz', in *Journal of Contemporary History*, Vol. 5, No. 1 (1970), pp. 73–86.

Cnaani, D., *Kibbutz and Other Communes* in Shenker (1971).

Diamond, S., 'Kibbutz and Shtetl: The History of an Idea', in *Social Problems*, Vol. 5, No. 2 (Autumn 1957), pp. 71–100.

Etzioni, A., 'The Functional Differentiation of Elites in the Kibbutz', in *American Journal of Sociology*, Vol. 64, No. 5 (March 1959), pp. 476–87.

Evens, T. M. S., 'Ideology and Social Organisation in an Israeli Collective', Ph.D. Thesis, University of Manchester, 1970.

Gazit, Z. *Values and Value Change* (2 parts), Hashomer Hatzair, Hanhagah Elyonah, English Speaking Dept, Israel, n.d.

Golan, Sh., 'Collective Education in the Kibbutz', in *Psychiatry*, Vol. 22, No. 2 (May 1959), pp. 167–77.

Golomb, N. 'The Kibbutz in the Seventies' (Hebrew), in *Heidim*, No. 101 (June 1974) pp. 135–54.

Hertzberg, A. (ed.), *The Zionist Idea: A Historical Analysis and Reader* (with 'Introduction'), Atheneum, New York, 1970.

Ichilov, O. and Bar, S., 'Extended Family Ties and the Allocation of Social Rewards in Veteran Kibbutzim in Israel', in *Journal of Marriage and the Family*, Vol. 42, No. 2 (May 1980) pp. 421–6.

Krausz, E., *Studies of Israeli Society, Vol. II, The Sociology of the Kibbutz*, Transaction Books, New Brunswick, 1983.

Krook, D., *Rationalism Triumphant: An Essay on the Kibbutzim of Israel*, in P. King and B. C. Parekh (eds), *Politics and Experience*, University Press, Cambridge, 1968.

Neubauer, P. B. (ed.), *Children in Collectives: Child-Rearing Aims and Practices in the Kibbutz*, Charles C. Thomas, Springfield, 1965.

Oz, A., *In the Land of Israel*, Fontana, London, 1983.

Rettig, S. and Pasamanick, B., 'Some Observations on the Moral Ideology of First and Second Generation Collective and Non-Collective Settlers in Israel', in *Social Problems*, Vol. 11, No. 2 (Autumn 1963), pp. 165–78.

Rosenfeld, E., 'Institutional Change in the Kibbutz', in *Social Problems*, Vol. 5, No. 2 (Autumn 1957), pp. 110–37.

Shenker, B. (ed.), *Kibbutz: A New Society?* (incl. his own 'An

Interpretation of Kibbutz Values'), Ichud Habonim, Tel Aviv, 1971.
Spiro, M. E., *Children of the Kibbutz*, Schocken Books, New York, 1965.
Spiro, M. E., *Kibbutz: Venture in Utopia*, Schocken Books, New York, 1970 (augmented edn).
Talmon-Garber, Y., *Family and Community in the Kibbutz*, Harvard University Press, Cambridge, 1972.
Viteles, H., *A History of the Co-operative Movement in Israel*. Vol. 2 (1967): *The Evolution of the Kibbutz Movement*. Vol. 3 (1968): *An Analysis of the Four Sectors of the Kibbutz Movement*, Vallentine, Mitchell, London.

4   Therapeutic communities

Apte, R. Z., *Halfway Houses: A New Dilemma in Institutional Care*, G. Bell & Sons, London, 1968.
Caine, T. M. and Smail, D. J., *The Treatment of Mental Illness – Science, Faith and the Therapeutic Personality*, University of London Press, London, 1969.
Clark, D. H., *Social Therapy in Psychiatry*, Penguin Books, Harmondsworth, 1974.
Fairweather, G. W. *et al.*, *Community Life for the Mentally Ill – An Alternative to Institutional Care*, Aldine Publishing Co., Chicago, 1969.
Greenblatt, M., 'The Rehabilitation Spectrum', in M. Greenblatt and B. Simon (eds), *Rehabilitation of the Mentally Ill: Social and Economic Aspects*, American Association for the Advancement of Science, Washington, D.C., 1959.
Jansen, E., *The Therapeutic Community Outside the Hospital*, Croom Helm, London, 1980.
Jones, K., *Mental Health and Social Policy 1845–1959*, Routledge & Kegan Paul, London, 1960.
Jones, M., 'The Treatment of Personality Disorders in a Therapeutic Community', in *Psychiatry*, Vol. 20, No. 3 (Aug. 1957), pp. 211–20.
Jones, M., *Beyond the Therapeutic Community: Social Learning and Social Psychiatry*, Yale University Press, New Haven, 1968a.
Jones, M., *Social Psychiatry in Practice: The Idea of a Therapeutic Community*, Penguin Books, Harmondsworth, 1968b.
Karger, H. J., 'Burnout as Alienation', in *Social Service Review*, Vol. 55, No. 2 (June 1981), pp. 270–81.
Laing, R. D., *The Divided Self*, Penguin Books, Harmondsworth, 1965.
Manning, N., 'Values and Practice in a Therapeutic Community', in *Human Relations*, Vol. 29, No. 2 (Feb. 1976), pp. 125–38.
Rapoport, R. N., *Community as Doctor: New Perspectives on a Therapeutic Community*, Tavistock Publications, London, 1960.
Raush, H. L. and C. L., *The Halfway House Movement: A Search for Sanity*, Appleton Century Crofts, New York, 1968.

Richmond Fellowship, Staff Manual, London.
Rothwell, N. D. and Doniger, J., 'Halfway House and Mental Hospital – Some Comparisons', in *Psychiatry*, Vol. 26, No. 3 (Aug. 1963), pp. 281–8.
Sharp, V., *Social Control in the Therapeutic Community*, Saxon House, Westmead, 1975.
Shenker, B., 'Studying a Therapeutic Community', in *Self and Society*, Vol. 5, No. 5 (May 1977), pp. 129–38.
Shenker, B., 'Community and Individuality', in *Self and Society*, Vol. 6, No. 3 (March 1978), pp. 65–76.
Shenker, B., 'Therapy as Sport?', in *Contact*, Vol. 74, No. 1 (1982), pp. 19–24.
Stanton, A. H. and Schwarz, M. S., *The Mental Hospital – A Study of Institutional Participation in Psychiatric Illness and Treatment*, Basic Books, New York, 1954.
Sugarman, B., *Daytop Village: A Therapeutic Community*, Holt, Rinehart & Winston, New York, 1974.
Sugarman, B., *Reluctant Converts: Social Control, Socialization and Adaptation in Therapeutic Communities*, in Wallis (1975, above, general bibliography).
Szasz, T., *Ideology and Insanity*, Penguin Books, Harmondsworth, 1974.
Wootton, A. J., 'Sharing: Some Notes on the Organization of Talk in a Therapeutic Community', in *Sociology*, Vol. 11, No. 2 (May 1977), pp. 333–50.

Index